ANXIOUS
ABOUT
EMPIRE

ANXIOUS ABOUT EMPIRE

*Theological Essays on the
New Global Realities*

Wes Avram, EDITOR

BrazosPress
Grand Rapids, Michigan

Published by Brazos Press
a division of Baker Publishing Group
P.O. Box 6287, Grand Rapids, MI 49516-6287
www.brazospress.com

Second printing, January 2005

Printed in the United States of America

Library of Congress Cataloging-in-Publication Data
Anxious about empire : theological essays on the new global realites / Wes Avram, editor.
     p.   cm.
  Includes bibliographical references.
  ISBN 1-58743-119-X (pbk.)
    1. Christianity and politics—United States. 2. United States—Foreign relations —2001–3. Christianity and international affairs. I. Avram, Wes, 1959– II. Title.
BR526.A58 2004
261.8′7—dc22   2004007724

Chapter 1 was previously published in *Commonweal Magazine*, September 2002. Reprinted by permission.

Chapter 2 first appeared on OrionOnline, the website of *Orion Magazine*, as part of its "Thoughts on America" series. See www.oriononline.org. Reprinted by permission.

Chapter 10 originally appeared in *Ethics and International Affairs* 17, no. 2 (Fall 2003). Copyright by Carnegie Council on Ethics and International Affairs, 2004.

Contents

Acknowledgments

Much passion, strong critique, and ready assistance have contributed to this volume. Deep thanks to all who have played a part. We have striven less to be comprehensive than provocative. In any publication of this sort, there is more missing than present, but it is the hope of everyone represented here that readers will use our ideas to move outward into further discussion and debate on the ideas raised here—to correct our mistakes, to extend our insights, and to clarify our judgments. Beyond those who have contributed, thanks also go to Rodney Clapp and Rebecca Cooper at Brazos Press, John Thorpe, Sarah Scherschligt, David Bartlett, and David Wood.

Introduction

This book attempts to provide a modest "word in edgewise" in the midst of a time of swirling rhetoric in our nation and abroad. Demonstrators in London pull down an effigy of President Bush in mockery of the televised toppling of the statue of Saddam Hussein in Baghdad, while on the shelf at KB Toys I notice a presidential action figure with the GI Joe-styled commander and chief decked out in the flak jacket the president wore on May 1, 2003, to declare victory in Iraq on the U.S.S. Abraham Lincoln. I ask if I can have one of those dolls and am told that they're sold out. The moment of victory that doll commemorates was also a moment when, by no contest whatsoever, it was safe to say that more Iraqi civilians had been killed at American hands since September 11, 2001, than American civilians were killed at the hands of terrorists that awful day. The times are tense and, for many, confusing. One can mark this moment back to that day in 2001 if one wants, and for good reason. Much, indeed, has changed since then. But as much as things have changed, it would be a mistake to assume that what our nation is now sorting out is altogether new. Our national argument, our ways of mourning our losses and reshaping our place in the world in response, our organized attempts to protect our families and bolster our national morale for a common defense, and our actions in the world on behalf of these priorities all find their origin in ways of thinking about the destiny, privilege, and responsibility of America that both predate September 11, 2001, and will outlive the politics of one season or president. It is worth considering these things carefully, particularly as American Christians.

This book is an invited gathering of Christian voices expressing a certain anxiety in our time and so beginning to imagine something else than what is ruling the day. The gathering began in conversation with a colleague at Yale Divinity School not long after the president's address to the Congress (which was in fact an address to the world) after September 11. My colleague is a veteran of attempts to imagine the church as a gathering that sues for justice and works for peace. He is a longtime participant in work to make that vision real in places such as Israel and Palestine. And he was a bit dumbfounded. "What can we do?" he asked. "I've no idea," I glibly replied. The horror seems too stark, the threat too real, the history of our own dangerous adventurism in foreign lands too close, the near inability of the American political culture to have reasoned and nonpartisan debates about things that matter too entrenched, and the hazards too great to trust the old ways. And things are moving too fast to discern *new* ways. It's not enough to cry "peace, peace" when folks who would give their lives to breed fear commandeer jet planes to meet their ruthless goals. Nor is it enough to cry "war, war" when the definitions of harm, threat, purpose, and even enemy are so slippery and ambiguous in our time. And for a person of serious faith trying to unravel it all? What must that person cry, once crying for the victims has paused?

In that conversation with my colleague I suggested that perhaps we *could* continue to do what has been given us by the church to do. As pastors and as academics we have, in some way or another, been given time, words, and arguments. We've been given access, if we've chosen to take it, to a diversity of perspectives. We've been given the space for some sort of reflection. So we must do that, gathering with friends to pray, think, and speak—even if we have good-faith disagreements. And so came the idea of a collection of essays by folks not so much famous as thoughtful. The charge was to sort out what Christian people in particular, and the church as their gathering, must think about in these times. This book is the result.

The conversation gathered here is not the product of face-to-face encounters. How wonderful it would be if it were. Nor is the friendship shared among all contributors with each other. That would also be fine, if it could be arranged. Some know each other, some do not, for the book is the touchstone for the friendship that shapes the gathering, as each writes by my invitation as editor. I invited folks I thought would be interesting and who I suspected would have some strong and thoughtful things to say to Christians now. Some accepted my invitation passionately. Some said they weren't ready. Some said yes but in the end found they still lacked the words or the time to shape them. Some came into the book by way of recommendation from other participants. One even contacted me at his own initiative after hearing about the project and expressed a desire to participate. When sparked by the Spirit, that kind of initiative shows one nice mark of Christian conspiracy—surprise.

In the end, not all of the writers agree with each other. Most take a strongly critical stance toward recent actions of the American government, but not all. What is shared in common is a yearning for clarity in this time and a desire to root our thinking in the church. What is also shared is a sense that the church is about a business far more urgent, and more vast, than being a naive agent of either rogue revolutionaries, on the one hand, or nation-states, on the other. There is an assumption of catholicity that runs through the essays, by which I mean a universalism that sees the church as a gift to the *whole* world and knows it to be made up of persons of all ethnicities, races, and nations—including the powerful as well as the powerless, victims as well as victimizers, hopeful as well as fearful. It may be that religion, through church, synagogue, mosque, or temple, may hold some insights now required to imagine a human future.

In preparation for this book, each participant offering an original essay received a copy of *The National Security Strategy of the United States of America*, issued by the White House of President George W. Bush in September of 2002. The *Strategy* is best known for developing what has been called the Bush Doctrine into a platform statement that is partly a policy paper and partly a confession of faith. It is worth reading. I asked these writers to have the document in mind as they reflected *theologically* about how Christians might think about America's role in the world and how we might effect that role Christianly. I didn't ask for a specific response to the document itself so much as a sense of its significance.

As things would have it, at about the same time as I made these initial requests, noted sociologist Robert Bellah published one of the first responses to the *Strategy* in the Roman Catholic publication *Commonweal*. In that early response, Bellah asserted that this document presents the blueprint for an American empire in ways American influence has not been described in the past. He called on *all* Americans to read and ponder the document. Not long after this, I received a printed copy of the document in my faculty mailbox, as did each of the faculty of my institution. The document was accompanied with a letter signed, one by one, by the members of our alumni council. The letter noted the signers' shared sense of the significance of this document and urged us to serve the church by reading and responding to it in some public fashion. Though the origin of this book lies elsewhere, it is fair to say that the gathering of these essays is in its own way a response to each of these calls. Professor Bellah's call, reprinted from *Commonweal*, is offered as the book's first chapter.

Does this mean these essays make no claim beyond the current debate over the *National Security Strategy* of the Bush White House? No. For while the essays explore themes that the Bush Doctrine may occasion, the essays stretch toward concerns that any citizen, in church or government, must grapple with in the coming years. This will be the case no matter who is our president.

The book is divided into five sections, with an appendix. Each section is led by a question. The first section is headed by a rhetorical question, to which each of the four essays within it answers "yes" in one way or another. Is it time for Christians to pay attention? Yes, indeed.

The first two chapters of this section come from essays that have appeared elsewhere. Robert Bellah says "yes" in the early reading of the Bush Doctrine just noted. Bellah argues that current U.S. policies drive toward a new American empire with "crystal clarity." And he is made nervous by this fact. After tracing both America's flirtation with and repulsion from empire during its history, he describes one view of how a new empire is taking shape today. And his central point is as clear as what he sees in the White House *Strategy*, that the "American polity is in no way prepared for this world-historical role that has been thrust upon us, making it doubtful that we can sustain the hegemony the national security document asserts."

The second essay is contributed by the editor and takes a simple and quite personal tack. In it, I provide a commentary on the preamble to the White House *Strategy* and try to see through it to a handful of issues that might be at stake for Christian thinking in this time. There are other interpretations prevalent, to be sure, but this one sees in the *Strategy* fundamental errors that take its ideas onto dangerous ground. These errors are seen not *first* in its policy recommendations, but *first* in its silence about a difficult challenge essential to Christian ethics—that is to listen to one's enemy even as one judges his actions. I suggest that we must forgo the fear of "rewarding" terror if we have any hopes of quieting it. Such action requires courage, however, and such courage may require divine aid.

The third essay, reprinted from *Orion* magazine, is presented as a set of twenty-seven thoughts by agrarian philosopher, essayist, and novelist Wendell Berry. In "Thoughts in the Presence of Fear," as in all that he has written since September 11, Berry calls for a cultural renewal and a critical reflection on our deeper values in light of the threats before us. And he refuses to limit those threats to terrorism, for terrorism, he insists, cannot be seen in a vacuum. Berry writes: "In a time such as this, when we have been seriously and most cruelly hurt by those who hate us, and when we must consider ourselves to be gravely threatened by those same people, it is hard to speak of the ways of peace and to remember that Christ enjoined us to love our enemies, but this is no less necessary for being difficult."

The fourth essay, by the dean of Vanderbilt University Divinity School, Rev. James Hudnut-Beumler, offers one view of what unintended effects might come when a *policy* of preemptive war is operationalized. The possibility of such unintended effects gives reason enough for serious Christian reflection in this time. He asks about effects on American identity, on the military, and on freedom. Preemption without cooperation is self-defeating, he claims, as he argues within a classic Christian refusal to collapse means and ends. Pursue freedom with freedom's methods, he begs, not those of freedom's enemies.

The next section is led by the question "What must we know?" In it, David Johnston and Michael L. Budde explore intriguing and often misunderstood terrain. Dr. Johnston was, for fifteen years, a teacher and pastor in the Middle East. In his essay, he uses Christ's call to love of neighbor in the parable of the Good Samaritan from the Gospel of Luke to describe Christian responsibility in this time. Considered globally, our neighbors are Muslims, and so learning to love our neighbors as a way to peace may begin with understanding more about the internal dynamics of Muslim life and thought. So to provide important groundwork for this kind of rapprochement, Johnston offers a summary and review of contemporary perspectives on democracy and social order operating among Islamic intellectuals. He brings out nuances often lost in the popular media and, perhaps, also lost among policy makers. He concludes with thoughts on Christian responsibility before these neighbors.

For his part, Michael Budde, professor of political science at DePaul University and director of DePaul's Center for Church/State Studies, asks us to pause in our debates about America's role in the world to both remember and empirically observe the catholicity of the church. The ties that bind Christians throughout the world run counter to the claims that nationalism would make on our primary loyalties. And alongside the spread of terror that seems to accompany the process of Western-led economic and technological globalization is what he calls a "reglobalization" of the church. This can be seen as the church struggles through practical action to become free of the national identities that dominated the modern era. What comes of this movement as a new kind of patriotic, if not economic, nationalism emerges in the wake of the War on Terror? Two sentences from his essay give a taste of his approach: "Christians who ignore the corrosive effects of resurgent nationalism in all its expressions overlook the war on the churches that is part and parcel of the renewed glorification of America. Nationalism, especially when armed and on the march, ought be seen as a sectarian heresy in conflict with the universality of the Christian gospel and God's construction of a new people from all peoples and nations, and whose allegiance is to the kingdom of God rather than to the fragmented lesser powers of the modern state system."

The next section, marked by the question, "How Might We Talk?" includes three essays loosely exploring the fate of language and argument during these days. The first is by Stephen Chapman, who teaches the New Testament at Duke University Divinity School. Professor Chapman looks quite specifically at how the speeches of President Bush since September 11, 2001, use Scripture to craft a sense of America's identity and mission. More than offering a standard rhetorical criticism of how church and state relationships are rendered in presidential speeches, Chapman sees a shift in presidential rhetoric that should alert Christian hearers. In light of this essay, one might wonder whether the president's early gaffe in calling our military moves against the Taliban and al-Qaeda a "crusade" (invoking strong ire among Muslims who remember the European crusades of Christians against Muslims), was an accidental gaffe at all. There is a novel use of New Testament imagery in the current presidential rhetoric that suggests a serious response by Christian believers.

Eugene McCarraher, a Roman Catholic political theorist at Villanova University, uses perhaps the strongest language in the book. He calls for a transformation of what is often called "public theology." He wants to move it from its recent interest in constructing political and economic structures to maintain "civil society" in response to Christian ideas of the common good to a more iconoclastic approach. He wants Christian intellectuals to unmask the idols and powers that he sees ruling the moment. He calls on Christian intellectuals to "assault the winter palaces of embedded ideology, revitalize and enlarge the political community called church, and rekindle the political imagination called theology." "Against the totems and sacraments of empire," he believes, "we must hurl the most intolerable and virtuous of insults." Professor McCarraher begins his essay with a quote from Randolph Bourne, who wrote in opposition to American entry into the First World War that "in an age of faith, skepticism is the most intolerable of insults." It is skepticism for which McCarraher calls.

A question presses upon us, however: What if, despite all of our attempts to reframe our situation in theological terms and follow the values and lessons of Christian Scripture in charting a path ahead, we still have a problem called terrorism that requires response? What if the path from our present place to a Christian ideal still needs stepping stones constructed of the stuff of *present* politics? And what if there is more of Providence at work in these times than our critiques allow?

While answers to those two questions may come in different forms, Professors Stephen Webb and Jean Bethke Elshtain offer their own compelling responses that run somewhat counter to the flow of the other essays in this gathering.

Stephen Webb, professor of religion at Wabash College, bases his analysis in an open question. What if God may be about something in the current time that is not yet clear; and what if America has a unique role to play, quite despite itself and its weaknesses, in something new being born? "Trusting in providence," he says, "has always been one of the hardest aspects of the Christian life. Theologians should have a lot to say about the destiny of the world, but it is far from clear what role American globalism will play in God's plan." He suggests that most liberal theologians miss the point in responding to visions recently laid out because they misunderstand what he calls the "evangelical Kantianism" influencing the Bush administration. By this he means that it may be a mistake to find contradiction between the president's affirmation of both the lordship of Jesus Christ and the universal desire of all people for human rights and democracy. That these two assertions can be held to be related but separable is no surprise to the mainstream of evangelical Christianity, Webb asserts. And holding the two together need not provide the prescription for violent imposition. In this, Professor Webb's piece can be read as a counterresponse to Professor McCarraher's. He believes intellectuals tend to miss what makes simple sense to most Americans. The confusion, he concludes, likely lies with the intellectuals. Perhaps so.

Professor Elshtain, the Laura Spelman Rockefeller Professor of Ethics at the University of Chicago, provides a piece of constructive political theory rooted in the church's tradition of just war thinking in her essay. Her anxiety about empire is in large part anxiety about how criticism of American imperial design in the world might cloud reasonable debate about prudential action in the face of genocide, failed states, and real terror. "The obligation is a concrete one," she insists, "compelled by one's profession of faith that works from basic human experience outward, so to speak." America has a unique role to play in the world and requires guiding principles for intervention. Attempting to break from an ethic of empathy or compassion that warrants "humanitarian" intervention in cases of genocidal terror such as seen in recent years in Kosovo, Liberia, or Rwanda, Professor Elshtain asks whether there is a more proactive stance we must take before simply stopping the insanity once it's started and then mopping up the mess. Must we not reengage the notion of "equal regard" at the heart of the Christian just war thinking and find there a way of rethinking our responsibility? Oppressed people deserve not our pity, but our honor as persons of value equal to ours. They deserve equal regard in their claims of harm and their calls for outside intervention in their behalf. And it's simply the case that the U.S. will remain the power most able to intervene to serve an order that assures at least minimal justice where tyranny reigns. One might either celebrate or argue with Professor Elshtain's application of her argument, but one cannot avoid her claim if one wants to take seriously what the Christian ethical tradition might say to our time. Her piece was originally commissioned by the Carneige Council on Ethics and International Affairs.

The final section of the book gathers three essays asking what might come of the church in these times. The first of these is by Allen Hilton, a pastor at Congregational Church of New Canaan, Connecticut. Dr. Hilton asks two guiding questions that he believes to be fundamental to any Christian interpretation of these days. The first question is both secular and political: whether the nation-state as we know it is capable of "other-interested" policy and action. He believes not. The second question is about the church, whether given its spotty history it can hope to transcend the limitations to which governments and nation-states are subject. He believes it can, but only if it recognizes that it is formed by a different constitution. American Christianity's habit of hoping to effect Christian good in the world through the government's foreign policy is ineffective and violates the essential identity and mission of the church as a people "for" others, Hilton claims. He concludes that as a people formed by the biblical story of God's activity in ancient Israel and Christ's church, Christianity can aspire to transcend the self-serving of nation-states and be a people "for" others in ways states cannot. By asking whether the nation is capable of applying Christian norms of other-regard, Pastor Hilton's essay shapes an engaging response to Professor Elshtain's.

Arthur Boers, a Canadian Mennonite pastor who served a congregation for several years before joining the faculty of the Associated Mennonite Biblical Seminary, writes about pastoral leadership during these times. His essay begins with an account of his experience as a rural pastor in Ontario during the days after the Trade Center towers fell. "I reject the claim that 'everything changed' or everything should change because of that day," he writes. "Rather, I see it in its truest sense as an *apocalyptic* moment, an opening or revelation where truths are made clear and are suddenly hard to ignore. The truths revealed, however, are not necessarily those being drawn by political leaders, the military, the media, or even many church folks, alas." Through this very personal account, taken then through more abstracted observations, Professor Boers arrives at an urgent call to the historic peace churches. He asks them to stake their claim among the churches during these days. Even for ones making a home in Christian denominations who do not share the pacifist history of the Mennonites, overhearing one "peace" pastor calling on his colleagues to be most true to themselves is an inspiring and instructive overhearing. It might change us all.

The final essay of the book comes from the Reverend Lillian Daniel, pastor of the Church of the Redeemer (United Church of Christ) in New Haven, Connecticut. Pastor Daniel asks what difference ordinary Christian living might make for thinking through these times. Recognizing that even while addressing such strong and urgent things as current events demand, our ordinary lives are still filled by day-to-day obligations that seem to trump other kinds of action. From that practical place, she wonders where we might yet find inspiration and enticement toward a new reality. She finds such inspiration, quite surprisingly, in the Sunday morning order of worship enjoyed in her congregation. There, in the rhythms of gathering and calling, announcements and prayer requests, confession, passing of the peace, hearing and interpreting the Word through preaching, sharing the Communion, taking up an offering, benediction, postlude, and the work after "church," she finds a kind of imagination that cuts deep into the principalities and powers that attempt to rule. There is a logic in Christian worship that when investigated washes its participants in a more subversive possibility— turning the world upside down and replacing it in ways unimaginable in Washington, or London, or Moscow, or Paris, or Beijing, or other centers of worldly authority. Christian faithfulness in these times, she shows, begins in worshiping well. May we all.

An appendix to the book contains the official text of *The National Security Strategy of the United States of America*, issued by the White House on September 17, 2002 (and printed in New York by William Drenttel, 2003). As I've already noted, while the book transcends the confines of the *Strategy* toward more timeless concerns, arguments such as those in the *Strategy* still loom behind these pages. It is included, therefore, in response to the call that initiated this gathering in the first place: take up, read, critique, respond. And in it all, pray.

Is It Time to Pay Attention?

1

The New American Empire

The Likely Consequences of the "Bush Doctrine"

Robert N. Bellah

I have been pondering for quite some time just how to describe the new American Empire, but now, quite suddenly, my task has become much simpler. On September 17, 2002, the White House issued George Bush's *The National Security Strategy of the United States of America,* which describes the new Empire with crystal clarity.

America will strike any nation or any group that it deems dangerous, whenever and however it feels necessary, and regardless of provocation or lack thereof. America invites allies to join in these ventures but reserves the right to act with or without allies. No nation will be allowed to surpass or even equal American military power, and indeed other nations are advised to limit or destroy any "weapons of mass destruction" (WMD) they may have, and that includes Russia, China, and India. Only the United States will have large reserves of WMD, apparently because only we can be trusted to use them justly. Although the document several times uses the time-honored phrase "balance of power," it is very unclear what that phrase can mean in a situation where we have all the power and no one else shall have the capacity to provide a balance. On top of the declaration of absolute military supremacy throughout the globe, the document reiterates, in the epigraph to section 3, Bush's intention to "rid the world of evil," first uttered on September 14, 2001, in the National Cathedral. Apparently what even God has not succeeded in doing, America will accomplish.

One may wonder how the George Bush who as a candidate in the 2000 electoral campaign so often sounded like an isolationist (we're not into nation-building) now sees himself as world ruler. Even more problematically, we can wonder how a nation whose third president advised it to avoid "foreign entanglements" finds itself the sole center of the entire globe. Actually there is a deep relation between these apparently contradictory stances: individualistic nationalism or national individualism. We will go it alone, either by withdrawing from the world, or by dominating it.

In human history empires are a fact of life; they have not been all bad. In his interesting book *War before Civilization*, Lawrence Keeley argues that the Roman Empire was one of the most peaceful periods in history—fewer men under arms, and fewer civilians killed in war than in most of history. The British Empire during its heyday, roughly from the Napoleonic Wars to World War I, maintained a degree of tranquility in the world that encouraged unprecedented economic growth. But both the Romans and the British *intended* to build an empire; the Americans, on the other hand, have become an empire almost by default, leaving us in no way prepared for imperial responsibilities.

I can only suggest here the course of empire that the United States has taken. Continental expansion was indeed "manifest destiny," intended to allow our growing population to occupy the continent. Beyond that, however, compared to other empires in history, our aims for direct rule were modest, peaking in the acquisitions that resulted from the Spanish-American War of 1895, and modestly diminishing (with the independence of the Philippines) since. The American Empire has grown through the extension of what has classically been known as spheres of influence rather than direct rule. The first and perhaps archetypal step was the Monroe Doctrine that declared the entire Western Hemisphere free from European expansion. It was motivated as much by our deep-seated isolationism, our desire not to be encroached upon, as by a wish to dominate, though economic, political, and, on occasion, military domination did indeed follow.

After another episode of isolationism between World Wars I and II (symbolized by our refusal to join the League of Nations that our own President Wilson had designed), we found ourselves after World War II as one of only two great powers in the world, and again, I would argue, we were more concerned that the Soviet bloc not encroach on the "free world" than in dominating the latter, although here, too, the record is ambiguous. So for forty-five years after World War II our imperial sphere of influence was the entire non-Communist world, quite an expansion compared to the Monroe Doctrine. It is the third great expansion of our sphere of influence in the midst of which we now live. After the collapse of the Soviet sphere in the period 1989–91 we became the only great power, and our sphere of influence became the globe.

America's rise to world dominance was, however, not only military and political. It was economic and cultural, and again, I believe, without anyone ever quite intending it. Based on our relatively undamaged economy at the end of World War II, when the economies of all our rivals were in ruins, we became the economic dynamo of the postwar era. Even when Japan and Europe (especially Germany) became serious economic rivals, it was our model of economic life that exerted pressure on all other nations, as it does today in the so-called Washington consensus embraced by the World Bank and the International Monetary Fund.

Our economic freedom, which has ambivalently fascinated the world, is closely related to our cultural freedom, which rouses similar ambivalence. Václav Havel, the president of the Czech Republic, in his 1995 graduation address at Harvard, made a telling observation:

> One evening not long ago I was sitting in an outdoor restaurant by the water. My chair was almost identical to the chairs they have in restaurants by the Vltava River in Prague. They were playing the same rock music they play in most Czech restaurants. I saw advertisements I'm familiar with back home. Above all, I was surrounded by young people who were similarly dressed, who drank familiar-looking drinks, and who behaved as casually as their contemporaries in Prague. Only their complexion and their facial features were different—for I was in Singapore.[1]

In one sense what Havel is talking about is globalization. But if you think about it, where, if not from America, did the rock music, the familiar-looking drinks, the clothes, and even the casual behavior originate? Informality and individuality are American trademarks, but so are consumerism, mass entertainment, and the ideology of the free market. There are certainly parts of the world that have not been touched by these cultural influences, such as Afghanistan under the Taliban, but it is remarkable how soon the transistor radios and the beauty parlors reappeared in Afghanistan once the Taliban were gone. There is almost no major city in the world where a scene such as that described by Havel could not be found. And although the language spoken in most of those restaurants would not be English, if you entered one, and spoke in English, chances are you would be understood.

So, on top of global military, political, and economic power, the United States has hegemonic cultural and linguistic influence. How are we to interpret this many-dimensional American globalization? One way would be to say that everyone in the world now has two nationalities: the one they were born with and American.

Or we could go farther and say we are not *a* country, we are *the* country. When Timothy Garton Ashe visited Belgrade and Pristina right after the Kosovo War, he asked young soccer players about their beliefs. Much as they hated each other, they agreed on one thing: both groups wanted to be like Americans. When MSNBC's Ashleigh Banfield interviewed young Iranians in Tehran in February of 2002, she asked if they hated America. They said no; they love American things and want to be like Americans. But this love of American things is profoundly ambivalent, and mixed with envy stimulated by the many American things they know they don't have. The Oxford Catholic scholar Nicholas Boyle has put this situation in Hegelian perspective:

> [I]t precisely corresponds to the Hegelian model in that a universal process—the establishment of a global free market—is understood, and is correctly understood, as legitimating the particular features of the national life and being actualized through them. World-historical developments, according to Hegel, are realized only in the history of particular states, and if globalization is the dominant world-historical process of the last century and a half, Americanization—first of America and then of the world—is the particular form in which it is realized. . . . The universal process of globalization has to become concrete in a particular form and it does so in the particular form of Americanization. Beyond individual statehood, for all of us, lies America.[2]

Yet the central point I want to make is that the American polity is in no way prepared for this world-historical role that has been thrust upon us, making it doubtful that we can sustain the hegemony the national security document asserts. We remain a profoundly provincial, monolingual nation. Most Americans are not interested in the rest of the world and certainly don't know much about it. Foreign news has been in decline as a proportion not only of television news, but even of newspaper reporting for decades. Our degree of national pride is unmatched in the world. Even before September 11 the National Opinion Research Center found that 90.4 percent of Americans agree with the statement "I would rather be a citizen of America than of any other country in the world" (rising to 97.2 percent after September 11). Only slightly fewer Americans agreed with the statement that "America is a better country than most other countries." After September 11 almost half of our people agreed with the statement "The world would be a better place if people from other countries were more like the Americans." In his cover letter to the *National Security Strategy* document Mr. Bush asserts that there is "a single sustainable model for national success: freedom, democracy, and free enterprise." The document itself makes it clear that all other nations not merely should, but must, follow this single model—or else.

It is one of the ironies of history that the national culture that embodies the world spirit today is hostile to government and committed to the enhancement of the freedom of individuals to pursue their self-interest with as little interference as possible. The trouble is that when this American ideology gets translated into the international realm it means that the United States must be allowed to act freely, unfettered by international institutions, including specifically the United Nations, but also unfettered by any other compact, covenant, or international agreement. Does Bush realize that when he calls the United Nations "irrelevant" and compares it to the League of Nations should it not bow to our will, he is doing just what the Germans, Italians, and Japanese did in the 1930s: making the League of Nations "irrelevant" by refusing to abide by its decisions? The list of the agreements that we have either broken or refused to sign is too long to list here. The reason why even the most innocent-sounding of them, such as the treaty to protect the rights of children, are rejected is that they encroach on American sovereignty; the absolutely sovereign American self must not be fettered.

The nemesis of empires has always been overextension: military failures abroad and bankruptcy at home. The doctrine spelled out in the *National Security Strategy* document seems to be headed exactly in that direction. Nicholas Boyle, after saying that "beyond individual statehood, for all of us, lies America," goes on to say: "And that is true for Americans too, though for them it is true in a special, paradoxical, and not necessarily comfortable way. To be the chosen intermediary of the world spirit is to be chosen in the end for destruction," a destruction to which "America is not immune."[3] It does not take a Hegelian to know that the assertion of absolute power provokes the assertion of absolute counterpower. The day after September 11, a front-page editorial in the French newspaper *Le Monde* stated and restated the phrase, "We are all Americans now." But a year later, on September 10, 2002, the same writer, Jean-Marie Colombani, observed that "the solidarity reflex of one year ago has been drowned in a wave that leads one to believe that, in the world, we have all become anti-American." Even if an "anti-American" is still a kind of "American," it is not the kind that should give us cheer.

Is there any way to reverse, or even slow, the fateful course upon which we appear to be set? Could we use our vast imperial power to transcend the idea of empire? *Imperare* means "command," and in the modern world, the idea of government by command has been replaced, at least in principle, by government by the consent of the governed. Could we give up command and replace it by the profoundly American principle of consent arising from public discussion, not force? Instead of decreeing the "single model" that the whole world must follow, could we instead work for a network of treaties, agreements, even international police forces, in which all the plurality of nations can participate? Instead of sabotaging every treaty, could we not promote as the principle of international order the democracy we claim to support—not "I am the king of the mountain and you will do what I say"—but all of us bound by a thousand ties of interdependence?

Some may think my argument unrealistic in a world where nation-states often place their own interests above all else. I would argue that in the present world the very idea of national interests needs to be rethought. It is in the ultimate best interest of every nation that transnational institutions replace nation-state power politics. China and/or India could become economic superpowers in the next half-century, and our military dominance could falter. It is surely in our interest to connect all nations, great and small, in agreements that limit weapons and mandate arbitration rather than assume we will always have the capacity to dominate the world by force. My great fear is that this latest American outburst of "the arrogance of power" will mobilize most of the world against us. But to look at the headlines or watch the evening news, it does not appear that many at the highest level of United States government share such a fear. We have embarked on an endless "war on terrorism" in which the invasion of Iraq is only one step—until exhaustion sets in.

A chance for another course, another role for America in the world, depends ultimately on the reform of our own culture. A culture of unfettered individualism combined with absolute world power is an explosive mixture. A few religious voices have been raised to say so.[4] The question of the hour is whether our fellow citizens, not to mention our leaders, are ready to hear such voices.

Notes

1. See www.znak.com.pl/eurodialog/ed/0/havel.html.en.
2. Nicholas Boyle, "Beyond the State: The Limits to World History," *Ethical Perspectives* 7, no. 4 (December 2000): 251.
3. Ibid.
4. See, among others, Stanley Hauerwas and Frank Lentricchia, eds., *Dissent from the Homeland: Essays After September 11*(Durham, NC: Duke University Press, 2003).

2

On Getting Past the Preamble

One Reading of the Strategy

Wes Avram

> In the war against global terrorism, we will never forget that
> we are ultimately fighting for our democratic values and way
> of life. Freedom and fear are at war, and there will be no quick
> or easy end to this conflict. (*Strategy*, section III)

*T*he National Security Strategy of the United States of America, issued by the White House on September 17, 2002, is almost 13,000 words, divided into nine sections and a preamble. Each section is led by an epigram, as if a Scripture heading, with a statement drawn from one or another presidential speech since September 11, 2001. The document appears in the form of a classic Protestant confession of faith, as if it is a doctrinal guide to orthodox interpretation and application of general statements of principle. In this case, the words to interpret and apply are not the words of Jesus Christ or the apostle Paul from Christian Scripture, but the words of a sitting president. The first of these nine sections provides an overview of America's international strategy. The

27

next eight sections are termed as if charges to be followed. We must *champion* aspirations for human dignity, *strengthen* alliances to defeat terror, *work* with others to diffuse regional conflicts, *prevent* enemies from threatening us and our friends with weapons of mass destruction, *ignite* a new era of global economic growth through expanding free markets and free trade in ways that model the West, *expand* the circle of development by opening societies and building democratic structures, *develop* agendas for cooperative action with other centers of global power such as NATO, the Pacific Rim, China, Japan, India, and completely *transform* America's national security institutions. These headings suggest noble intentions, in their way, but as the old saying goes . . . the devil may be in the details.

I rest my response largely within the preamble. For it is there both in what is said and what is noticeably left unsaid, that I see the concerns that express themselves in the details later on. An equivocation between generalities and specificities begins there, as does a certain slippage between world-concern and presumptive nationalism. I also see there an absence of other-regard and a refusal to define certain key ideas that should give any Christian reader pause. Before asking any questions, however, one should give credit to the White House for offering the public such a document to ponder and critique. That itself remains a testimony to American strength.

A Certain Equivocation

The *Strategy* moves back and forth between affirmations of guiding principles, abstracted generalities for application of those principles in certain contexts (such as affirming international organizations *in general*), and almost incongruously specific suggestions in other cases (such as refusal to recognize jurisdiction of the International Criminal Court over U.S. armed forces or invoking the recent free trade agreement with Jordan in 2001 and pledging to complete similar accords with specifically Chile and Singapore, then Morocco and Australia). What is noticeable here is a disparate level of detail across themes. This would make sense if the generalities were affirmed first and their principles applied to specific situations, but that order is not followed consistently through the document. It is more unpredictable than that. This imbalance may suggest areas not yet clarified, which is surely understandable. It may also reflect a sense that some problems require more immediate attention, while other problems can be named but left for later consideration. However, these disparate levels of detailed application can also leave a reader wondering what of this is by design. What is being purposely left out? Are more potentially controversial applications of this broad strategy hidden behind generalities and couched underneath less controversial affirmations?

Take the equivocation between American self-interest and world-concern as one place where one is left to ponder between the lines. At the beginning of the *Strategy* we learn the following: "We [meaning the U.S.] will defend the peace by fighting terrorists and tyrants. We will preserve the peace by building good relations among the great powers. We will extend the peace by encouraging free and open societies on every continent."[1] We also find that this work of defense, preservation, and extension is coterminous with the spreading of prosperity, freedom, and democracy. And we further see that these are identical, because the Western-style values that sustain them are "right and true for every person, in every society—and the duty of protecting these values against their enemies is the common calling of freedom-loving people across the globe and across the ages."[2] These lofty ideals are then shaved closer by the recurrent corrective found throughout the *Strategy* that defense of the U.S. is the first priority of American policy and that all actions in support of international benevolence are subservient to the primary purpose of protecting and advancing U.S. interests, for "defending our Nation against its enemies is the first and fundamental commitment of the Federal Government."[3] Such priority to kin and kind is understandable where a rough balance of power measures international relations. However, where no rival is to be allowed in any sphere and American leadership is to be proactively defended on all fronts, in the service of the very values noted above, one wonders if the federal government has not reshaped its moral responsibility in ways that render that so-called first commitment rather dangerous—like smoking at a filling station and assuming we won't blow up because we own the station. Gasoline fumes have a way of equalizing power in the presence of a flame.

For an example of how the assumptions that hide behind this ambivalence might sound, one might ask how we are to read generalist affirmations of economic openness for developing countries. These affirmations are accompanied by specific calls for extending Western-style, capital-intensive free enterprise to all nations. Are protectionist walls to be torn down in *their* interests or in *ours*? The *Strategy* is clear that the U.S. will work aggressively to create conditions favorable for foreign investment throughout the globe and that such efforts will be defended by our military. For in a logic that asserts at one time that a particular economic policy, such as "free trade" as organized through the WTO and World Bank, is vital to the War on Terror, and that the War on Terror will be won only through uncontested American strength and leadership, and that American strength and leadership will be backed up by a transformation and strengthening of American military might and concerted multidirectional effort to be sure that no country, region, or movement can challenge the U.S. in any terms other than those we agree to, and that all these actions are finally meant to support American security *first* and world security only inasmuch as it supports American security, one is left a bit dizzy.

If I were a citizen of any land but this, I'd feel rather threatened by such logic. Why would I accept, simply by the power of its assertion, that an enthusiastic American supremacy that is designed, first, for America's sake is, on the face of it, best for me? I'd wonder how free, or at least how independent, I'll be in this new order. Not very, unless I agree that freedom comes in a certain vassalage to American values. Since I am not a foreign national, perhaps this shouldn't trouble me. Yet I am one of many millions baptized into a church that claims my solidarity with all persons in all places before my allegiance to this particular people in this particular place, even as I am bound to this people and love this place. Might there be arguable policies folded into ostensibly generous principles here? I think so.

Unasked Questions and Coded Silences

As forthright as the document presents itself to be, there is a lot of "coded" language there that one must wade through, interpret, and speculate on. And so, sadly, the stated purpose of the document to chart a new and open path for American policy based in plain speaking and truth telling is undermined, and the credibility of the document severely weakened.

One slippery silence surrounds the very definition of terrorism at work. As long as we never define what terrorism is, we can avoid any self-critique in our fight against it. We all know that it is *they*, after all, and not *us*, who terrorize! And we all know, after all, that it is only the underbelly of the world that can blow as a bellow to the flame and never the breath of more established powers. As long as we don't define terrorism, any debate about it is stifled.

The unstated definition of terrorism in the document might be terrorism as acts of violence intentionally targeted against civilians or their possessions. But military and government officials are quick to label roadside bombs targeting military convoys as terrorism, so the presence of civilians must not be a necessary condition for something to be terrorism in the view that informs the *Strategy*. Perhaps, then, the idea of terrorism is less and less about what is done or to whom it is done than it is about who does it. Any act of politically charged violence committed by a group other than the standing army of a recognized nation-state or officially sanctioned authority and at any time other than during a recognized military conflict would then be terrorism. We are now a ways from the more obvious view of terrorism held by most folk, which would generally involve that first notion of terrorism as acts of violence against people who are not combatants for the purpose of achieving dubious political gain. Yet even that definition, if we were to return to it, is incomplete.

Consider the word itself as a key to its definition: *terrorism*, the blending of ideology with terror. As a tactic, then, terrorism would be the attempt to manipulate people or policy through the cultivation of terror among those considered either directly or indirectly responsible for a harm against the persons, people, or cause of those sowing the terror. Against the powerful, it works through capitalizing on fear of anarchy. Against the weak and oppressed, it works by controlling a population through the threat of escalating domination and arbitrary authority. Cultivated terror preoccupies a people with fear for their own safety and security. That definition, or one like it, would allow a more nuanced view of our situation. For it forces us to ask if terrorism also includes the systematic destruction of a land and a people while withholding effective mechanisms for them to claim their harm and seek redress. It forces us to resist pervasive road blocks in an occupied land, or systematic destruction of homes of the relatives of suspected terrorists, or strafing civilian neighborhoods with gunfire from Apache helicopters even while we rightfully condemn hijackings and random bombings. It even forces us to ask whether certain economic activities in parts of the world, such as attend predatory capitalism or the expropriation of native resources, can add up to terror. They certainly evoke rage, and so fuel the fire. Gradations are possible, of course, but we still need enough clarity in our discussions of terrorism to have a more thoroughgoing view than the one we've been getting. The *Strategy* lacks that clarity.

No doubt we must police the thugs, no matter where they're found, and remove their tools. However, responses to terrorism as I have defined it would also include strong and careful shoring up (not systematic undermining) of international organizations and other structures by which persons, peoples, and groups can make claims regarding harms they believe done to them and seek binding redress for their grievances. However flawed, the United Nations, the International Court of Justice, the War Crimes Tribunal, are among those most available now. We must honor those organizations, fund them, strengthen them, and even allow them to judge *us* when necessary. Sadly, the *Strategy* imagines doing just the opposite.

The churches are in a unique position to provide another venue in which the aggrieved of the world can express their grievances and seek relief. It has done this historically and must ever strengthen that work. And so the many efforts of the churches in respectful mission, interfaith dialogue, and truth telling remain urgent.

Another silence worth noting is the near absence of critical, political, or ideological analysis of the enemies "freedom, democracy, and free enterprise" now face. This leaves the impression of a desperate child flailing arms at a threatening but indescribable phantom in the night shadows. But such is not our situation, even if it feels that way to some. We can know far more about the character, aspirations, and odd intelligence of the foes we face than what we can know of a mere ghost. And we'd be well served to not stereotype those foes for fear of missing the point. A phantom will always win, unless through the wise use of knowledge, and not just the random application of what passes for "intelligence," we straighten ourselves out. This begins in acknowledging at least the possibility that we've played a dangerous role in creating the shadowy monster in the first place and working hard to stop feeding it.

An Obscured Enemy

What does the monster want? And how might some knowledge of his yearnings—more than merely a loaded description of his acts—assist us in creatively addressing our threat? The question remains unasked in the *Strategy* at any level past caricature. Two brief passages in the preamble seem to suffice for describing the threat and its perpetrators. They provide a warrant for all that follows. The first is this statement:

> Enemies in the past needed armies and great industrial capabilities to endanger America. Now, shadowy networks of individuals can bring great chaos and suffering to our shores for less than it costs to purchase a single tank. Terrorists are organized to penetrate open societies and to turn the power of modern technologies against us.[4]

The second is this, cited in one of the president's speeches and reiterated in the preamble:

> The gravest danger our Nation faces lies at the crossroads of radicalism and technology.[5]

Three observations on these statements. *First, one need only to think back to the early years of the so-called Cold War to recognize very quickly that the first statement is rather inaccurate.* Images of shadowy networks ready to unleash great chaos from within our body politic and so wound us from behind shaped early public images of the communist threat as strongly as did grosser military confrontations and the arms race. Could the House Un-American Activities Committee have done its work as it did had there not been a pervasive sense of terror in the land at least similar to what this document describes as unique to the post–September 11, 2001, world? Before that, how could the nation have put thousands of Japanese Americans into internment camps without due process or just cause if the fear of terror had not trumped better American values? Fear of violent anarchy is not new to us, and it is that very fear that contemporary terrorism evokes and so exploits. And, sadly, I fear that this document seeks to evoke the same fear, and so exploit it as warrant for accepting its proposals at face value—free of any critical analysis of the threat itself. If our situation is so novel, then we've nothing to learn from twentieth-century experience. I'm simply not convinced.

A second observation about this odd warrant regards the equivocal use of the image and idea of technology in it. It is in the very nature of technology to have unintended consequences and "off-label" use (both positive and negative), and too little of our cultural confidence in technology recognizes that challenging fact. There is no technological development that can, finally, be harnessed or controlled. And the bigger and more extravagant the product of technological innovation, the bigger and potentially more extravagant its unintended use (and misuse).

Once the terrible loss of life is weighed, and the loss of property is counted, one of the more horrific aspects of what happened on September 11 is how decidedly crude were the tools that were used against us: conviction to the point of psychosis, careful and patient planning, falsified documents, flight manuals, and box cutters. These actors did not gain sophisticated technology; they simply borrowed it for a horrifying moment. The California fires of 2003 show the kind of destruction a simple match or two, or a signal flare, can sow.

The *Strategy* insists that our enemies' first choice to equalize their power against our superiority is the procurement of weapons of mass destruction.[6] Yet no such weapons have been used in any of the cases of terror we've seen, except for the sarin gas released in the Tokyo subway in 1995 by a Japanese cultist. The WMD threat should not be minimized, of course, but it should not be stressed to the point of *overtechnologizing* the threat that terror wields. Great havoc can be wrought by simple acts, and there is little defense against these except redressing legitimate grievances, confronting social psychosis, and effective and ethical policing. We can't just assert that we're in charge, wield a stick or two to prove it, and expect that to remove the threat.

Christians have affirmed the fragility of life all along—"like a grass that withers," so Psalm 90 says. However, we have too often failed to affirm with equal vigor the fragility of our handmade creations. This is practical wisdom rooted deep in Christian tradition, and wisdom we might be smart to urge upon world leaders. There is no technological fix to the harm that human imagination can concoct and human tools produce. There is no fix without a basic transformation of our commonly accepted trust in and dependence on technology itself. This is not to suggest we stop screening passengers before they get on airplanes, but it is to insist that more screening of passengers, and more snooping on e-mail, and more spying on neighbors, and more listing of enemies, and more hiding of prisoners without trial, and more striking at targets, and more swinging at phantoms will not make us safer until core human concerns are more quickly addressed. I take this to be the argument of Wendell Berry since September 11, and I agree.[7]

The *Strategy* relies on an unfettered transformation of military, intelligence, political, and economic technique—guided by American ingenuity—to resolve this lurking and ever present threat that modern technology will be used to spread rage and chaos. Yet if the unfettered and unqualified spread of technological culture quite despite local context and local needs accounts for even a part of the web that produces the rage that spreads into chaos, we are indeed at a crossroads. I refer not just to the spread of technological devices, but also of all the cultural and economic realities that tend to come with technology—in the name of free trade and economic development.[8] For might not the increasing refinement of technique in the face of technique's misuse, and the increasing centralization of control over that refinement into the hands of one capital of one nation open the door to increasing the rage? And might not the new techniques and developed technologies we use to assure the continuing free expansion of technological culture also provide new things to be manipulated into service of the rage they produce? The *Strategy* seems to assume much the opposite.

One might call the analogy naïve, but I remember conversations among compassionate and responsible administrators at the small liberal arts college where I served as chaplain for six years about responding to pervasive binge drinking on campus and the sexual violence, vandalism, and self-destruction that went with it. The problem was on the rise. Now these were smart and well-qualified students. Our expectations of them were high, and all the benefits of the world were in arm's reach—as long as they performed. The campus was well managed (perhaps overmanaged), with an active office of student affairs overseeing student activities, psychological services, crisis support, academic development, and security. Student lives were filtered and organized all the way down. And so solutions to the violence were proposed in the image of this existing organization. Better-managed parties, better information gathering on problematic dorms or individuals, better treatment programs, redescribed disciplinary policies, more effective monitoring, more educational programs. And yet nothing helped. I wondered if the problem lay, at least in part, in the solution. For as many programs as were proposed, few presented anything really other than more management. I would speculate that part of what our students were telling us in their binge drinking was that they didn't want to be managed. Only in such self-abuse, and the other-abuse that often attended it, could students say that they would not be controlled by an increasingly perfected, and ironically impersonal, system. Sick, yes, but partially explainable.

Perhaps the answer lay in a new kind of religion rooted by a different kind of listening, a serious and painfully respectful face-to-face confrontation and an alternative moral imagination of how that small world could be ordered. The problem of terrorism, like the problem of pervasive self-abuse, is not new, and yet the response proposed in the *Strategy* appears to be a perfection and reorganization of old techniques and old patterns of power and influence. And this is offered in the name of a new approach. Perhaps we need something *quite* new. Perhaps we need to courageously and creatively move to *break* the cycle, not feed it. The thinkers behind the *Strategy* believe they are doing just that. But I believe they are looking at the wrong problems, and so tragically missing more radical and appropriate solutions available.

Losing the Question in the Answer

The question, "Why do they hate us so much?" had a predictably short-lived currency in popular media after September 11, 2001. While responses to the question were often incomplete, the permission the situation granted to at least ask the question gave some hope that a nuanced and broad public conversation was at least possible. While a robust conversation of that sort still goes on, in tribute to lingering democratic strength, the conversation seems to have largely retreated out of the open public square and into smaller religious and academic circles. One hopes that it still goes on in some diplomatic circles as well. But as far as governmental and mainstream discourse is concerned, the first question was soon replaced by purely strategic considerations. And critical conversation about these strategies was quickly co-opted by international wrangling over the first *major* test case, in Iraq, of the strategic unilateralism asserted by the *Strategy*. Did the president, the defense secretary, the national security advisor, and the secretary of state lie to the world regarding their intelligence on Iraq's weapons of mass destruction? Or were they merely deceived? If they lied, what intentions were they lying to cover up? What were we not told about this invasion, or told in such oblique terms that little public debate was admitted? Or if they were deceived, can we trust any statement made or preemption imagined on the basis of supposedly incontrovertible intelligence again?

Questions about Iraq, while quite legitimate, replaced the *first* question. What is happening in the world to prompt what we now call this great threat against us? Do we simply face rogue tyrants or spoiled rich ideologues hell-bent on sewing chaos for chaos' sake? That seems to be what this document assumes. Now, accepting that interpretation of our situation as a genuine possibility, should we not also entertain other possibilities—if only for the sake of exhausting all our options in case we make a fatal error? Should we not entertain the possibility, if only for a moment, that there may also be *design* at work in the terror we see? What if such careful calculation as we have seen in our new enemies, effective enough to remain both spectacular and outside our control, is *both* evil *and* interpretable?

A Thin Evil

Stereotypical depictions of Satan aside, Christian theology has always maintained a far more subtle understanding of evil than that presumed in recent presidential rhetoric and implied in the *Strategy*. Christianity understands that one can at one time seek the good *and* do evil—and that is true of both the constitutionally malevolent and the constitutionally good-willed. The Augustinian heritage sees in evil a perversion of the good. It cautions believers to discern the good lurking within evil impulse as a place to begin to see how God might work redemption. Claiming that tradition need not mean suggesting that our president simply wait for the hearts of Osama bin Laden and his ilk to be warmed (though it couldn't hurt to pray for them as earnestly as we plot their destruction). But it does suggest that one need not fall into some trap of "moral equivalency" to admit that while malevolent, Osama bin Laden may yet require a close hearing to decide whether despite his crimes we might still be able to respond to the grievances that played a role in *making* him.

However short shrift, the *Strategy* does give some attention to the political conditions of "failed states" that breed terrorists.[9] It tries to provide techniques for redressing the problem. But what it provides is not enough, in my view. For the *Strategy* still fails to pay any attention at all to the claims these enemies would make on us. Christians must, even if governments may not. And so Christians have a better way set before them, even if more difficult. For it takes a great deal of courage, and some power from beyond, to listen to those who hate you and, even while judging their actions, admit they may have an argument worth hearing in their tragic rage. It's terribly difficult to do this, because it requires thinking more than one thing at once and bearing the burden of such complexity. But the peace and well-being of the world might now depend on it. This is not for the purpose of understanding in order to empathize, but of understanding in order to credibly figure out how to ease the threat for everyone—even while punishing the crime.

Perhaps we should treat Islam with more respect. Perhaps we *should* provide Palestinians self-determination and a human future as we rightly insist on for Israel. Perhaps we *should* get out of Saudi Arabia. Perhaps we *should* do less harm in the name of free trade and liberal economy. Perhaps we should do even more. And should we not entertain the possibility that in the eyes of at least some in the world we are more the creators of their terror than are our enemies? Surely a Palestinian whose house is destroyed by an American-made bulldozer bought with American loan guarantees and operated by a military funded and developed in close association with the United States might feel that way. And surely an Afghan whose daughter was killed by a misdirected U.S. bomb might feel that way. And so also might a Jamaican banana picker whose benefits and wages were decimated when an international corporation bought out his plantation because the trade protections that defended his enterprise were struck down by American action in the name of "free trade."

The Fear That Stops Response

The mantra reappears, however, that to "listen to terrorists" is to "reward" their actions. For as with never granting victory to a tantrum-throwing child, we exclude anyone from a hearing who no longer makes their claim of harm in the idiom we expect of them—whether we've summarily dismissed them in their attempts to make a claim in the past or not. Yet I know as a parent that dealing with a problem need not be confused with approving or "rewarding" the tantrum. Communication can, in fact, break down. I need not approve of the tantrum's frustration or accept its view of the world, but if I do not listen, I may make long-lasting and serious mistakes in my response.

The stakes are obviously much, much higher in the political arena, for there we are not simply dealing with a bad-tempered child or a binge-drinking adolescent. There we are dealing with folks who, apparently, will bring the house down with them if no one listens. But isn't that also true of adults acting out in whatever world they can make for themselves? The world of terror is just much, much bigger. And so also are the stakes in how we respond—Western states and Muslim leadership alike. As a Christian preacher I must preach that I neither reward terror nor dishonor the dead when I ask *why* in such a way that my *why* is directed toward what's happening with me as well as with others, and allows that there yet may be a logic at work, however perverted, that is worth sorting out. Asking such questions is precisely what the memory of the dead—in New York, in Baghdad, in Gaza, in Istanbul, in Jerusalem—demands.

A Complicated Arrogance

There is little sign of such listening or such questioning in the *National Security Strategy*, at least in my reading of it. What we get, instead, is the evocation of "radicalism" as a self-contained discussion-stopper. If it is "radical," it need not be attended to. It need only be defeated. Yet, again, we risk not only missing the moral point but also making serious strategic error. We risk feeding right into the hands of the very threat we seek to eliminate. What if, after all, we are now doing exactly what al-Qaeda wants us to do? What if we are being goaded into overplaying our hand in a rash assertion of American might in a reckless bet that we'll make a mistake that will open a gaping hole through which Islamists will have a much better chance of achieving their designs?

The possibility is more real than speculative, I fear. And it begins with our own complicated arrogance, repeated throughout this document in the argument that American power (1) is identical to American state and economic interests within the international system of nation-states and trade, (2) is and must remain unmatched and unchallenged for peace and prosperity to reign, (3) must be the yardstick by which all social and economic orders (secular or religious) are measured, and (4) must be unfettered by any limiting accountability that we do not freely accept. What if from the position of such complicated arrogance we make just one well-placed mistake, let alone several? What if we unintentionally open the possibility for an Islamist state in Iraq, or give the Israeli right wing a free hand to ethnically cleanse the West Bank and expropriate that land, or accumulate mishaps like bombing a wedding party in Afghanistan, or torturing prisoners, or humiliating the wrong people and undo the wrong state or undermining the wrong economy at the wrong time in the name of our security?

A Dangerous Wager

The document seems to work within a remarkable and, I would suggest, hazardous algebra that admits no room whatsoever for such misstep or error. The farm is bet, as it were, and the wager promises either unprecedented reward or devastating loss. If we can just get the technology right—military, economic, political, ideological—we will not err and our reward is sure. Yet where there are no sustainable structures whereby alternative ways of imagining human flourishing may be put forth, critiqued, and tolerated without falling into unacceptable violence, unintended consequences of our hegemony will surely follow. And where there are few if any sustainable forums or practices of engagement whereby claims of injustice done *in the name* of freedom, democracy, and free enterprise can be redressed, then only rage will result. And we have already seen how, in a technological age, rage can find tools to break free of its confines. And we have seen how legitimate rage can be turned, however so slightly, toward uncontrollable destructiveness.

The question must be asked, then, whether the wager as it has been presented is worth the risk. If what is bet on this proactive American hegemony is global stability, international economy, freedom from fear, and the peace of the world, what is offered as collateral? For one, the pocket books of every American (and indirectly, those of all in the world who will support the debt we will incur to underwrite our control). For another, the military-aged children of every American household and the households of those nations who might join us here or there along the way of this gamble. For another, the freedom of peoples to pursue well-being through patterns of religious, political, and economic life that we haven't thought of first. And for another, anyone who accidentally gets in the way. Pity the mothers who lost their conscripted sons on the battlefields of Iraq, or their daughters in the marketplaces wrongly attacked. We were liberating them, after all. And pity all those whose blood is shed on the way to a promised future that may only be deferred into ongoing war.

Hope from Elsewhere

The preamble to the *Strategy* begins with a gloss on the last century by stating that "the great struggles of the twentieth century between liberty and totalitarianism ended with a decisive victory for the forces of freedom."[10] I've no doubt this is true, and I thank God for it. What is implied here, however, is that this victory was finally won by the force and wit of the nations now in power. After all, it is a statement of dogma for many of those interpreting policy that it was the Reagan administration's belligerence toward the Soviet Union that finally won the Cold War.[11] Because this assumption often warrants the kind of adventurism advocated in the *Strategy*, it is worth at least a passing glance at the conclusion of this essay.

Ignore for a moment that even Reagan's approach was developed after the logic of an internal and shadowy threat of communism destroying us from within had been put to rest, and that his strategy was roughly a crude instance of what Zigmut Bauman sees as the character of contemporary power, namely, "subterfuge and the art of the dodge"—mirroring the very thing we now seek to overcome.[12] Note that at no time did the U.S. invade the Soviet Union, and that there had been decidedly mixed results in cases where the war was fought in proxy lands or by proxy fighters (Korea, Cuba, Vietnam, El Salvador, Israel, Afghanistan). And finally admit, at least for the sake of argument, that the Soviet Union may have largely collapsed under the weight of its own contradictions and through the surprisingly peaceful demonstration of dissent born within its own polity. One of the great ironies of the twentieth century is that a violent and totalitarian system such as the Soviet Union was able to create a political culture and sustain an internal political movement that ended up undoing it, and with relatively little violence.

It took something *other* than American power to undo the Communist threat. It took something that included the force of proclamation from a Polish-born bishop of Rome called Pope John Paul II, and the wit of a Catholic Christian dock worker named Lech Walesa, and the courage of a Russian leader, who was secretly baptized by his believing grandmother, named Mikhail Gorbachev, and the eloquence of a Czech playwright who claimed Jesus over Marx named Václav Havel. And it took more like them. It took patience, and faith, and hope, and a kind of power that cannot be measured by military budgets or tactical plans. And it happened under the radar screens of U.S. intelligence.[13]

Is this a counsel to inaction? Not at all. But it is a counsel to a *chastened* proactivity, far more respectful of international constraints on our own power than this *Strategy* envisions and far less sure that only we can lead. We are, indeed, the most powerful military and economic power in the world at the moment, but this does not mean that we can dominate as this document imagines. There are other kinds of power, other kinds of subterfuge, and other kinds of dodge that we in all our power will never, finally, control. And if we are not undoing such powers through a counterforce of *good* and an overarching sense of responsibility for those who so strongly depend on us, then we may yet lose the war.

History is full of overwhelming powers who were undone from without by wit and passion, or bankrupt from within by nervous self-protection.

We must mind those lessons and find another way. Is it a more fully Christian way we must find? That must be left to the churches to give witness to. I pray we might.

Notes

1. Appendix, 190.
2. Ibid., 189.
3. Ibid., 190.
4. Ibid.
5. Ibid., 190, 199.
6. "In the Cold War, weapons of mass destruction were considered weapons of last resort whose use risked the destruction of those who used them. Today, our enemies see weapons of mass destruction as weapons of choice" (*Strategy*, section V).
7. See "Thoughts in the Presence of Fear," in this volume.
8. See Albert Borgmann's writing on this, including *Crossing the Postmodern Divide* (Chicago: University of Chicago Press, 1992) and *Power Failure: Christianity in the Culture of Technology* (Grand Rapids: Brazos, 2003). Also see Jacques Ellul's classic statements on related matters, especially *Violence* (New York: Seabury, 1969) and *The Technological Bluff* (Grand Rapids: Eerdmans, 1990).
9. Appendix, 207–209.
10. Ibid., 189.
11. See, for example, Paul Wolfowitz, "Statesmanship in the New Century," in *Present Dangers: Crisis and Opportunity in American Foreign and Defense Policy*, ed. Robert Kagan and William Kristol (San Francisco: Encounter Books, 2000), 307–36.
12. Zigmut Baurman, *Liquid Modernity* (Malden, MA: Blackwell, 2000).
13. For a fascinating discussion of the organic religiosity that has undone power in ways no state could imagine, see Robert Inchausti, *The Ignorant Perfection of Ordinary People* (Albany: SUNY, 1991).

3

Thoughts in the Presence of Fear

Wendell Berry

I. The time will soon come when we will not be able to remember the horrors of September 11 without remembering also the unquestioning technological and economic optimism that ended on that day.

II. This optimism rested on the proposition that we were living in a "new world order" and a "new economy" that would "grow" on and on, bringing a prosperity of which every new increment would be "unprecedented."

III. The dominant politicians, corporate officers, and investors who believed this proposition did not acknowledge that the prosperity was limited to a tiny percent of the world's people, and to an ever smaller number of people even in the United States; that it was founded upon the oppressive labor of poor people all over the world; and that its ecological costs increasingly threatened all life, including the lives of the supposedly prosperous.

IV. The "developed" nations had given to the "free market" the status of a god and were sacrificing to it their farmers, farmlands, and communities, their forests, wetlands, and prairies, their ecosystems and watersheds. They had accepted universal pollution and global warming as normal costs of doing business.

V. There was, as a consequence, a growing worldwide effort on behalf of economic decentralization, economic justice, and ecological responsibility. We must recognize that the events of September 11 make this effort more necessary than ever. We citizens of the industrial countries must continue the labor of self-criticism and self-correction. We must recognize our mistakes.

VI. The paramount doctrine of the economic and technological euphoria of recent decades has been that everything depends on innovation. It was understood as desirable, and even necessary, that we should go on and on from one technological innovation to the next, which would cause the economy to "grow" and make everything better and better. This of course implied at every point a hatred of the past, of all things inherited and free. All things superseded in our progress of innovations, whatever their value might have been, were discounted as of no value at all.

VII. We did not anticipate anything like what has now happened. We did not foresee that all our sequence of innovations might be at once overridden by a greater one: the invention of a new kind of war that would turn our previous innovations against us, discovering and exploiting the debits and the dangers that we had ignored. We never considered the possibility that we might be trapped in the webwork of communication and transport that was supposed to make us free.

VIII. Nor did we foresee that the weaponry and the war science that we marketed and taught to the world would become available, not just to recognized national governments, which possess so uncannily the power to legitimate large-scale violence, but also to "rogue nations," dissident or fanatical groups and individuals—whose violence, though never worse than that of nations, is judged by the nations to be illegitimate.

IX. We had accepted uncritically the belief that technology is only good; that it cannot serve evil as well as good; that it cannot serve our enemies as well as ourselves; that it cannot be used to destroy what is good, including our homelands and our lives.

X. We had accepted too the corollary belief that an economy (either as a money economy or as a life-support system) that is global in extent, technologically complex, and centralized is invulnerable to terrorism, sabotage, or war, and that it is protectable by "national defense."

XI. We now have a clear, inescapable choice that we must make. We can continue to promote a global economic system of unlimited "free trade" among corporations, held together by long and highly vulnerable lines of communication and supply, but now recognizing that such a system will have to be protected by a hugely expensive police force that will be worldwide, whether maintained by one nation or several or all, and that such a police force will be effective precisely to the extent that it oversways the freedom and privacy of the citizens of every nation.

XII. Or we can promote a decentralized world economy which would have the aim of assuring to every nation and region a local self-sufficiency in life-supporting goods. This would not eliminate international trade, but it would tend toward a trade in surpluses after local needs had been met.

XIII. One of the gravest dangers to us now, second only to further terrorist attacks against our people, is that we will attempt to go on as before with the corporate program of global "free trade," whatever the cost in freedom and civil rights, without self-questioning or self-criticism or public debate.

XIV. This is why the substitution of rhetoric for thought, always a temptation in a national crisis, must be resisted by officials and citizens alike. It is hard for ordinary citizens to know what is actually happening in Washington in a time of such great trouble; for all we know, serious and difficult thought may be taking place there. But the talk that we are hearing from politicians, bureaucrats, and commentators has so far tended to reduce the complex problems now facing us to issues of unity, security, normality, and retaliation.

XV. National self-righteousness, like personal self-righteousness, is a mistake. It is misleading. It is a sign of weakness. Any war that we may make now against terrorism will come as a new installment in a history of war in which we have fully participated. We are not innocent of making war against civilian populations. The modern doctrine of such warfare was set forth and enacted by General William Tecumseh Sherman, who held that a civilian population could be declared guilty and rightly subjected to military punishment. We have never repudiated that doctrine.

XVI. It is a mistake also—as events since September 11 have shown—to suppose that a government can promote and participate in a global economy and at the same time act exclusively in its own interest by abrogating its international treaties and standing apart from international cooperation on moral issues.

XVII. And surely, in our country, under our Constitution, it is a fundamental error to suppose that any crisis or emergency can justify any form of political oppression. Since September 11, far too many public voices have presumed to "speak for us" in saying that Americans will gladly accept a reduction of freedom in exchange for greater "security." Some would, maybe. But some others would accept a reduction in security (and in global trade) far more willingly than they would accept any abridgement of our constitutional rights.

XVIII. In a time such as this, when we have been seriously and most cruelly hurt by those who hate us, and when we must consider ourselves to be gravely threatened by those same people, it is hard to speak of the ways of peace and to remember that Christ enjoined us to love our enemies, but this is no less necessary for being difficult.

XIX. Even now we dare not forget that since the attack on Pearl Harbor—to which the present attack has been often and not usefully compared—we humans have suffered an almost uninterrupted sequence of wars, none of which has brought peace or made us more peaceable.

XX. The aim and result of war necessarily is not peace but victory, and any victory won by violence necessarily justifies the violence that won it and leads to further violence. If we are serious about innovation, must we not conclude that we need something new to replace our perpetual "war to end war"?

XXI. What leads to peace is not violence but peaceableness, which is not passivity, but an alert, informed, practiced, and active state of being. We should recognize that while we have extravagantly subsidized the means of war, we have almost totally neglected the ways of peaceableness. We have, for example, several national military academies, but not one peace academy. We have ignored the teachings and the examples of Christ, Gandhi, Martin Luther King, and other peaceable leaders. And here we have an inescapable duty to notice also that war is profitable, whereas the means of peaceableness, being cheap or free, make no money.

XXII. The key to peaceableness is continuous practice. It is wrong to suppose that we can exploit and impoverish the poorer countries, while arming them and instructing them in the newest means of war, and then reasonably expect them to be peaceable.

XXIII. We must not again allow public emotion or the public media to caricature our enemies. If our enemies are now to be some nations of Islam, then we should undertake to know those enemies. Our schools should begin to teach the histories, cultures, arts, and language of the Islamic nations. And our leaders should have the humility and the wisdom to ask the reasons some of those people have for hating us.

XXIV. Starting with the economies of food and farming, we should promote at home, and encourage abroad, the ideal of local self-sufficiency. We should recognize that this is the surest, the safest, and the cheapest way for the world to live. We should not countenance the loss or destruction of any local capacity to produce necessary goods

XXV. We should reconsider and renew and extend our efforts to protect the natural foundations of the human economy: soil, water, and air. We should protect every intact ecosystem and watershed that we have left, and begin restoration of those that have been damaged.

XXVI. The complexity of our present trouble suggests as never before that we need to change our present concept of education. Education is not properly an industry, and its proper use is not to serve industries, either by job training or by industry-subsidized research. Its proper use is to enable citizens to live lives that are economically, politically, socially, and culturally responsible. This cannot be done by gathering or "accessing" what we now call "information"—which is to say facts without context and therefore without priority. A proper education enables young people to put their lives in order, which means knowing what things are more important than other things; it means putting first things first.

XXVII. The first thing we must begin to teach our children (and learn ourselves) is that we cannot spend and consume endlessly. We have got to learn to save and conserve. We do need a "new economy," but one that is founded on thrift and care, on saving and conserving, not on excess and waste. An economy based on waste is inherently and hopelessly violent, and war is its inevitable by-product. We need a peaceable economy.

4

Shock and Awe

Life in Mr. Rumsfeld's Neighborhood

James Hudnut-Beumler

At the opening of the United States military campaign against Iraq in 2003, military leaders told the press that instead of overwhelming force, superior firepower would carry the day. Rejecting the Powell Doctrine as outdated, Defense Secretary Donald Rumsfeld described his war-making technique reliant upon high-tech weapons as "Shock and Awe." The Iraqis, faced with the use of lethal, precise weapons to hunt down and decapitate their leadership, would quickly admit defeat and accept the freedom that was America's to give. So much for the theory.

Shock and Awe did not work out the way it was planned. The Iraqis did not quit and welcome the United States and British forces with open arms. Low-intensity war continued to claim the lives of Iraqis and armed forces personnel while civilian life in Iraq became anything but the high-tech Western miracle promised in March of 2003. Shock and Awe did not work on the Iraqis, but it worked on me. I am *shocked* that my country is using preemptive war as a tool of maintaining its global hegemony. I am *shocked* that it is being wrapped up in a package of "Iraqi freedom." I am not only shocked, I am also *awed*. I am *awed* by the sight of Democrats lined up to say, "Me too." "Let's support our troops." "Let's make sure we win big-time."

This is the reason for my awe: it is as though no one in the government is taking the long view on preemptive war in a global context. Fundamentally, if one really cares about

- the long-term future and safety of the United States,
- the movement toward true freedom in oppressed nations ruled by dictators and dictatorial regimes,
- the women and men who serve to defend the nation,

then the posture that must be adopted is one of resistance against the new rules of Mr. Rumsfeld's neighborhood, and of any similar approach that follows his. The fact that no one of sufficient stature in governmental leadership has stood up against the underlying policies and actual foreign adventures of the Bush administration to slow down those policies and actions simply leaves me more acutely aware of the need for leaders in other walks of life and citizens in all places to speak up for peace. Peace is such a soft and wistful word in the minds of many these days. I prefer to think of peace in our context as a form of restraint against our own post-9/11 fears and the arrogance of power in our land as we think beyond sovereign borders. I think of peace as a chain-link fence that keeps us from mistaking another's land for our own and that forces the genuine exercise of judgment in our nation's use of armed force. For now, and to no one's real benefit, the fence of peace is rent with a gaping hole.

In the middle of my university's spring term, I saw a cartoon in the *Vanderbilt Hustler* that pretty well depicted a campus whose students were mostly amused to see their middle-aged professors so passionate about the war. The cartoon showed aging peace protesters holding their predictable signs. One protester says to another, "Psst, what's the latest news in the war?" The clear implication of the cartoon was that peace-oriented people should not have cared or paid attention to what happened to coalition forces or to Iraqis. That such a cartoon was drawn, run, and drew laughs on my and other college campuses means that the voices of peace are not communicating effectively. Most peace people wanted Iraqis free from Baathist oppression. Most of us wanted minimal casualties and for our troops, at least, to behave decently toward prisoners of war and civilians. But, and here's the big *but*, peace people know deep down there is a real danger in this war that we may have attained victory but lost the peace. We are, right now, undermining credibility with the

Arab world and our allies. A clear victory in a preemptive war is a clear and present danger to our values, to our statecraft, and to our troops. It appears that George W. Bush still believes he did nothing wrong, while our world neighbors of states and people are deeply concerned that we are a danger to ourselves and others as a juggernaut out of control.

Supporting the Troops

Before continuing to address the issue of U.S. statecraft abroad, let us take up the matter of what preventive war does to our own citizens, the men and women of the armed forces who are its de facto agents. I hear a great deal in my southern and patriotic setting about "supporting our troops." I think, if anything, I have more empathy for the men and women in our armed forces than I ever did before. I watched with tears like many Americans as Jessica Lynch was rescued and evacuated. I look at pictures of her and of other people who have been killed or wounded, and I note that they often look too young to even be Vanderbilt students. Like many of us, I have learned what they make for a living. These people who are risking their lives for their country are starting out at $12,000 a year. After ten years as sergeants in the army, they may be making $24,000. So for a third of what some of my students' parents pay in a year for a Vanderbilt tuition bill, their peers, the youth of my country, are risking their lives. Campus activists care about livable wages for Vanderbilt food service and grounds crew staff. But the troops we say we want to support are making even less. How is that for a livable wage?

Why do the people serving in the military do it? Well, there's an implicit bargain they take on. They believe they will give part of their lives, even at the risk of their lives, in order to defend a country they have come, by age eighteen, nineteen, or twenty, to love. Our troops believe that their job is to protect and defend the country, not to foster the hegemonic wishes of its ruling class. American armed forces (in our mythic version of ourselves as America-the-good) are supposed to end wars, not start them. So then, here is my worry about those troops we are supposed to support: if this works, Paul Wolfowitz, Dick Cheney, Donald Rumsfeld, or their successors will send them to Korea, to "take out the threat," then to Iran, and so on.

If Mr. Rumsfeld's neighborhood rules come to be enforced by his smaller military that is deployed more of the year, undesirable things are likely to happen to our children who wear the blue and green uniforms of our nation. The career of the United States soldier, sailor, or aviator will increasingly become like being a mercenary in the Hundred

Years War, or in the religious wars of the sixteenth century. Is that any way to support our troops—to sign them on for this war making again and again?

From Military Policy to Statecraft

Sometimes, however, I wonder if Americans, freed from the prospect of the draft, really care, as long as some kid from small-town Texas, Michigan, or Tennessee will take that bargain. Americans readily accept the safety their service provides. Think about that attitude for a moment. I will not even question its moral cynicism. That kind of attitude—"It's not my war; as long as our leaders keep me safe and prosperous, I won't say anything"—has propped up Hitler, Stalin, Saddam, and countless others like them through time. So leaving aside whether a warrior society is good for the warriors, I wish now to consider the long-term consequences of making war an easy instrument of our statecraft. Everything nations do has consequences—win, lose, or draw, we've already scared our neighbors. That fact alone has made us less safe in the long run.

Here is why.

The twenty-first century is shaping up to be a struggle between people and groups who want to be free to believe and live as they wish and those who want to force people to live "the right way." This is the challenge of radical Islam to the secular West. The big picture is freedom versus force; not really faith against faith. Muslims can be good Americans, and God knows, Christians can be very puritanical toward others.

If we want to be on the side of freedom, we need the support and cooperation of the other global neighbors who hate terrorism and getting what you want at gunpoint. But, to the contrary end, Team USA has scared its natural allies.

The situation is like this:

Let us say that you live in a nice suburban neighborhood. Picnics, smiles, barbeques abound. But in one house on the street there's a tyrant. You and the neighbors frequently hear him yelling at his kids and his wife. The kids are sullen, depressed. His wife sometimes has bruises. Concerned, some of you have called in the police. The UN inspectors . . . I mean the *police* . . . come in, don't find anything, can't get the wife or children to make a complaint, and do nothing. The terror goes on.

Now on Friday night, one of your neighbors invites ten of you to his home and says, "What's going on in that house is wrong. Those kids are going to grow up and terrorize the neighborhood; that man tortures his own household. The police haven't done anything, but something must be done, and I've got a plan." He pulls out his extensive collection of guns, stun grenades, night vision goggles, and body armor. He tells you, "We own the night." He asks who's with him and who's against him. Somebody asks what about the dog; he says one dog is a small price to pay for a family's freedom. Someone else asks what if the stun grenade catches the house on fire or the tyrant hides behind his innocent family. Your neighborhood Rambo says, "Freedom is never free."

Put yourself in my fictional situation. Do you feel safe in this neighborhood? Or are you worried about what comes next? Obviously, my argument is that the rest of the freedom-loving countries wonder if we Americans, in our zeal, have gone off our rockers. They wonder what is next. They feel about as safe as you would if someone you work with kept a loaded and recently fired gun next to the mouse pad on his desk.

Freedom is not free; propagating freedom by a calculated policy of easy resort to force is self-defeating.

But many will say, There is a war on; what can I, who neither sent nor can recall troops, do? My answer is simply to take advantage of the fact that this still remains a democratic republic when it comes to life within the United States. If we are not content with Mr. Rumsfeld's plans for the neighborhood, then we must use our voices to keep the pressure up. The time is short but still at hand for patriotic citizens to delegitimate the strategy of preemptive force so that all Americans might get leaders who will pursue freedom with freedom's methods and not by parroting our long-term foes. The war in Iraq was a bad idea when it was rolled out like a new car model in September 2002. It will be an even worse idea next September.

America, God's New Israel?

There is another dimension of America's identity crisis in the new century, and that is that our national self-understanding often plays into the hands of those who would preserve and protect American hegemony at any cost. Americans understand themselves as good and well-intentioned, so much so that any and every international policy or action must be, ipso facto, good.

Often in their national history, Americans have tried to see themselves and their nation as exceptional. Exceptional in the sense of more fortunate, surrounded by a superabundance of good land, minerals, defensible borders, waterways, and hardworking people, to be sure. But Americans have wished to see themselves as exceptional in another sense as well, that of the providentially favored nation. Indeed in this view, which goes all the way back to John Winthrop's speech to his fellow Puritans aboard the *Arabella* on their way to found Massachusetts

Bay Colony, America is the place God favors, because God has great expectations for a holy commonwealth. "Wee shall be like a Citie on a Hill," said Winthrop. This nation was to be a new creation: "God's New Israel," a place where God could make a fresh start with a new chosen people, just as of old.

As a historian, I cannot hear the words "Old Europe" without thinking of this second kind of exceptionalism that so often takes the form of smug national self-assurance that we alone know what is right since the apocalyptic candle of God's great interaction with humanity has been passed from the tired "old world" to a new one, innocent of trickery, deceit, kings, and compromises. Let us never mind the fact that Winthrop's own speech spent an extraordinary amount of time on the dangers that can befall a people who play false with God's favor, since the city on a hill displays its fools and evildoers all the more clearly for others to see. Since some speechwriter helped Ronald Reagan resuscitate the metaphor of the city on the hill (purged of any sense of danger of failing to be good), this kind of American exceptionalism has only grown. And lacking either irony or its own original sense of moral peril, the belief that the American nation is favored by God as a beacon of freedom for the globe is more dangerous than ever before.

America has wanted to be God's New Israel in the sense of some romanticized version of the Davidic monarchy. I think instead that the metaphor of America as the New Israel has ironic bite, for the nation that twenty-first-century America is in danger of becoming is not ancient Israel, but modern Israel. What characterizes contemporary Israel? An occupation in which it can neither succeed nor allow itself to stop. Having gone to undeclared war to put things right by its own lights, it cannot come to grips with the fact that the forces of pacification are hated by the occupied. Violence directed at these forces of occupation begets more violence by the occupiers. How is the contemporary occupation in Iraq all that different from Israel's occupation? The United States told its own people and others that we were going after something threatening to us. We believed we were justified and in the right; and now the local residents are, in many cases, regarding us as an unwelcome addition to their lives. So much for the similarities. American defenders of "Operation Iraqi Freedom" would be quick to point out differences between U.S. and Israeli occupations and the precedents for U.S. intervention in other countries. They would point to the successful occupations and democratic transformations of Germany and Japan after World War II, or the largely successful Bosnia and Kosovo occupations of the 1990s. How, might they ask, is Iraq and the ultimate goal of transforming the

Middle East different from those instances of American power being used for the good?

How indeed? The postwar transformation of Germany and Japan was the result of an unconditional surrender by defeated nations that had previously declared war on the United States and its allies and were now, by virtue of that defeat, in submission to their victors. Iraq had not attacked the United States, nor did the U.S. seek the total victory required to subject the people to total control. As I have argued above, either of these actions would have been problematic in the context of the global neighborhood. Comparisons to the postwar era are misleading in other ways as well, but the most striking feature of the current go-it-alone American mind-set is that we have carried out what to many Iraqis must appear to be a home invasion and now expect to be received as dinner guests.

As for the comparisons to the humanitarian rescues in Bosnia and Kosovo, the situation in those regions was one of humanitarian disaster, where both those in the situation and peoples beyond their national borders agreed that rescue was moral—perhaps even required of other states and people possessing the means for rescue. Iraq lacked such an internal will for liberation by the United States, except perhaps in the Kurdish north. A final difference is that of culture, for in the Islamic world the United States is not viewed as a liberator, as a peer, or as worthy of admiration. Perhaps even more than any other example of forced democratization (including the tragedy of Vietnam, the Spanish American War, the Grenada Invasion, and the most recent "liberation" of Haiti) the desire for American-style democratic capitalism is absent. What America represents and has to offer is not wanted, as much as we would like to give it.

At the beginning of a new century, there can be no doubt that the United States is a global titan. It is able to project and protect power like no other nation in recorded history. Yet Americans have never wished to be an empire despised by others, and that is the fate of all empires. Our American self-conception stands in need of a reality check. The way is clear to be a good, even admired, neighbor among other nations in the global neighborhood *or* a distrusted, violent, and self-absorbed empire. Self-assertions of goodness by a nation that acts abroad in naked and narrow self-interest are worse than laughable; they are dangerous to us and to others. May our dangerous self-deceptions be cleared away before this *pox Americana* destroys our way of life and all we hold most dear for all of humanity and not for just ourselves.

WHAT MUST
WE KNOW?

5

Loving Neighbors in a Globalized World

U.S. Christians, Muslims, and the Mideast

David L. Johnston

Francis of Assisi departed from Italy with twelve brothers on his way to the front lines of the Fifth Crusade in Egypt. The sources are unanimous: his first two goals were martyrdom for Jesus' sake and the conversion of Sultan Malik al-Kamil, who was then engaged in a series of battles with the Crusaders' army. No direct statement in the contemporary sources leads us to cast this encounter as a peacemaking strategy, but, considering the wider context of his ministry and thought, this would be a likely supposition.[1]

Thus, in 1219 two bare-footed monks, St. Francis and his companion, after a severe beating managed to convince the Muslim sentries that they must see the Muslim ruler. Upon their entry into the sultan's ornately decorated tent, St. Francis immediately impressed on Malik al-Kamil that he had come to save his soul from certain destruction. Though the sultan did not convert to Christianity, we do know that he (being known for his mystical leanings) listened and discussed a good while with the monks—thus forcibly dismissing his Muslim jurist advisers, who had reminded him that the Islamic *shari'a* (Islamic law)

stipulated the death penalty for anyone daring to denigrate the Holy
Qur'an. So impressed was he, in fact, that he offered his guests rich
presents (which they earnestly turned down) and granted them escort
back to their military camp.[2]

This historical encounter—a "meeting on the cusp of history"[3]—reflects
a useful paradigm for concerned Western Christians today. Individuals
can facilitate the needed dialogue between civilizations, or they can fail
by remaining trapped by their own cultural stereotypes. The conversation between Islam and the West—at all levels—is even more urgently
needed today, and yet may be just as difficult as it was for St. Francis.
Instead of an unpolished medieval Christian culture entering into dialogue
with an Islamic civilization blossoming in its fifth century,[4] the towering
U.S. world power is seen by a majority of contemporary Muslims as the
vanguard of a new Christian Crusade to control the Muslim heartland,
now in its fifteenth century, from Palestine to Iraq. Though the Crusades
made little impact militarily or culturally on Islamdom,[5] they have been
painfully planted in the Middle Eastern collective memory. Since the 1991
Gulf War they have sprouted up into a potent symbol of the neocolonial
juggernaut imposed on them by the United States.

Fuad Nahdi is the publisher of the British Muslim magazine *Q-News*
and a regular contributor to the British press. He is considered neither
radical nor extremist. His words before the recent Gulf War are worth
pondering:

> Fellow marchers, of whatever faith and none, understand why we oppose
> the war against Iraq. It is not support for Saddam Hussein's murderous
> regime: the Baathist leader is directly responsible for more Muslim deaths
> than anybody in history.
>
> Yet most Muslims see the coming war as anti-Islamic and anti-Muslim.
> The other justifications just don't hold water. Every Muslim child can tell
> you that Iraq does not have a monopoly of weapons of mass destruction,
> that Israel has flouted at least 64 UN resolutions and that one of the most
> despicable leaders in the region, namely Ariel Sharon, leads a govern-
> ment that has unmatched political and financial support from the United
> States.
>
> Whatever the spin, we find it difficult to understand the war except as
> another Crusade. It is not just that George W. Bush pledges that he and
> his administration will act to serve "a just and faithful God." They also say
> they want to build a better Iraq. How can we take them seriously when
> Afghanistan still smolders with violence, death and anarchy and they turn
> a blind eye to the atrocities and injustices of Chechnya and Kashmir? And
> what about Palestine? The occupied territories, as Edward Said put it,
> today are witnessing the onset of mass famine; there is a health crisis of
> catastrophic proportions; there is a civilian death toll that totals at least

a dozen to 20 people a week; the economy has collapsed; hundreds of thousands of innocent civilians are unable to work, study or move about as curfews and at least 300 barricades impede their daily lives; houses are blown up or bulldozed on a mass basis [60 last week]. And all of it with US equipment, US political support, US finance.[6]

All of this is easily substantiated, and having lived in North Africa and the Middle East for sixteen years, I could add more of these legitimate grievances to the Muslim list. It is a matter of urgency that we American Christians listen to what our Muslim neighbors are saying. The purpose of this chapter, then, is threefold: first, to present a brief theological grounding to Jesus' call to love neighbors and enemies in the global context of the twenty-first century; second, to offer a glimpse into some current debates in the Muslim world; and third, to propose several ways in which Western followers of Jesus (and St. Francis) may concretely express their love to Muslims—especially, but not exclusively in the Mideast—in today's climate of global terrorism.

Of Cain, Neighbors, and Enemies

After Cain murders his brother Abel he complains to God about his terrible punishment: "[A]nyone who meets me may kill me" (Gen. 4:14). Israeli rabbi Arik Ascherman, cofounder of Rabbis for Human Rights, comments on this passage by saying that his first reaction is always that Cain deserves whatever happens to him.[7] Yet before the story reveals whether Cain in fact repents, "God provides Cain with a mark of protection. Two wrongs will not make a right." Ascherman then proceeds to tell the story of one of many days in which Jewish and Palestinian peace activists and international volunteers went to help Palestinian villagers harvest their olives. Not that these peasants would normally have needed help, but either their land was suddenly declared a "military zone" by the Israelis in order to help local Jewish settlements expand, or the settlers themselves forced the Palestinians to leave at gunpoint. In this case the settlers had been stealing the crop for three days.

This time, the soldiers watched over them without hindering the volunteers' efforts. But more and more armed settlers gathered and kept jeering the soldiers for defending the "shahidim" (Hebrew plural of the Arabic *shahid*, or "martyr"). At one point, the security forces ordered the international harvesting team to abandon the first row of trees, but then the efforts at negotiation by the Israelis in the group completely broke down, and the settlers got their way: the soldiers forced the peasants and their friends off their own land.

Sadly, muses Ascherman, Palestinians are seen by Israeli society as Cain—all are terrorists or support terrorists, and therefore deserve any bad treatment meted out to them, when in fact it is the Israeli occupation with the accompanying construction of settlements on Palestinian land that is the main motive behind Palestinian violence to begin with. Further, "those of us working in the field knew a year and a half before the Intifada that human rights were leading average Palestinians to lose faith in the peace process and that Israelis were shooting for a day and a half before the first Palestinian shot was fired."[8]

This situation of conflict must lead us to reflect theologically, continues Ascherman. We must differentiate between Noah, who sought to save only his own family, and Abraham, who interceded for any ten innocent people who still might be in Sodom before its judgment. He concludes:

> If we are all to survive in this Land, we must truly become worthy of our heritage as the children of Abraham. That heritage is more than land, which we fight over. It is also the spiritual and moral heritage of one who was willing to put his personal feelings and "He deserves it" aside, and remind God that even God must deal justly with all—friends and foes, enemies and strangers.[9]

Now to the writings of the "New Covenant." In the telling of the parable of the Good Samaritan, Jesus takes the lesson of Cain and Abraham a step further. Two surprises awaited his Jewish contemporaries in this story. First, the saint to emulate was neither the Levite nor the priest, but a Samaritan, or a Palestinian in Ascherman's narrative. Stereotypes are shattered. Before people belong to a particular social or ethnic grouping, they are created in God's image. Each one is "my neighbor." But this is not enough, warns Jesus. The second shock is that God holds us accountable for how "neighborly" we are. Simply cataloging people will not do. And of course, when this is coupled with Jesus' command to love enemies, we begin to appreciate his radical call to discipleship. The Great Commission is about spreading the good news to all, but it already includes the command to love neighbor and enemy in word and in deed. Somehow, as Christian citizens of the United States, we should resist the trap of thinking "we are good and they are evil." A repentant heart humbly reviews its own sin before accusing others. Terrorism—"premeditated, politically motivated violence perpetrated against innocents"[10]—morally wrong and reprehensible, is hardly the monopoly of one group. One need not be a pacifist to acknowledge that many civilians are killed in wars in ways that arguably could be avoided.

It is plain to see how those on the receiving end of such casualties consider this, too, as terrorism.

And what about the repressive measures of regimes who respond to terrorism with "disproportionate force"? U.S. allies such as Morocco, Egypt, Israel, Saudi Arabia, and Pakistan routinely use torture and incarcerate thousands with no trial.[11] Israel assassinates those it considers leaders in the terrorist network and, worse yet, deprives the entire population in the occupied territories of their most basic human rights. A recent Christian Aid report states:

> The Palestinians are currently living in a state of extreme, worsening poverty and fear for their future. . . . Almost three quarters of Palestinians now live on less than US$2 a day—below the United Nations poverty line. . . . The international community must either find the political will to tackle this situation, or witness a further descent into abject poverty, despair and hopelessness—a potent mix that will blight the lives of millions of people for years to come.[12]

Much of our reluctance to "be neighborly" stems from ignorance, which in part can be traced to U.S. media that have consistently favored Israelis over Arabs, offering little criticism of governmental policies beyond the usual bipartisan squabbles.[13] To love our neighbor—who may be defined by many as our enemy—we must gain a global perspective and a holy curiosity, in this case, about Muslims and the state of Islam today.

Islam Today: An Unstable Mix of Variant Readings

To his credit, President George W. Bush quickly differentiated between Islam and the practices of those who committed the atrocities of September 11, 2001. He characterized Islam as "a faith based upon peace and love and compassion" committed to "morality and learning and tolerance." Dana Milbank writing for the *Washington Post* describes "this rare disagreement with conservatives" as crucial to any kind of success in the war against terror: "The administration, and moderate governments in Arab and Muslim nations, are struggling to prevent the war on terrorism from becoming what Osama bin Laden wants: a war of civilization between the Judeo-Christian West and a resentful and impoverished Muslim world."[14]

My argument in this section is twofold: that the government is partly right but the total picture is more complex. And second, that if we pursue the policies laid out in the *National Security Strategy*, the balance could easily shift to the advantage of the more aggressive and violent proponents of Islam.

It is well known that under the impulse of his "revelation" and religious community building in Medina in the last ten years of his life (622–32), the Islamic prophet Muhammad had set his sights not only on the unification of the Arabian peninsula but also on the north, where the Persian/Zoroastrian Sassanian and Christian Byzantine empires had both grown weak after decades of war. In twenty years the lion's share of the Mideast as we know it today fell under the military and political sway of his successors.

There is no soft-pedaling the fact that Islam initially spread through the force of military might. Yet the common phrase, "Islam spread by the sword," can also be misleading. The Byzantine Empire, just to name one Christian political entity at the time of Muhammad, routinely used force against non-Chalcedonian believers, and thus the Coptic Orthodox Church of Egypt (the non-Chalcedonian Monophysites) at first welcomed the Arab invaders. By A.D. 750, even as the second dynasty of Muslim rulers established itself in Baghdad, only 10 percent of the population of the vast Islamic empire was Muslim. Forced conversions did occur but were more the exception than the rule. In other words, one should compare standards of religious tolerance within similar periods. Between the Crusades, the Inquisition, the forced conversion of many native peoples by the colonial powers in Latin America, and the European Thirty Years War in the eighteenth century, Christian states were arguably more violent than many Muslim states at the time.

More pertinent in our understanding of "Islamic terrorism" today, however, is that Islam expresses a multifaceted phenomenon: at least five historical tendencies compete for dominance.[15] The first tendency springs from a group called the Kharijites, which broke off from among the supporters of Ali, the fourth caliph (which means "successor," "deputy"), who was Muhammad's cousin and son-in-law. The Kharijites had Ali assassinated, and the caliphate moved from Medina to Damascus. The Kharijites are the purists of Islamic theology. They have remained a small and opposed minority, but at times are capable of mounting serious military attacks against central powers. Their theology points to salvation by works, whereby only those upright people who faithfully follow the original teachings of the Prophet can be considered true Muslims. Finally, as the most democratically oriented, they insist that the leaders of the Muslim community be elected (no dynasties) and exemplify the same virtues as the Prophet.

Though the Kharijites disappeared as a group, their mind-set has resurfaced at different periods. The Wahhabis ruling Saudi Arabia display many of their ideals, even though Osama bin Laden opposes the

Saudi corruption, hereditary rule, and perceived compromises with the "Christian" West on the same puritan basis. A contemporary Muslim leader exemplifying this Kharijite tendency was the author of the most influential qur'anic commentary in the twentieth century, Sayyid Qutb, a member of the Muslim Brotherhood executed by Egyptian president Nasser in 1966. Qutb believed most Muslims belong to the pre-Islamic "era of ignorance" (al-jahiliyya), and foremost among them are the elitist leaders of Muslim countries, in reality propped up by the West.

A second movement arose to counter the extremist tendencies of the Kharijites: the Murji'ites. Those of this tendency, like a silent majority that never took official power, stood clearly for faith, rather than works, determining Islamic identity and salvation. With their main goal of unity among the disparate streams of early Islam, tolerance surpassed every other virtue.[16]

Third, a movement spearheaded by a class of religious scholars (ulama)[17] gradually evolved into the Sunni mainstream of Islam in the ninth and tenth centuries. It borrowed a great deal from the Murji'ites and developed a truly ecumenical approach to theology and politics. For the ulama, salvation was by faith as well as works, while Muslims who committed grave sins, if they repented, were forgiven and thus remained Muslim. For all intents and purposes, the great majority of Islamic history demonstrates this Sunni tendency with a de facto separation of religion and state. Corrupt and oppressive rulers were to be tolerated as long as they vouchsafed a public sphere, at least Muslim in name, in which Muslim institutions operated unhindered. The institution of the caliphate stood till the Mongols sacked Baghdad in 1258, but the caliph increasingly had become a religious figurehead, and either the Sultan or local warlords held the reins of political power. The Shi'ites (roughly 16 percent of Muslims today) separated from the Sunnis over the issue of succession, as they felt that the caliph, or imam of the Muslim community, must come from the family of the Prophet. Today those historical differences are receding.[18]

A fourth tendency, that of mystical Sufism, must be mentioned, though it has minimal contemporary political influence.[19] It is thanks to many brotherhoods and Sufi orders of all stripes prevalent during the medieval period that Islam spread so rapidly in Africa and Asia. Also during that period significant cross-fertilization took place among Muslim, Christian, and Jewish mystics. The Crusades acted as a catalyst, not only for the spreading of Islamic philosophy and science into Europe, but also for elements of Islamic theology and spirituality spreading west. Yet today, apart from the fact that most Euro-American converts to Islam come through the Sufi door, Islamic mysticism is not a rallying cry for any sizable number of Muslims.

The fifth and last movement is that of the Muslim rationalists, the Mu'tazilites. Against the emphasis of the last two groups on predestination, they championed free will and the role of human reason in articulating the content of revelation. They drew heavily on Greek philosophy, and we know that Thomas Aquinas found much inspiration in the Muslim theological works drawn up from this perspective. For almost forty years of the ninth century their views prevailed, but then their influence waned considerably until the nineteenth century, when as a result of forced interaction with the colonizing West, issues of rationalism, free will, and, eventually, human rights, became hotly debated in Muslim circles. This reform movement initiated in nineteenth-century Egypt by Jamal al-Din al-Afghani and Muhammad Abduh gained momentum in the twentieth century. Yet with the abolition of the caliphate (held by the Turkish Ottomans for nearly 400 years) in 1924, the seeds of contemporary Islamic fundamentalism, or Islamism, were sown. In such a climate of upheaval the penetrating question begged a reply: Could the message of Islam be adapted to contemporary political and social norms, or must Islamic law in its classical medieval formulation still by and large hold today?

On one level, the question posed seems merely political: can Islam sanction any kind of government, including a rule of democratic pluralism? But it is more far-reaching than that; it goes to the nature of Islam itself. Is Islam a religious law that must rule supreme in a land (and globally, in the view of some) in order for Muslims to be truly themselves, or is Islam simply a set of religious beliefs, rites, and values?

We are familiar with the fundamentalist, or islamist, answers to this question—from the Taliban to al-Qaeda, to the Islamic resistance movements in southern Lebanon (Hizbollah) and Palestine (Hamas and Islamic Jihad).[20] Yet they are not unique, for many others at the grass roots are considering the weight of this islamist response. Egypt, for one, has witnessed a dramatic religious revival from the bottom up. Since President Sadat's signing the Camp David Accords of 1979 and his successor Hosni Mubarak's continued pro-American policies, which have been accompanied by an increasing gap between rich and poor in Egypt, a "soft islamism" largely sympathetic to the more moderate[21] Muslim Brotherhood party now dominates Egyptian civil society. As such, if the political and military stranglehold of Mubarak's single-party regime were broken to allow for a democratic system to prevail, the islamists would likely gain a majority in the Egyptian parliament. This same phenomenon is true for many Mideastern regimes. Interestingly, however, if such conservative regimes come to power and their citizens are given freedom, as has been witnessed in Iran, governments become progressively more open and liberal with time.

Jordan, another key U.S. ally, now teeters on the edge of public re-
bellion against King Abdullah's pro-American stand on all key issues.
He did not dare intervene when his State Security Court handed down
a prison sentence to three journalists for "defaming the prophet Muhammad,"[22] though while giving a speech at the Economic Forum in
Davos, Switzerland, Abdullah boasted of Jordan's "freedom of expression, speech, and thought, including a free media." We remark that in an
increasingly conservative Islamic atmosphere, the Muslim proponents
for a more secular version of society can be muzzled—even if one of
them be the king!

And lastly, the situation presents even more dramatically in Pakistan
where the government that has fallen in line with the Bush "war on terror"
is a military government with little political legitimacy. Consequently,
the oldest islamist party, the Jamaat-i-Islami, has grown in popularity
by leaps and bounds.[23]

In concluding this look at those grassroots movements that embrace
the islamist expression of Islam, one needs no prophetic gift to predict
an ominous clash on the horizon unless the U.S. changes its foreign
policies in this part of the world.[24] Since the Afghan war to topple the
Taliban, many have begun to characterize the U.S. strategy as "the Karzai effect"—propping up docile regimes, like that of Hamid Karzai in
Afghanistan, that are pro-American without reflecting the will of the
people. If the U.S. truly worked toward the implementation of democracy
and human rights, it would gain respect by practicing what it preaches
and win the battle of the minds in the long run. In this case Egypt and
Saudi Arabia would be candidates, neither of aid nor of strategic alliance, but of sanctions. Thus the U.S. slogan of "liberation" to justify its
attack on Iraq fell on deaf ears in the Arab world, not because people
didn't agree that Saddam Hussein was a ruthless dictator, but because
American hegemony over the region (including the control of Iraq's oil
fields) seemed to them to be the first U.S. concern.

Besides the islamists, a growing number of Muslim intellectuals are
calling for a bold reinterpretation of the Islamic tradition. *New York
Times* columnist Thomas L. Friedman recently called attention to Iran's
Hashem Aghajari, a college professor who after his arrest and subsequent
death sentence provoked massive student protests around the country.[25]
Aghajari had compared the necessary rethinking of traditional theology to
the Protestant Reformation in Christianity. Friedman argues that "what's
going on in Iran today is precisely the war of ideas within Islam" and
that this is the most important war of all. I would agree. Actually, the
most widely read Iranian reformer today is Abdelkarim Soroush. While
his more than twenty books are in Persian, a recent book in English
provides a fascinating and readable introduction to the work of one of

today's most creative Muslim thinkers: *Reason, Freedom, & Democracy in Islam: Essential Writings of 'Abdolkarim Soroush*.[26] His main thesis is that religious knowledge is humanly constructed and therefore fallible and subject to constant revision in light of new circumstances and contexts. The divine *shari'a*—for him the qur'anic text and the principles of Islamic law—is flawless and eternal, but Islamic jurisprudence, because it is a human effort to adapt *shari'a*, must continuously evolve.

For lack of space I will offer just two more illustrations of Muslim thinkers reinterpreting Islam for the contemporary context. Abdulaziz Sachedina, at the University of Virginia, is a typical Muslim American professor—liberal and ready to cooperate with any group interested in issues of peace and human rights. Unlike many others who lecture on Islam either in Middle East Studies or Religion departments, Sachedina writes about these issues theologically. His recent book *The Islamic Roots of Democratic Pluralism* reclaims the Mu'tazilite heritage as he reexamines the traditional dogmas of Islam in their sociopolitical and cultural context. "The project's guiding tenet," he announces from the start, "is the value of preventive diplomacy in promoting democracy, communication, and pluralism as antidotes to the tragic violence that wracks the globe."[27] He holds that the mistake of most Muslim apologetic works on human rights written from a conservative standpoint is that they ignore the epistemological implications of transposing a historically conditioned religious, legal, and political system to the contemporary nation-state. By concentrating on the "ethicoreligious concepts which directly impact our contemporary concerns for pluralism and individual autonomy," Sachedina states, "the history of the Muslim community's movement toward a just and equitable society provides creative and fertile ground for an evolving interpretation of the divine purposes indicated in the Koran."[28] Humanistic secularism has not found the way to unite people around values of democracy and human dignity. Space must be found for religious values, contends Sachedina, to contribute their strength and enduring qualities to the global discussion, and in this sense the Islamic community can, alongside other religious communities, provide leadership in the twenty-first century. His conclusion is simple:

> The challenge for Muslims today, as ever, is to tap the tradition of Koranic pluralism to develop a culture of restoration, of just intrareligious and interreligious relationships in a world of cultural and religious diversity. Without restoring the principle of coexistence, Muslims will not be able to recapture the spirit of early civil society under the Prophet. The principle of 'equals in creation' can serve as the cornerstone of Muslim civil society.

The principle must be implemented globally to restore fractured human relations through forgiveness and compassion.[29]

How many Muslims actually read and are affected by his thoughts? Admittedly, mostly Western-educated Muslims like himself—certainly a growing number around the world—have little chance of gaining the ear of the masses who struggle to eke out an existence in harsh, impoverished urban conditions around the Muslim world, and who are becoming ever more convinced that their suffering is in part due to the Christian West's crusade to keep Muslims weak and backward.

Khaled Abou El Fadl may represent the exception here. He holds the Chair of Islamic Law at UCLA, after growing up in a family of legal specialists (*ulama*) in Kuwait, steeped in qur'anic and Islamic law from his early years. He came under fire for his writings on democracy there, so then came to the U.S. on an ambitious study program in 1982. First he graduated from Yale with a bachelors degree, then from the University of Pennsylvania with a law degree, and finally from Princeton with a Ph.D. in Islamic Studies. A prolific book collector, reader, and writer, he devoted his energies to refuting the "puritan" ideology of the islamists. He has received many death threats, mainly because of his positions on the equality of the sexes and tolerance in Muslim society. But what makes Abou El Fadl a most formidable foe to islamist thinkers is his ability to quote from a dizzying array of traditional sources. Many of his books are banned in the Gulf countries, which only makes them more popular.

Though Abou El Fadl's English works are valuable sources for specialists in Islamic law, one book serves as an enlightening introduction to his perspective and thought: *And God Knows the Soldiers: The Authoritative and Authoritarian in Islamic Discourses*.[30] First, he offers a good deal of autobiographical material—an eye-opening perspective on the Muslim community in America and abroad and his personal frustration with their reactionary reflexes. Second, the whole book is a gloss on an event that took place in 1996 on an NBA basketball court when a Muslim player refused to stand up to the national anthem. Amidst the flurry of Muslim commentaries and controversies on the issue, Abou El Fadl not only looks at the detail of a particular *fatwa* (legal ruling) on the subject in the light of established Islamic legal practice, but also sets out to deconstruct that text in light of its sociocultural context—demonstrating his competence in postmodern methodology and thought.

Representing God's law to other human beings is truly an onerous burden. The burden is not simply to represent the evidence of God's particular injunctions, but to internalize God's goodness and morality within oneself. The burden is one of diligence and honesty, not just with the textual sources, but with oneself—to bring the intellect and conscience to bear upon how we evaluate and understand the evidence . . . to sift through the evidence in order to identify the indicants that have become tainted with human ugliness or that were initially articulated as concessions to human weaknesses, and then to rise above this ugliness and weakness so as to articulate a vision of the law that reflects the beauty of Godliness. In all of this, the most challenging burden is to consistently be mindful of the fact that despite all the efforts and investigations, no person can rest with the assurance of being forever right.[31]

This vision of law, no doubt, leaves little patience for the rigid, arrogant, and self-righteous versions of *shari'a* articulated by the "authoritarians," whether in Nigeria, Saudi Arabia, or Malaysia. But, as with other such voices, this vision will have little chance of gaining ground as long as the U.S. underwrites despotic Muslim allies to further its interests and asserts its right to change other regimes by force. I can attest to the fact that this "internalization of God's goodness and morality within oneself" is taking place in more radical Muslim circles as well. In my doctoral research conducted in the West Bank and Gaza in 1999, I interviewed Shaykh Ahmad Yasin, the spiritual leader and founder of Hamas who was assassinated by the Israeli military in 2004, and engaged in several conversations with one Hamas leader in Hebron who outwardly condemned suicide bombings.

Following in the footsteps of Brother Andrew (founder of Open Doors), who had deliberately befriended many of these Hamas leaders, I was pursuing a theological dialogue. My main interest was in the qur'anic notion of humanity's caliphate, "trusteeship" or "deputyship," of God on earth. Both shaykhs clearly supported the growing emphasis in Muslim circles on the inalienable dignity of the human person created by God and placed by God on earth to manage its resources, both natural and human. Though the Qur'an does not teach that God created Adam and Eve in his image, the notion of humankind's stewardship (*khilafa*, from the word *khalifa*, "caliph") easily undergirds a notion of human rights that applies to all people, as individuals and nations, and that is congruent with the UN's Universal Declaration of Human Rights (UDHR, 1948).[32] The Muslim literature on this topic in the last twenty years has been voluminous, and one can now say that the gap between some of the earlier Islamic writings on human rights and the UDHR is narrowing progressively. Shaykh Yasin assumed that this was the case: Jews, Christians, and Muslims—and all people of good will—should be able to work together for justice and respect for the human rights of people. On the other hand, he has been known to waver on whether the 1967 borders would be sufficient for a Palestinian state. As with the issue of suicide bombing, the Hamas position concerning this point has hardened considerably during this second intifada. The Islamic movements feel justified in killing Israeli civilians just as their own civilians are being killed on a daily basis. Sadly, theological reflection in a context of violence and oppression tends to veer toward exclusion of the other.

Time is needed—as it was in the U.S.—for these nations to develop a solid tradition of pluralistic democracy and human rights. To pursue a multilateral approach that submits to and applies international law along with the rest of the international community serves as the best antidote to terrorism, and thus entails a determination to be impartial toward nations that flout UN resolutions—toward both Israel and Iraq, for instance. Freedom requires justice and law to usher in deliverance from grinding poverty, equitable trade relations between rich and poor countries, and zero tolerance for oppression and human rights abuses. With these freedoms in place radical fundamentalism will begin to drain from those countries that teem with volunteers for suicide operations against American targets. Though not a solution of force, it lends itself to long-term effectiveness. More importantly, Jesus reminds us of the consequences inherent with militarism, that those who live by the sword will die by the sword.

Suggestions on Loving Our Mideast Neighbors

In the post–Cold War world of the twenty-first century, U.S. global hegemony is felt across the board—in the military, political, economic, and cultural spheres. The White House *Strategy* documents the reality of this globalized world. Regarding alliances, it states: "In exercising our leadership, we will respect the values, judgment, and interests of our friends and partners." Missing, however, is any concept of a global dialogue of civilizations. Only "friends and partners" are worthy of consultation, and that only as our interests dictate, as the next sentence confirms: "Still, we will be prepared to act apart when our interests and unique responsibilities require."[33]

The *Strategy* astutely declares that a battle, or "struggle of ideas," exists within the Muslim civilization. One could only applaud a U.S. policy that would aim to support the views of progressive Muslim intellectuals who are currently losing ground. However, the avowed policies of the *Strategy* guarantee the opposite effect. Specifically, with its doctrine of absolute military supremacy and limited multilateral patience,[34] the paternalism of "supporting moderate and modern government" and reserving the right to "convince or compel states to accept their sovereign responsibilities"[35] becomes apparent, especially in the Muslim world. The cynical reading of this text by Arabs is certainly reinforced by the reality they experience on a daily basis, as the closest U.S. Arab allies are also some of the most undemocratic and oppressive regimes.

In view of the far-reaching implications of the *National Security Strategy* and of the realities I have described in the world of Islam, and in the Mideast in particular, I conclude with a few practical suggestions—food for thought and prayer—for concerned American Christians seeking to follow their Master's command to be neighborly to all:

1. We are first citizens of the kingdom to come. "My kingdom is not from this world," Jesus said to Pilate (John 18:36). Only secondarily are we citizens of an earthly realm. Citizenship in this first kingdom mandates us as twenty-first century Christians to find practical ways of loving all the people of our second citizenship, thus working for a more peaceful and righteous world. With Jesus we act and pray, "Thy kingdom come. . . ."

2. We prefer negotiation and conflict resolution in recognized international bodies as the means to arbitrate between nations and groups (including "terrrorists") over the recourse to military action. I believe we ought to embrace international law, by signing all the relevant treaties for arms reduction and providing leadership for the progressive destruction of all nuclear weapons; by joining and coming under the jurisdiction of the newly formed International Criminal Court in The Hague, as well as engaging in stewardship of the earth by signing the Kyoto Treaty on the reduction of carbon dioxide emissions. As former president Jimmy Carter has urged us, we also should take these steps because we are fast losing credibility in the eyes of even our allies.[36] Gulf War II is a logical application of the *Strategy* but will tragically demonstrate for many the recklessness of a unilateral policy. Equally, the U.S. should not have shouldered the military occupation of Iraq alone, but worked directly with the UN on establishing a credible peacekeeping force under UN auspices (as it should have done in Afghanistan).

3. We pray and lobby for a consistent U.S. foreign policy driven by the priorities of democracy and human rights, with more pressure brought to bear on U.S. "allies": Morocco, Algeria, Tunisia, Egypt, Gulf states, and especially Saudi Arabia, and now Central Asia.

4. We pray and lobby for a just solution to the Israeli-Palestinian conflict, along the lines of the Saudi proposal of March 2002, guaranteeing the security of Israel behind its 1967 borders (with the exception of Jerusalem, which would be the shared capital)

and the dignity of the Palestinian people in a viable state, with due compensation for the refugees of 1948 and 1967.

Saint Francis dared to go beyond the crusading paradigm of his time and share his faith with the leader of the Muslim realm his army was fighting. In America today we are challenged by his example to rethink the political implications of our faith in order to follow Jesus, who excluded no one but embraced all in his cross, calling us to be true neighbors to everyone in today's world, and in particular to Muslims here and in the Mideast.[37]

Post Scriptum

In light of the U.S.-led invasion and occupation of Iraq, I would recommend three articles that confirm the principles enunciated in this chapter. The first is a report by the United States Advisory Group on Public Diplomacy for the Arab and Muslim World, led by former ambassador and Arab specialist Edward P. Djerejian and commissioned by the Bush administration. They write that the "United States must drastically increase and overhaul its public relations efforts to salvage its plummeting image among Muslims and Arabs abroad" and that "hostility toward America has reached shocking levels."[38] I would go further than simply recommending more investment in U.S. propaganda abroad and becoming an active participant in the Middle Eastern media. Though the commission cites U.S. policy as partly responsible for the sharp rise in anti-American sentiment globally, it falls short of advocating a change of policy—the need for which is underscored by the second article. A prize-winning British journalist traveled through Iraq in August and September of 2003 and wrote a long article on her findings, "A Land Ruled by Chaos."[39] Though mainstream American journalists eventually began to question the wisdom of the invasion in the first place, they come nowhere near to this degree of honesty and depth of analysis. The last article confirms Middle Easterners' worst accusations: the participation of an extreme-right Israeli politician in the "reconstruction of Iraq."[40] The situation in the Mideast now presents more danger and, at the same time, more opportunities for U.S. Christians to partner with their brothers and sisters from many other parts of the world in showing "neighborly" love to all parties involved, and especially to Muslims. Yet they cannot be content to give out tracts or plant underground churches. They must also protest the wanton killings of civilians by both Israelis and Palestinians, the destructive power of the "Great Wall of Israel," and the U.S. hegemonic designs on this strategic and volatile part of the world.

Notes

1. Out of hundreds of books written on St. Francis, only a handful have been written exclusively on his encounter with Islam—and so far I have not discovered any in English. A French one, *Rencontre sur l'autre rive* ["A meeting on the other bank"] emphasizes how in the violent context of the Crusades, this astonishing act of two monks could only be seen as the antithesis of war and a conscious modeling of being "neighborly" to the "enemy." The author, Gwenolé Jeusset, is a Franciscan, and he sees his book as an encouragement for Christians to get beyond the violent and fanatical stereotypes Westerners have entertained about Muslims over centuries (France: Les Éditions Franciscaines, 1996).

2. The sultan had invited him to stay longer, but Francis replied that he would do so only if he converted. In the end, he did stay several days and was received lavishly.

3. David F. Forte uses this encounter to introduce his collected studies entitled, *Studies in Islamic Law: Classical and Contemporary Application* (Lanham, MD: Austin & Winfield, 1999). I recommend this book as a nonspecialist introduction to the nature of Islamic law, a crucial aspect, yet sadly ignored, of our contemporary twenty-first-century world civilization.

4. Forte writes that as the First Crusade took Jerusalem, the "barbaric" Europeans "had thrust into civilization at its height. The Islamic realm in 1099 was more developed in medicine, in the decorative arts, in the science of metallurgy, in architecture, in commerce, and in cuisine. At that time Islamic law was at least five centuries in advance of the West, while Greek philosophy was being read and Arabic philosophy was being written. Except in religion, the Crusaders in the Levant quickly adopted much of the culture of their hosts" (ibid., 6–7).

5. If one looks at the immense Islamic legal literature, the Mongol invasions of the thirteenth century (with the sacking of Baghdad in 1258) left a much greater and lasting impact on Muslim thought and civilization.

6. "On the Brink of War No One Seems to Understand Muslim Fears," *Independent*, Feb. 15, 2003 http://argument.independent.co.uk/commentators/story.jsp?story=378439.

7. From a mailing. A significant Jewish movement worldwide has risen up against Israeli policies toward the Palestinians. See, for instance, Gush Shalom's website and related links, http://www.gush-shalom.org, and The Jewish Voice for Peace, http://www.jewishvoiceforpeace.org. In September 2002 representatives from eighteen European Jewish peace groups gathered in Amsterdam and founded a new organization called European Jews for a Just Peace. All these groups oppose the Israeli occupation of the territories taken in 1967 (Gaza and the West Bank) and advocate a two-state solution to the conflict, with Jerusalem as their shared capital.

8. Quoted from a mailing. The impression one gets from the U.S. media is that the Israeli army stumbles into human rights violations in its defensive measures against Palestinian suicide bombings. The stepping-up of military offensives in Nablus and Gaza since Sharon's reelection reveals an overall strategy at work now for years: the design to "transfer" the Palestinian population to Jordan and elsewhere. See Robert Blecher's excellent study on this policy of ethnic cleansing sanctioned at the highest levels of Israeli leadership: "Living on the Edge: The Threat of 'Transfer' in Israel and Palestine," *Middle East Report* 225 (Winter 2002): 22–29. See also the theoretical underpinning of the current campaign to boycott Israeli products as a way to undermine the apartheid of the

last colonial state: Kaylin Goldstein, "Reading Palestine-Israel on Coloniality and Other Paradigms," *Middle East Report* 225 (Winter 2002): 50–2.

9. Quoted from a mailing.

10. *The National Security Strategy of the United States of America*, http://www.white house.gov/nsc/nssall.html, 5. See the appendix to this volume.

11. Such violations of human rights are regularly documented by NGOs such as Amnesty International, Human Rights Watch, and in the Israeli case, especially by B'Tselem. For a candid article on Mubarak's sham democracy, see Jackson Diehl's "Gorbachev on the Nile?" *Washington Post*, Feb. 10, 2003, A21. On the regular use of torture against Egyptian political opponents, see Mary Anne Weaver, *A Portrait of Egypt: A Journey through the World of Militant Islam* (New York: Farrar, Straus & Giroux, 1999).

12. See http://www.christianaid.org.uk/news/media/pressrel/031027p.htm. In this January 27, 2003 report, Christian Aid also recognizes the Palestinian Authority's failure to tackle this poverty and calls for its reform. On the other hand, it would be nearly impossible for any Palestinian government to alleviate the economic plight of a population herded in little enclaves and kept under curfew months on end.

13. By way of comparison, the British press is much more nuanced and informative. Compare, for instance, the *Guardian*, the *Economist*, the *Independent*.

14. "Conservatives Attack Portrayal of Islam," Nov. 30, 2002, A4. Milbank quotes Pat Robertson as saying, "Adolf Hitler was bad, but what the Muslims want to do to the Jews is worse." Also, Jerry Falwell called Muhammad a "terrorist" but later apologized.

15. The main ideas of this section are taken from Forte's *Studies in Islamic Law*, 235–48.

16. One has to realize how troubled the first thirty years of Islamdom (after Muhammad's death in 632) was: out of the first four caliphs (officially, the only "rightly guided" ones), three were assassinated by discontents. The first candidate for "golden age" was the ten-year rule of the Prophet in Medina, and the second (rather far behind in Muslim judgment) is the first two hundred years of the Abbasid caliphate (750 on).

17. In a first stage they were the *hadith* specialists, that is, the collectors and expert critics of the hundreds of thousands of reports on Muhammad's sayings and deeds. Since the Qur'an contains precious little legal material, Islamic law developed mainly from the work of these *hadith* specialists. By the ninth century, however, there arose from among them a class of specialized legal scholars and a number of schools of Islamic law. Only four of those stood the test of time, still functioning today, though the tendency now is to unify the schools as much as possible.

18. The Islamic revolution of Iran (1979) not only sparked religious and political revival throughout the Sunni world, but brought with it several innovations, the greatest of which is the installation of a "republic" with a constitution.

The popular mood has now turned against the power wielded by Shi'ite clergy, and that power struggle, if the U.S. can keep its distance, will turn to the favor of a constitutional democracy.

19. Sufism is not in Forte's list, but I add it because it represents such a great portion of the Islamic heritage and could well be revived at a future date.

20. I am among those who do not capitalize "islamist" or "islamism," as they reflect an ideology and not the religion of Islam itself—like "capitalism" or "fundamentalism." The most comprehensive and up-to-date discussion on radical Islam and the growing liberal reaction in Muslim circles is Hebrew University professor Emmanuel Sivan's "The Clash within Islam," *Survival* 45, no. 1 (Spring 2003): 25–43.

21. By "moderate" I mean that they denounce violence as a way to change government policy. Instead, they advocate a democratic process of free elections and a multiparty political system. For an excellent glimpse into "progressive" islamism, see Azzam

S. Tamimi's *Rachid Ghannouchi: A Democrat within Islamism* (New York and Oxford: Oxford University Press, 2001).

22. "Jordan Blasphemy Verdict Shakes the Free Press," *Christian Science Monitor*, Feb. 18, 2003, http://www.csmonitor.com/2003/0218/p.07s02–wome.html. The authors had "speculated on Muhammad's sexual potency after marrying Aisha, the favorite of his 14 wives." The same article also showcases the courageous protest of award-winning Palestinian evangelical journalist Daoud Kuttab, who published an article decrying this judgment in the English-language *Jordan Times*.

23. Rory McCarthy, "Building an Islamic Future," Feb. 21, 2003, *Guardian*, http://www.guardian.co.uk/elsewhere/journalist/story/0,7792,900086,00.html.

24. For a useful summary of the dangerous implications of U.S. policy in the Mideast, see Mahmood Monshipouri, "The Paradoxes of U.S. Policy in the Middle East," *Middle East Policy* 9, no. 3 (September 2002): 65–84.

25. "An Islamic Reformation," Dec. 4, 2002, A31, col. 5.

26. Abdelkarim Soroush, *Reason, Freedom, & Democracy in Islam: Essential Writings of 'Abdolkarim Soroush*, trans. and ed. Mahmoud Sadri and Ahmad Sadri (New York and Oxford: Oxford University Press), 2000.

27. Abdulaziz Sachedina, *The Islamic Roots of Democratic Pluralism* (Oxford and New York: Oxford University Press, and Washington, D.C.: The Center for Strategic and International Studies, 2001), 13.

28. Ibid., 17.

29. Ibid., 138–39.

30. Khaled Abou El Fadl, *And God Knows the Soldiers: The Authoritative and Authoritarian in Islamic Discourses* (Lanham, Md.: University Press of America, 2001).

31. Ibid., 154.

32. "He created Adam in His image" is a saying of the prophet Muhammad attested in two of the canonical collections. For a detailed discussion on the issue of the human caliphate and the UDHR, see my article "The Human *Khilafa*: A Growing Overlap between Islamists and Reformists on Human Rights Discourse," *Islamochristiana* 28 (2002): 35–53.

33. All these quotes are from *The National Security Strategy of the United States of America*, Appendix, 217.

34. Only twice in the 24 pages of the *Strategy* is the United Nations mentioned by name (7), and though the *Strategy* mentions the idea of enlisting international support several times, the multilateral style is vastly overshadowed by the self-proclaimed right to act preemptively against terrorists or any hostile state (Appendix, 195, 201–3) by the adamant contention that the U.S. military is above international law (Appendix, 216), and by the clear implication that world peace depends on unchallenged American military superiority (esp. Appendix, 214–15). Ironically, one of the five characteristics given for "rogue nations" is disregard for international law (Appendix, 200).

35. *Strategy*, Appendix, 195–6. Brian Whitaker describes how Ariel Sharon found much receptiveness with John Bolton (undersecretary of state) in suggesting that after Iraq the U.S. should change the regimes of Iran, Syria, and Lybia ("Conflict and Catchphrases," *Guardian*, Feb. 24, 2003, http://www.guardian.co.uk/elsewhere/journalist/story/0,7792,901982,00.html). Finally, George Monbiot argues that as the U.S. gradually pulls out of international agreements, it is sowing the seeds that could in time destroy its imperial rule ("Out of the Wreckage," *Guardian*, Feb. 25, 2003, http://www.guardian.co.uk/Columnists/Column/0,5673,902365,00.html).

36. "The Troubling New Face of America," *Washington Post*, Sept. 4, 2002, http://www.washingtonpost.com/wp-dyn/articles/A38441-2002Sep4.html. See also, from his

former national security adviser, Zbigniew Brzezinski's editorial in the *Washington Post*, Feb. 18, 2003, http://washingtonpost.com/wp-dyn/articles/A27771–2003Feb18.html.

37. The allusion here is to the theological work of Miroslav Volf, so easily applicable to all the conflict situations on the globe (*Exclusion and Embrace: A Theological Exploration of Identity, Otherness, and Reconciliation* [Nashville: Abingdon, 1996]).

38. Steven R. Weisman, "US Must Counteract Image in Muslim World, Panel Says," *New York Times*, Oct. 1, 2003, http://www.nytimes.com/2003/10/01/politics/01DIPL.html ?ex=1066021829&ei=1&en=7b1315cc0377ac8e.

39. *Guardian*, October 4, 2003, www.guardian.co.uk/international/story/0,3604,1055697, 00.html.

40. Brian Whitaker, "Zionist Settler Joins Iraqi to Promote Trade," *Guardian*, Oct. 7, 2003, http://www.guardian.co.uk/Iraq/Story/0,2763,1057561,00.html.

6

Selling America, Restricting the Church

Michael L. Budde

Transnationalism is not a new element in Christian life and practice. From its beginnings Christianity balanced a concern for the local church with a lived sense of the unity of the church across political and ethnic borders. From Paul's collection for the Jerusalem church to the hospitality extended (sometimes at substantial risk) to evangelists and delegates from faraway sister churches, the Christian movement contextualized local allegiances with membership in the universal body of Christ.

Such is important to remember amid contemporary enthusiasms for matters global. Pundits now assess the global expansions and linkages of everything from terrorism to basketball, cartoons to bond traders. If these and other features of life are "globalizing" as a result of long-term changes in communications, economics, transportation, data management, and the like, it is important to recognize that—to the extent that these affect the churches—they are part of the "*re*globalization of Christianity" (as I describe it) rather than creating something never before seen.

The so-called era of Christendom maintained, among other things, "a true overarching unity and a focus of loyalty transcending mere kingdoms or empires—Christendom offered a higher set of standards and mores, which alone could claim to be universal."[1] This form of Christian transnationalism collapsed under the assault of secular nationalism, itself both cause and consequence of the coercive variety of Christian expansionism pursued by the Spanish, Portuguese, and other European colonialists.[2] What emerged was our current circumstance of churches in principle tied to one another, but in practice identifying their religious duties as coterminous with those of "their" national states or local political/ethnic authorities. The willingness of Christians—Catholic, Protestant, Orthodox, and "other"—to kill their brothers and sisters in Christ on orders of national authorities is but one expression, played out countless times, of how being a loyal citizen has trumped being a Christian as a primary allegiance and identity.

This circumstance is finally showing possibilities for transformation, ironically in part thanks to the instruments of corporate globalization (the aforementioned innovations in travel, media, and awareness). Space considerations require I assume rather than demonstrate my contention that there are now more and/or deeper institutional, congregational, interpersonal, and affective ties between Christians in many countries (outside traditional immigrant diaspora networks, e.g., Polish Catholics in Warsaw and Chicago). From sister-church ties between individual congregations to two-way flows of mission personnel, Christians are finding more reminders of the transnational quality of the Jesus movement at every turn. In the parts of the world where Christianity is growing fastest, in which the majority of the world's Christians now live, several commentators point to the potentially greater importance of universal and transnational loyalties—*ecclesial* loyalties—compared to the more narrow (sectarian, perhaps?) claims of the nation-state.[3]

While clearly uneven, irregular, and unstable, this "reglobalization of Christianity" is already beginning to play itself out in socially and politically significant ways. Consider, for example, the worldwide opposition of the Christian world to the U.S. invasion of Iraq—a litany of church-to-church statements and exhortations that called upon Christians to oppose the war, even in opposition to the positions of their national leaders (as in Britain and the United States). Pope John Paul II, no pacifist himself, spoke out repeatedly in advance of (and in opposition to) the invasion of Iraq, forcing some Catholics in the United States to choose between their ecclesial and political leadership.[4] The neo-imperial policies prevailed, but secular elites were required to expend significant resources (public and private) in reasserting the primacy of national allegiances over transnational religious calls for solidarity and opposition to militarism. Secular prerogatives prevailed, but the potential for future problems caused by an emerging Christian transnationalism has attracted the attention of leaders for whom the American future contains the application of military force on a regular basis. These applications may be in terms of the "war on terrorism," against so-called rogue states, or against movements opposed to the stipulated U.S. definition of "political and economic liberty."[5]

Shoring-Up National Allegiance

The reglobalization of Christianity poses potential political problems for aggressive American ambitions that presuppose certain minimal levels of public support for armed interventions and attacks. For more than two decades, American elites worried about a "crisis of patriotism" among large sectors of the polity—insufficient zeal for American symbols and stories, pools of cynicism and apathy, and inadequate appreciation for "being American" as one's ultimate allegiance and identity. Official U.S. policy is now committed to an open-ended war to "rid the world of evil," in President Bush's words to a prayer service that sounded as much like a war rally on September 14, 2002. This policy promises aggressive steps to preserve and extend U.S. national interests and "values."[6] Given this, or similar policies that might follow, the need to reaffirm state loyalties is more evident than ever, and the incipient reglobalization of Christian solidarity is an obstacle to be overcome. For if Christians in the United States become more reluctant to kill their brothers and sisters in Christ who live under another national banner, the capacities of American power projection become uncertain. Christians who begin struggling with orders to kill other Christians are but one short step from hesitating to kill non-Christians, whom Christians believe are also children of a loving and generous God.

In this context, governmental and private initiatives to boost patriotism also aim to encourage a narrow, truncated ecclesiology within the Christian world. Christians who ignore the corrosive effects of resurgent nationalism in all its expressions overlook the war on the churches that is part and parcel of the renewed glorification of America. Nationalism, especially when armed and on the march, ought be seen as a sectarian heresy in conflict with the universality of the Christian gospel and God's construction of a new people from all peoples and nations, and whose allegiance is to the kingdom of God rather than to the fragmented lesser powers of the modern state system.

Reasserting Patriotic Imperatives

Issued just before the second anniversary of the September 11 attacks, a report from an education policy group met with praise from across the conservative-liberal divide. "Education for Democracy," issued by the Albert Shanker Institute, claims that American students don't get a sufficiently positive picture of American history, politics, and society. In announcing the report, former congressman (and chair of the Permanent Select Committee on Intelligence) Lee Hamilton noted, "We're not conveying to young people forcefully enough the American heritage, the American way of life." The claim of insufficiently pro-American curricula was rejected by Peggy Altoff of the National Council for the Social Studies, who claimed that public schools strive for balanced presentations rather than "emphasizing the negative."[7]

Reports like this remind us that a central purpose of public schooling in the United States and elsewhere has always been indoctrination of the young (and their parents in an indirect fashion) into nationalist ideologies and identities. This indoctrination has intended to diminish and dilute the integrity of particularistic communities (like the church) in order to replace it with a love of country and an exaltation of its leaders, purposes, and destiny. However much they disagree on other things, the mainstream of American leaders have agreed that

> for democracy to survive, it requires the education of each generation to the ways of knowledge and active participation in the preservation of a way of life. These are not innate behaviors, they are learned. Thus the role of the school becomes paramount in preserving the Republic.[8]

Before September 11, persons committed to the primacy of the state in matters of allegiance and ideology bemoaned the shortcomings of school-based civic formation. With increased ethnic and cultural diversity the norm in many parts of the country, liberals and conservatives alike began calling for new programs of civic formation and patriotism (varying to the degree that "tolerance" is idealized and inflected as an American value) in the schools in order to corrode more particularistic identities that might exist as alternatives to fidelity to America. While the U.S. Supreme Court prohibits crudely coercive measures like state-compelled participation in the Pledge of Allegiance,[9] it allows a whole host of indoctrination measures, "unofficial" compulsion, and other approaches to cultivating nation-worship. For example, teachers can be required (under penalty of dismissal for noncompliance) to start the school day with the Pledge of Allegiance or some other patriotic exercise, and the federal courts have no objection to a history course designed to promote patriotism . . . by teaching only history that would tend to inspire patriotism. As long as naked compulsion is not used, government schools may seek to invade the sphere of intellect and spirit.[10]

It is this sort of curriculum that the Shanker Institute and similar bodies, public and private, want to increase as means of patriotic nurture after September 11 and the invasion of Iraq. At all levels of government, and involving private actors of many sorts, the reassertion of nationalism via schools includes initiatives and proposals like the following:

- At the federal level, in 2002 President Bush implemented a number of directives intended to increase patriotism among the nation's primary and secondary school children. These included recommended programs of mass recitation of the Pledge of Allegiance, the use of military veterans to teach "Lessons of Liberty,"[11] and grant programs to bring historic American memorabilia to school districts across the country.
- State and local measures included passage of a new law in Pennsylvania requiring the pledge on a daily basis, and a resolution by the New York City school board to require the pledge during the school day and at all school-wide assemblies and events.[12]
- Private measures ranged from prayer services at the base of school flagpoles (a favorite among evangelical Christians) to a threat leveled against a suburban Minneapolis school district by the American Legion (withdrawing a $100,000 contribution unless it required recitation of the Pledge of Allegiance).[13]
- The armed forces have taken advantage of federal legislation—one old law, one new one—to increase access to the nation's high schools and universities for recruiting and public relations purposes. After September 11, military attorneys adopted a more rigorous interpretation of the Solomon Amendment, under which the government can withdraw all federal funds from law schools that bar military recruiters (or universities that remove ROTC programs against the military's wishes). Many law schools—including Harvard and Yale—barred military recruiters on the grounds that the armed forces violated the schools' antidiscrimination policies with reference to homosexuals. Faced with the loss of hundreds of millions of federal dollars ($350 million for Yale, for example), the schools have now opened their doors to military recruiters without restrictions.[14]

The new law through which the military uses schools for public relations and recruiting is the so-called No Child Left Behind law passed in 2002. A little-known section of the law prohibits school districts from denying student records and recruiting access to the military if it provides such to colleges and universities. The law is expected to force more than 15 percent of American high schools to reverse policies banning military recruitment, according to supporters of the measure.[15]

Government use of the military to inculcate patriotism has escalated dramatically in recent years—from the upsurge of JROTC programs in inner-city high schools (including running entire high schools in Chicago and elsewhere) to significant increases in military advertising budgets and promotional moves into youth culture via sophisticated "first-person shooter" video games aimed at young boys. Spending on recruitment, advertising, and promotion aimed at the young adds up to several billion dollars per year, according to several estimates.

Additionally, the military has once again become a force in Hollywood, with the Pentagon lending production assistance (including access to aircraft carriers, military installations, and fighter jets) to television programs and big-budget films that offer a pro-military story line and imagery. Having missed recruitment goals a few times in the late 1990s, several branches of the military have moved into entertainment media to enhance the attractions of military life and patriotism—assisting in films like *Pearl Harbor, Black Hawk Down,* and others. In exchange for its valuable cooperation, the Pentagon exercises close control over film content; as the Pentagon's "movie liaison officer" puts it, "Any film that portrays the military as negative is not realistic to us."[16]

The cumulative effects of this multilevel campaign to enhance American nationalism are already appearing. From 1975 to 2002, according to a recent Gallup poll, Americans expressing a "great deal" or "quite a lot" of confidence in religious leaders fell from 68 percent to 45 percent; those expressing the same views of Congress declined from 40 percent to 29 percent. At the same time, however, confidence in the armed forces rose from 58 percent to 79 percent. A comparable poll by the Harvard Institute of Politics in April 2003 found that 75 percent of 1,200 undergraduates interviewed trust the military "to do the right thing" either "all of the time" or "most of the time"; in 1975, a Harris poll of persons 18–29 years of age found only 20 percent expressing confidence in military leaders.[17]

The increased reliance on popular culture and advertising to sell nationalist allegiance invites consideration of another, thus far less successful, effort to market the preferred image of America to target audiences. Like practices of school-based propaganda, this initiative works to undermine traditional practices of Christian solidarity and ecclesial unity, albeit in paradoxical ways. At issue here is an array of programs, offices, and campaigns to promote a more favorable picture of "America" to the world, especially to peoples and countries perceived as hostile to American ambitions and power. This is the world of "public diplomacy" as practiced by the United States government and related private partners.

The centerpiece of these efforts has been the creation of the Office of Public Diplomacy within the State Department in 2001. Its founding director was Charlotte Beers, a legendary Madison Avenue advertising executive who had run two of the world's top ten advertising agencies before taking on the "American account." The mission given to Beers—get people to "stop hating America" through the use of slick advertising and promotional campaigns—testified to a widespread faith in the efficacy of American salesmanship and glossy presentation. That it has proven to be a complete failure thus far suggests that even high-quality sizzle cannot compensate for unpopular policies and actions—for example, trying to improve the U.S. image in the Arab world while leaving untouched policies that seem unfavorable to the Palestinians and others.

Before resigning unexpectedly in March 2003, Beers launched several high-profile advertising campaigns abroad—showcasing the freedoms and quality of life enjoyed by American Muslims, testimonials to the religious liberty enjoyed by Muslims in the United States, and promoting the launch by another State Department office of an Arab-language radio station (Radio Sawa) that combined youth-oriented music (by local and international artists) with news produced from a pro-U.S. standpoint. These various efforts involved partnerships to varying degrees with private advertising agencies and broadcasting companies, all aiming to win "hearts and minds" without changing the essentials of American foreign policy.

The Office of Public Diplomacy is only one agency created in recent years to deal in propaganda and salesmanship aimed at overseas and domestic audiences. Others include the White House-created Office of Global Communications, a steering group that sets the "line of the day," or the single message the Bush administration wants all government agencies to emphasize to the news media that day (used especially in the run-up to the Iraq invasion; governmental spokespersons are expected to seek out opportunities to reinforce and proffer the line of the day in their interactions with journalists, even if the latter initially seek information on other topics.[18] Additionally, the Pentagon established, then disbanded, then reestablished several offices and programs dealing with propagating a pro-U.S. message and views, including the Office of Strategic Influence (shut down before it started, over concerns it would plant false news stories in the media—a practice in place before and after its rise and fall). The Pentagon also proffered a huge domestic data-collection and -analysis initiative, Total Information Awareness (TIA), which would gather and collate personal information from individual purchases, transactions, event attendance, governmental and credit records, and more—to look for patterns suggesting possible terrorist activity. Like the Office of Strategic Information, the TIA met with vocal opposition upon its first public scrutiny; the TIA reemerged a few months later, however, with decidedly less fanfare, as the Terrorism Information Awareness program, the name under which it currently operates. Convicted Iran-Contra figure John Poindexter devised the TIA as part of the Defense Advanced Research Projects Agency (DARPA), the research-and-development hub of the Pentagon. In all of these, state action in pursuit of foreign policy objectives involves intentional practices of opinion formation, image management, and reinforcing notions of state-centered loyalty. (It is less clear how TIA fits this assessment, given the classified nature of much of its work, but its data-collection capabilities could conceivably be used to enhance propaganda campaigns in the same way that commercial advertisers use personal data to devise more effective appeals and pitches targeting consumers.)

The Office of Public Diplomacy, by most accounts, has performed poorly during Beers's tenure and since her resignation. A recent report for a congressional subcommittee detailed many shortcomings in American public relations policy and called for dramatic increases in funding and coordination among various federal agencies working to improve the U.S. image abroad, especially in Muslim countries. Efforts to date, according to the report, have been ineffective and perhaps counterproductive.[19]

Still, even poorly run campaigns of international attitude formation have implications for the transnational character of the church. First, by stressing the Americanized nature of all religious groups in the U.S. (the focus of the "Muslims in America" campaign), the government tells the rest of the world, including church members worldwide, that Christians in America are thoroughly assimilated and subordinated to national loyalties; persons acting on such a proffered impression may contribute to self-fulfilling practices that overlook or thwart possibilities for transnational ties between churches that would otherwise exist. Christians elsewhere may well put less trust in their American coreligionists if they perceive them as happy inhabitants of the imperial condominium. Second, to the extent that state public relations affects both domestic and international audiences, it reinforces the smooth blending of religion and nationalist loyalties at the center of indoctrination efforts in schools, the military, and popular culture. Other consequences are possible, depending on the direction such public diplomacy efforts take in the future, but most scenarios offer more to trouble Christians than to reassure them in their ecclesial identity.

Conclusion

Emphasizing the transnational nature of Christian discipleship is not akin to a naïve cosmopolitanism or an idealized "world citizenship" that knows no home or sense of place. Rather, it is a recognition that Christians are not Christians in isolation, that they depend on ties of brotherhood and sisterhood with others—dead and alive—to live out their baptismal vows while on sojourn in the earthly city. In theological terms, there is no contradiction between the local church and the universal church—they are the same body, whose health depends upon comity and mutual assistance among themselves. Indeed, the reglobalization of Christianity both advances and presupposes a greater degree of local rootedness and distinctiveness—akin to simultaneous globalizing-localizing dynamics observed with reference to economics, culture, and politics in our time. It may be that the territorial state, pulled simultaneously by transnationalizing and localizing forces, is now fighting for its institutional life by any means necessary.

Nationalism sunders Christian unity, putting in its place a sectarianism of the most violent kind—killing on behalf of a collective that is smaller than the church universal, indeed one that often requires killing other Christians in the interests of the state. It took the modern state system several centuries to domesticate the Christian movement into more or less fragmented groups who identified more with "their" country than with the body of Christ. That the body of Christ is showing signs of repairing its breaches, that Christians in many parts of the world are finding ways around, over, and through the barriers of separation and Reformation—all of this looks threatening to many states, but especially to the most powerful one. The American empire has been built upon the truncated and diminished loyalties of an Americanized Christianity; its apologists in the state and in the churches will not rest until the promise of a reglobalized Christianity is extinguished, or at least quarantined. Whether they will prevail against the Spirit of unity and hope, at least in the short term, remains to be seen; in the long term, Christians know that the church will endure after the empires of the world—including the American version—have passed away.

Notes

1. Philip Jenkins, *The Next Christendom: The Coming of Global Christianity* (New York: Oxford University Press, 2002), 10.

2. E.g., Andrew Walls, *The Missionary Movement in Church History: Studies in the Transmission of Faith* (Maryknoll, N.Y.: Orbis Books, 1996), 258–59.

3. E.g., Jenkins, *Next Christendom*, 11–12.

4. See, for example, Laurie Goodstein, "Catholics Debating: Back President or Pope on Iraq?" *New York Times*, March 6, 2003.

5. *The National Security Strategy of the United States of America*, 2002, Introduction. See the appendix to this volume.

6. These almost by definition cannot conflict, e.g., *National Security Strategy*, sec. 3, 9.

7. Ben Feller, "Report Criticizes Negativity in Civics Class," *Chicago Sun-Times*, September 10, 2002, 42.

8. John Cogan, "Civic Education in the United States: A Brief History," *International Journal of Social Education* 14 (1999): 1.

9. *Barnette v. West Virginia Bd. of Educ.*, 319 U.S. 624 (1943).

10. Tyl Van Geel, "Citizenship Education and the Free Exercise of Religion," *Akron Law Journal* 34 (2000): 1.

11. Cecelia O'Leary and Tony Platt, "Pledging Allegiance: The Revival of Prescriptive Patriotism," *Social Justice* 28 (2001): 3, 41.

12. "Pledging for Patriotism," *Newsletter on Intellectual Freedom*, 51, no. 1 (January 2002).

13. Ibid.

14. Kristin Eliasberg, "Legal Jeopardy," *Nation* 275 (2002): 15, 26.

15. "Should Your High School Tell the Military Where You Live?" *New York Times* Upfront, Jan. 24, 2003; David Goodman, "No Child Unrecruited," *Mother Jones* 27 (2002): 6, 18–19.

16. V. Dion Haynes, "Hollywood Boosts the Military," *Chicago Tribune*, May 27, 2001.

17. Robin Toner, "Trust in the Military Heightens among Baby Boomers' Children," *New York Times*, May 27, 2003.

18. This approach to "message management" was perfected by the Reagan administration team of Mike Deaver, David Gergen, and others in the 1980s—see Mark Hertsgaard's still valuable book *On Bended Knee: The Press and the Reagan Presidency* (New York: Farrar, Straus & Giroux, 1988) for the best treatment of the practice.

19. Steven Weisman, "U.S. Must Counteract Image in Muslim World, Panel Says," *New York Times*, October 1, 2003.

How Might
We Talk?

7

Imperial Exegesis

When Caesar Interprets Scripture

Stephen B. Chapman

". . . we Americans are the peculiar, chosen people—the Israel
of our time; we bear the ark of the liberties of the world."

Herman Melville, *White-Jacket* (1850)

On September 11, 2002, President George W. Bush engaged in an
official act of biblical interpretation, carefully choreographed
for television. Before a brilliantly illuminated Statue of Liberty, President
Bush ended his address to the nation on the emotional anniversary of
the previous year's terrorist attacks with these words:

Ours is the cause of human dignity: freedom guided by conscience and
guarded by peace. This ideal of America is the hope of all mankind. That
hope drew millions to this harbor. That hope still lights our way. And the
light shines in the darkness. And the darkness will not overcome it. May
God bless America.[1]

Left unsaid in Bush's speech (and unnoted in the official transcript), however, was that his stirring conclusion had involved a citation of the Gospel of John from Christian Scripture. Since every citation is also an interpretation, it seems important to ask about the kind of scriptural interpretation Bush offered the American people that night.

In the New Testament, the prologue to the Gospel of John reads:

> In the beginning was the Word, and the Word was with God, and the Word was God. He was in the beginning with God. All things came into being through him, and without him not one thing came into being. What has come into being in him was life, and the life was the light of all people. The light shines in the darkness, and the darkness did not overcome it. (John 1:1–5)

John's words here tell about Christ, of the deep mystery regarding Christ's relationship to God the Father and of the salvation Christ has brought to "all people." Christ himself is "life" and the "true light" (cf. John 1:9). Although threatened by the spiritual darkness of ignorance (John 1:9–10) and confronted with willful rejection (John 1:11), the light of Christ was not "overcome" (past tense!). Christ the Son appeared on earth as flesh and blood in order to reconcile creation with God the Father (John 1: 12–13) and perfectly to make known God's abiding will (John 1:18).

As can be seen even in this brief description, the logic of John 1 is intensely theological, communicating the very heart of the Christian gospel by means of highly symbolic language. What Bush offered in his speech, by contrast, was the cadence of the biblical passage, stripped from its actual context, as a means of giving rhetorical resonance to traditional American values like human dignity, freedom, conscience, peace, and hope. Bush also changed the tense, so that "light" became descriptive of America's present role within foreign affairs while the decisive victory against "darkness" was made into something still to happen in the future, although the end was not in doubt.

In all this, however, the application of religious language to political values is certainly nothing new. Moreover, many contemporary Christians would view such values as ultimately related—in some way—to the teachings of their faith. By employing this kind of religious language, was not the president authentically speaking out of his own orthodox Christian conviction, simply keeping his rhetoric appropriately abstract in recognition of the pluralism now found within U.S. society?

The answer must be "no" on both counts.

To be sure, there is a long history of using biblical language in U.S. political discourse.[2] Even in recent history, Ronald Reagan's "city on a hill" and Bill Clinton's "new covenant" stand out as prominent examples.

At one level, it is easy to dismiss such religious metaphors and tropes as the watery gruel of civil religion. Yet these tropes continue to be used precisely because they are still effective. Not only is there a lingering Christian consciousness within contemporary culture that yearns for a more vital link between faith and politics, there are many Christians and even non-Christians who look to their politicians for personal inspiration. Even if the specific beliefs of particular political leaders are not shared, the fact that such figures have beliefs at all continues to resonate strongly within a cynical citizenry. Americans, in fact, tend patronizingly to discount as "policy wonks" those politicians who speak in pragmatic terms alone. Curiously, at the same moment in history when capitalism appears to have won a global victory, people appear more in need than ever of appeals to transcendent values. Perhaps these two things are not unrelated.

From this perspective, therefore, a Christian might well greet President Bush's religious rhetoric as a courageous attempt to articulate the moral dimension of public policy. Richard Cizik, vice president of the National Association of Evangelicals, argues exactly along these lines:

> [Presidents] have every right to use theological language. Why? Because in our form of government, they're not just the head of [their] party but the head of the state. In that role, it's a president's job to be "national healer and consoler." To describe Saddam Hussein as evil—what some theologians have objected to—in my estimation, is entirely appropriate. It sets off [Bush's] opponents [who believe that] evil is a result of the failure of social institutions or the result of human ignorance but rarely that of the depravity of the human heart. Yet that is exactly what is the case with Saddam Hussein.[3]

For Cizik, the head of state actually has a duty to acknowledge and address the abiding verities of the human condition. To ask the president to withhold moral, even theological, judgments is fundamentally to misunderstand his role.

However, there are then further shoals to be navigated for Cizik and other advocates of this view. European allies and the Arabic world have not responded well to the president's theological rhetoric. They know from long experience that the language of "good" and "evil" makes fashioning compromise significantly more difficult. How can a politician risk appearing to strike a deal with "evil"? Such language rules out compromise almost by definition. Just as troubling is the all-too-easy assumption that America is "good," again almost by definition. Bush himself discovered this danger the hard way, eventually being forced to distance himself publicly from the rhetoric that conservative religious figures like Franklin Graham, Pat Robertson, Jerry Falwell, and Jimmy Swaggart had used to demonize Islam, although they were arguably just following Bush's lead in taking up such language. "Islam," Bush belatedly said, "as practiced by the vast majority of people, is a peaceful religion, a religion that respects others."[4] So one danger involved in the president's inclination to announce moral judgments is simply that they may prove in the end to have been politically counterproductive.

It follows that the president may well need to become more selective about the occasions when he speaks to America as its "healer and consoler" and more mindful of how his words will be received in the rest of the world.[5] An example of this kind of role confusion seems to lie behind the conclusion to Bush's call for new Palestinian leadership, on June 24, 2002. After urging Israelis and Palestinians to work together for peace, Bush finished his address with a reference to Deuteronomy 30:19: "I have set before you life and death; therefore, choose life."[6] For Muslim listeners, a concluding verse from Hebrew Scripture conveyed bias rather than fairness, but Bush's biblical citation was likely geared for internal consumption. (As has often been said, in America all politics is domestic.) Thus, another danger arising from the current style of presidential religious rhetoric is that the old American tendency toward isolationism from world affairs may be reinforced. A related, but further, danger is that such rhetoric may actually hamper U.S. efforts to play an increased global role as the only remaining superpower.

Even within domestic politics, however, the president's religious language may prove more divisive than unifying. The president and his staff are certainly not unaware of the pluralistic character of contemporary U.S. culture. Michael Gerson, Bush's chief speechwriter, claims that the president's addresses have intentionally steered clear of any explicit references to "Jesus" or "Christ," stating that "there is a responsibility for public officials to maintain a principled pluralism that respects the important role of faith, but does not favor any sectarian creed."[7] According to Gerson, Bush appropriately invokes religious categories by avoiding any specifically Christian references.

Richard Cizik makes a similar point: "We're not so pluralist that Hindu, Muslim, Christian and Jew don't all resonate to an appeal to transcendent values. The only people I hear squawking are in university settings."[8] Yet this seemingly populist claim of "principled pluralism" falls short in at least two crucial ways. First, this "pluralism" is in practice uniformly unidirectional, moving from traditional Christian categories to more abstract values only loosely based upon them (e.g., "freedom," "hope," etc.). The conceptual underlay of these categories is still Christian enough to be noticed and to prevent a straightforward translation into the categories of other religious systems.[9] Moreover, President Bush has yet to balance his quotations of Christian Scripture with citations from the Qur'an or the Bhagavad Gita.[10] It is fundamentally dishonest to state "pluralism" as a goal of the president's speeches but then smuggle into his discourse a succession of exclusively Christian categories, no matter how watered down.[11]

Second, as Bush's quotation from the Gospel of John makes evident, more is at work in his rhetoric than the expression of abstract Christian "values." Bush's use of John 1:5 involves an analogy in which the referent of the language undergoes a crucial shift. In John, the light of the world is Christ; in Bush's speech that same light is now America. To be sure, a long tradition exists in U.S. history of interpreting America as the "new Israel," a rhetorical move that invests America's national project with salvation-historical significance: America as a divinely-authorized mission to the world.[12] Bush, however, has taken this tradition of biblical typology one critical step further. Despite Gerson's assurances that particularistic Christian language has been assiduously avoided, by using John 1:5 Bush has applied unmistakably christological language to the United States of America, now investing the nation with *messianic* meaning. In other words, George Bush used the occasion of his September 11th anniversary speech to describe the U.S. with the same language that the New Testament reserves for Christ alone. As the president stood in front of the dazzling "light" of the Statue of Liberty, his symbolic substitution could not have been any more plain—or idolatrous.

Bush's nationalistic appropriation of John's Christology is also not an isolated incident. In his 2003 State of the Union address, Bush cribbed a line from a well-known evangelical hymn ("There Is Power in the Blood"), intoning, "There's power, wonder-working power, in the goodness and idealism and faith of the American people."[13] Evangelicals especially should be appalled at the way the real "power" praised in this hymn—"the blood of the lamb"!—was replaced in the president's version by a vague secular humanism. Even in Bush's 2001 inaugural address, his tendency toward a christological interpretation of America was signaled by his reference to the story of the "good" Samaritan:[14] "And I pledge our nation to a goal: When we see that wounded traveler on the road to Jericho, we will not pass to the other side."[15] In the biblical account of that story the point being made is how love for God is necessarily linked to love for neighbor. The two, rightly understood, are mirror expressions of each other and therefore inseparable. In Bush's version, however, care for the neighbor is abstracted from any kind of religious value system whatsoever and turned into a nationalistic welfare initiative.

As these examples show, Bush's use of religious language is neither genuinely pluralistic nor authentically orthodox. The tragedy of the situation is that George Bush apparently considers himself an evangelical

Christian, and yet he cannot recognize blasphemy for what it is. Michael Gerson also has an evangelical pedigree, having majored in theology at Wheaton College and once served as a staff writer for Charles W. Colson. No one should be more concerned to safeguard the uniqueness of Christ than evangelicals, whose theology and piety is so resolutely christocentric. Still, even assuming Bush and his supporters all have the best of intentions, the application of Christ language to America ought to be opposed by every Christian. If not outright idolatry, this kind of rhetoric is still blasphemous speech, speech in which crypto-Christian language is used to confer messianic significance upon the state. That is not at all the kind of "principled pluralism" Gerson claims to be pursuing as a matter of policy. The rhetorical move in question neither shows sufficient respect for the Christian faith nor avoids privileging it. Instead, coded Christian language is used to advance a political agenda at great remove from what Jesus actually taught. The state is ever alert for opportunities to use the authority of Christ as a talisman for its advancing armies. If Christians do not insist on safeguarding that authority, the state will be only too glad to put Christ to another use.

So why have Christian conservatives been so supportive of the president's debased religious rhetoric?[16] Some are probably just unwilling to criticize a Republican administration. Many, no doubt, are simply pleased to have a president who wants to quote Scripture at all—and are willing to overlook a lack of nuance from a man who has never claimed to be a biblical scholar or theologian. Even so, a certain anxiety has been evident, not least in dismissive treatments of Bush's critics as "squawkers."

Richard John Neuhaus, chief editor of *First Things*, actually did express an uneasiness with Bush's September 11 anniversary speech. While his sympathies are certainly with conservative politics, he is too fine a theologian not to perceive the danger of applying Christ language to the state. Neuhaus conceded that Bush's use of John 1:5 "goes right up to the line and threatens to go over it." He elaborated, "We are not the redeemer nation in a way analogous to [Christ] being the redeemer of the world." He wrote that he wished the president had instead said, "And this light, too, shines in the darkness," an adjustment he termed a "small, but crucial distinction."[17] But his adjustment appears to be a distinction without a difference. Did Neuhaus mean that America somehow *shares* in the messianic work of Christ?

He would certainly not be the first theologian to view a political empire as having a role in Christ's mission to the world. The early church historian Eusebius (263–339 C.E.) celebrated the Christian conversion of Constantine, emperor of Rome, as a key moment in the history of the church because from that moment onward the church of the outsiders became the church of the insiders, an establishment church that could be protected and promoted by all the structures of imperial power. This "Constantinian turn" had profound consequences for the church's later history, reaching arguably right up to the present day. As self-evident as Constantinian Christianity has usually seemed to be for Christians ever since, its accommodationist character cannot avoid doing violence to the teachings of Jesus in the New Testament.[18] Jesus himself rejected worldly power (Matt. 4:8–10; Luke 4:5–8), taught a lifestyle based upon loving self-sacrifice rather than legal rights (Matt. 5:38–48; Luke 6:27–30, 32–36), preached that faithfulness to God necessarily leads to civil persecution instead of social success (Matt. 10:17–25, 34–39; Luke 12:51–53; 14:26–27), and explicitly authorized his disciples to establish a communal order in which the hierarchical structures typical of secular power would be firmly rejected (Matt. 20:24–28; Mark 10:41–45; Luke 22:24–27). Self-styled "Christian empires," from Rome on down through history, including the U.S., not only lack such dominical characteristics within themselves, but also undermine the vitality of these characteristics within the church.

Within the New Testament, "Caesar" does not represent a potential ally for God; but God's competitor for control of the world. Caesar's power is realistically acknowledged, yet also, quite "unrealistically," diminished. Within the inverted order of God's kingdom, Caesar occupies a subordinate place. The confession "Jesus is Lord" carries with it the implicit challenge "and Caesar is not." All the more astonishing, then, to find that Eusebius declared messianic prophecies from the Old Testament as being fulfilled in the military conquests of the Constantinian empire. He applied important eschatological passages such as Micah 4:4; 5:4–5 (English); Psalm 71:7 (LXX); and Isaiah 2:2–4 to the time of peace inaugurated by Constantine's reign, thereby secularizing biblical prophecy as well as at the same time conferring messianic significance on Constantine's rule.[19] Even if recent scholarship is correct in stressing that Eusebius continued to view the church as the *primary* fulfillment of such Old Testament prophecies, and that the application of such messianic tropes to the *pax Romana* was largely a matter of rhetorical convention, the lasting effect of his influential historical work was still to muffle the church's authentic witness by underwriting a new gospel of worldly success.[20]

The further possibility exists that Eusebius's theological vision of empire may have been shared, or even have originated, with Constantine himself. In Eusebius's biographical work, *The Life of Constantine*, the emperor both is referred to and refers to himself as "a universal bishop appointed by God."[21] This kind of self-aggrandizement is what invariably happens within Constantinian Christianity; Caesar eventually becomes not only Scripture's chief interpreter, but also Scripture's chief subject. At this point the striking similarity between Constantine's *pax Romana* and Bush's *pax Americana* should be all too clear. George Bush's sense of America's divinely authorized mission is intimately bound up with his belief in his own divine calling, his "charge to keep."[22]

Again, tropes from Scripture have been used to undergird the American project since its inception, but these tropes have almost always worked according to an analogy based upon the biblical tradition of Israel's election: "America = Biblical Israel."[23] Now, however, the analogy favored by Bush is grounded in the New Testament's christological tradition, "America = Christ," which raises the stakes significantly for Christians who are concerned to prevent their faith from being taken hostage by the state. History teaches that this kind of messianic rhetoric never simply disappears once it has been found culturally acceptable, even if it lies dormant for some time. It survives into the future as an unexploded landmine of demonic pretension.[24]

From the standpoint of Christian theology, when the state takes on messianic ambitions, it ceases to be justly authorized (i.e., the kind of state described in Romans 13) and becomes essentially demonic (i.e., the kind of state described in Revelation 13). The only possible response for Christians then becomes civil disobedience. If George Bush is serious about America having a messianic role to play in world affairs, then he and his view must be opposed by every Christian. If George Bush does not really mean to say what he says, then he and his supporters have much to learn about using biblical language responsibly, from a political as well as a Christian perspective.

Senator J. William Fulbright once analyzed the political temptation toward messianism by noting that "power tends to confuse itself with virtue and a great nation is peculiarly susceptible to the idea that its power is a sign of God's favor."[25] This is exactly the trap into which falls Richard Land, head of the Southern Baptists' Ethics and Religious Liberty Commission, when he defends a view of "American exceptionalism," the idea that "there is a divine providence at work in the history and purpose of the United States," that the U.S. has "never been just a nation."[26] How does Land defend such a position biblically and theologically? Many nations have thought themselves to be divinely elected—what makes them wrong and the U.S. right? Is divine providence to be identified behind everything the U.S. does? If so, can the U.S. do no wrong in God's eyes? And if not, why is divine providence only selectively operative?

Moreover, as Fulbright insightfully explored, the "missionary instinct in foreign affairs" may prove problematic even on purely political grounds, because ultimately it stems just as much from national self-doubt as from self-confidence:

In America's case the evidence of a lack of self-confidence is our apparent need for constant proof and reassurance, our nagging desire for popularity, our bitterness and confusion when foreigners fail to appreciate our generosity and good intentions. Lacking an appreciation of the dimensions of our own power, we fail to understand our enormous and disruptive impact on the world; we fail to understand that no matter how good our intentions—and they are, in most cases, decent enough—other nations are alarmed by the very existence of such great power, which, whatever its benevolence, cannot help but remind them of their own helplessness before it.

Those who lack self-assurance are also likely to lack magnanimity, because the one is the condition of the other.[27]

In light of American confusion and belligerence in response to world opinion following the events of September 11, 2001, and the subsequent invasions of Afghanistan and Iraq, Fulbright's words from the sixties now appear almost prophetic.

Constantinian pretension must be openly rejected by Christians today for theological as well as political reasons. Christians must model instead a very different view of the state: a pragmatic nationalism shorn of quasi-religious mythology. Senator Fulbright was such a model in his generation. For Fulbright, the most important reason why the idea of the messianic American empire should be rejected is that

it never should have begun, because we are not God's chosen saviour of mankind but only one of mankind's more successful and fortunate branches, endowed by our Creator with about the same capacity for good and evil, no more or less, than the rest of humanity.[28]

This is the proper Christian stance toward American power, now more than ever.

There follow further implications for responsible biblical interpretation, both inside the church and within public discourse. On Christian theological grounds it is crucial to see that the election of biblical Israel has never applied *at all* to the U.S. or to any modern *nation* (including the modern state of Israel!). Rather, the true bearers of God's promises continue to be the *people* of Israel, the Jews, into whose special covenant the other peoples of the world have gained the possibility of inclusion through God's reconciling work in Jesus Christ (Rom. 11:17). In other words, even the church is only *secondarily* heir to God's promises for Israel. For these reasons, it is now necessary to be extra vigilant even about how "Israel" is interpreted and understood within local churches, especially given the lingering anti-Semitism often present there and because of the increased confusion between true biblical faith and its nationalistic appropriation by the Bush administration. America does not share in Christ's work; neither is it God's "new Israel."

The point here is not that nationhood itself is necessarily idolatrous. There are important pragmatic reasons for nations and civil rulers, which Christians can and should affirm, but only to a point. Jim Wallis explains:

> In Christian theology, it is not nations that rid the world of evil—they are too often caught up in complicated webs of political power, economic interests, cultural clashes, and nationalist dreams. The confrontation with evil is a role reserved for God, and for the people of God when they faithfully exercise moral conscience. But God has not given the responsibility for overcoming evil to a nation-state, much less to a superpower with enormous wealth and particular national interests. To confuse the role of God with that of the American nation, as George Bush seems to do, is a serious theological error that some might say borders on idolatry or blasphemy.[29]

In brief, God has not delegated a special responsibility for ridding the world of evil to the U.S. or its leaders, and religious communities should say so.

What American Christians must clearly articulate is a nonmessianic vision of nationhood that stresses openness instead of jingoistic defensiveness, cooperation instead of isolationism, generosity instead of retribution, responsibility instead of privilege, and modesty instead of imperial ambition—a robust vision of nationhood nevertheless haunted by the ultimate insignificance of all nations before God:

"Even the nations are like a drop from a bucket, and are accounted as dust on the scales; see, he takes up the isles like fine dust. . . . All the nations are as nothing before him; they are accounted by him as less than nothing and emptiness" (Isa. 40:15, 17).

Notes

1. http://www.whitehouse.gov/news/releases/2002/09/20020911–3.html#.

2. For important critical surveys, see S. Berkovitch, *The Puritan Origins of the American Self* (New Haven: Yale University Press, 1976); C. Cherry (ed.), *God's New Israel: Religious Interpretations of American Destiny* (rev. ed; Chapel Hill/London: University of North Carolina Press, 1998); M. I. Lowance Jr., *The Language of Canaan: Metaphor and Symbol in New England from the Puritans to the Transcendentalists* (Cambridge/London: Harvard University Press, 1980); E. L. Tuveson, *Redeemer Nation: The Idea of America's Millennial Role* (Chicago: University of Chicago Press, 1968).

3. As quoted by Nancy Haught in her article "Putting a Public Face on Private Beliefs," *Oregonian*, March 2, 2003.

4. See Debby Morse, "Dr. Strangereligion," *San Francisco Examiner*, November 21, 2002.

5. Cf. Michael Tackett, "Bush's Expressions of Faith Enter War Debate," *Chicago Tribune*, March 2, 2003.

6. http://www.whitehouse.gov/news/releases/2002/06/20020624–3.html.

7. As quoted by Laurie Goodstein, "A President Puts His Faith in Providence," *New York Times*, February 9, 2003.

8. As quoted by Bruce Nolan, "Seeing God as 'a Kind of Mascot,'" *Toronto Star*, February 23, 2003.

9. Jane Eisner, "President Bush's Religious Language May Be Heartfelt—But What If It's Also Exclusionary?" *Philadelphia Inquirer*, February 11, 2003.

10. Bush has cited the Qur'an at least once. By doing so, however, in a speech on September 17, 2001, specifically designed to pacify adherents of Islam, rather than in a major policy address, he perpetuated the very marginalization of Islam the speech was ostensibly directed against. See the entire text at http://www.whitehouse.gov/news/releases/2001/09/20010917–11.html.

11. For other prominent examples of such smuggling, see the reference to Psalm 23:4 in Bush's address to the nation on September 11, 2001 (http://www.whitehouse.gov/news/releases/2001/09/20010911–16.html), and to Rom. 8:38–39 in his remarks at the National Cathedral on September 14, 2001 (http://www.whitehouse.gov/news/releases/2001/09/20010914–2.html).

12. R. T. Handy, "The American Messianic Consciousness: The Concept of the Chosen People and Manifest Destiny," *Review and Expositor* 73 (1976): 47–58.

13. http://www.whitehouse.gov/news/releases/2003/01/20030128–20.html.

14. The biblical story appears in Luke 10:29–37. Although usually referred to as the story of the "Good Samaritan," the biblical account never actually calls the Samaritan "good." It says he "showed mercy." Thus, a more appropriate title would be the story of the "Merciful Samaritan."

15. http://www.whitehouse.gov/news/releases/inaugural-address.html.

16. For examples of such support, see the editorial "Free Speech for Politicians" (30–31) and the article "The Bush Doctrine," by Tony Carnes (38–40), both in *Christianity Today*, May 2003.

17. Richard John Neuhaus, "The Public Square," *First Things* (December 2002): 84.

18. Although the question is more complicated with respect to the Old Testament, I would maintain that "Constantinian" religion cannot do full justice to the entirety of the Old Testament's canonical witness either. To be sure, monarchy finally finds a foothold in Israel's tradition, and passages such as Daniel 2 acknowledge the divine authorization of foreign rulers (analogous to Matt. 17:27, John 19:11, and Rom. 13:1–2 in the New Testament). However, the monarchy is handled ambiguously throughout the Old Testament, and once it was lost, it was never reinstituted. Instead, the monarchic tradition is eschatologized, joining together with the developing messianic tradition. Never in the Old Testament does one find an indication that once the Messiah has come he will share his role with the foreign rulers of the world (Isa. 44:28–45:1 is not an exception). Rather, God's coming reign will replace them all (Zech. 14:9).

19. For an early but influential study, see E. Peterson, *Monotheismus als politisches Problem: Ein Beitrag zur Geschichte der politischen Theologie im Imperium Romanum* (Leipzig: Jakob Hegner, 1935), 75–78.

20. M. J. Hollerich, "Religion and Politics in the Writings of Eusebius: Reassessing the First 'Court Theologian,'" *Church History* 59 (1990): 309–25.

21. For the relevant passages and critical evaluation, see C. Rapp, "Imperial Ideology in the Making: Eusebius of Caesarea on Constantine as 'Bishop,'" *Journal of Theological Studies* 49 (1998): 685–95.

22. See Tony Carnes, "Bush's Defining Moment," *Christianity Today*, November 12, 2001. Cf. George W. Bush, *A Charge to Keep* (New York: Morrow, 1999).

23. Handy, "Messianic Consciousness."

24. See O. Friedrich, *Before the Deluge: A Portrait of Berlin in the 1920s* (New York: HarperCollins, 1972; 1995), 139.

25. J. W. Fulbright, *The Arrogance of Power* (New York: Random House, 1966), 3.

26. As cited in Nolan, "Seeing God."

27. Fulbright, *Arrogance*, 21.

28. Ibid., 20. Also cited in Handy, "Messianic Consciousness," 57.

29. J. Wallis, "Dangerous Religion: George W. Bush's Theology of Empire," *Sojourners* (September–October 2003): 20–26.

8

"The Most Intolerable of Insults"

Remarks to Christian Infidels in the American Empire

Eugene McCarraher

Writing in opposition to American entry into the First World War, Randolph Bourne reminded his fellow dissenters of the impending vituperation. "In an age of faith," he mused, "skepticism is the most intolerable of insults."[1] Having witnessed, in the invasion of Iraq, an extension of the American empire unprecedented in its arrogant chicanery, one should add that skepticism can also be the most indispensable of virtues. Certainly, given the War on Criticism waged in the press, Bourne's maxim has lost nothing in truth or portent. But the growing awareness of the Bush regime's deceit about the reasons for the war is the bitter but nutritious fruit of courageous, steadfast doubt. Thus, in our own age of misplaced faith, skepticism—unyielding, uncivil, and corrosive—must become the habit and tone of political criticism among Christian intellectuals. There are idols to be desecrated, priests to be ridiculed, an unholy trinity of guns, machines, and money to be identified and blasphemed. With a harsh and dreadful love, we must disparage the martial and pecuniary faith that animates history's richest, most well armed, and parochial superpower.

But our insults will have no force or effect until we measure the empire we inhabit. Two years ago, Ari Fleischer, then the Bush regime's press secretary, anointed the culture of American capitalism "our blessed way of life." Combined with the president's frequent references to the providential quality of American power, Fleischer's assertion now appears to be more than the eloquence of an apparatchik. The historical moment we are now enduring is indeed, as Tariq Ali has put it, a "clash of fundamentalisms."[2] It's time to realize that the American empire is a sacral order, a more beguiling and frightful incarnation of the earthly city described by Augustine in the *City of God*. Just as the Roman Empire embodied, in William Cavanaugh's words, "a dim archetype" of the church, so the American imperium is a parody of *ecclesia*, a "false copy of the Body of Christ," which captivates and mobilizes our celestial longings.[3] It worships a triune god of Caesar, Mammon, and Mars. It adheres to a covenant theology, which we might call the ecumenical-corporate dispensation. It possesses a soteriology and an ecclesiology—now labeled "democratic capitalism," "neoliberalism," or "globalization"—that defines redemption as participation in the liberal state and the capitalist market. It employs a clerisy of embedded intellectuals in the government, the media, and the academy who, while often discordant about particular issues, nonetheless police the imaginative boundaries of imperial culture. Its boldest creedal statement is *The National Security Strategy of the United States of America*, which openly calls for the missionary (and, on occasion, "preemptive") extension of liberal democracy and corporate capitalism.

This imperium contains, in the words of St. Paul, "the rulers of this age who are passing away" (1 Cor. 2:6, NASB). Paul's dismissal of imperial power—cold and passionate in its assurance of a victory already won—must now become our own, in all its austere and enormous hope. Indeed, our moment should remind us that Christianity is a revolutionary movement—the long, true, and only revolution, the annunciation and performance of a new order inaugurated in the death and resurrection of Christ. If, as Paul and Lenin would agree, no new order arrives without the practice of disciplined cadres, then unembedded intellectuals must assault the winter palaces of embedded ideology, revitalize and enlarge the political community called church, and rekindle the political imagination called theology. Against the totems and sacraments of empire, we must hurl the most intolerable and virtuous of insults.

Every revolution requires a history, and historians who write the narrative of our times need look no further than the writings of Michael

Novak for the cultural economy of imperial theology. Whether cast in the mold of "democratic capitalism" or the "theology of the corporation," Novak's economic thinking is essential for those eager to launder money in a baptismal font. (Though Novak, like other embedded intellectuals, presents himself as an oh-so-beleaguered rebel, he's cited, lauded, and lavished with the Templeton Prize.) Readily conceding the "wasteland" at the heart of capitalist culture, Novak rejoices at rather than laments this desert, whose barrenness "permits" individuals to undergo "alienation, anomie, loneliness, and nothingness." In fact, capitalism is "renewed" by these travails, these "experiences of human liberty." Where an older theology might have called these experiences "sin," Novak sees opportunities for growth, spiritual and accumulative. Novak gingerly disparages that older theology by pointing to "the empty shrine" erected at the spiritual core of corporate capitalism. Rehashing the liberal discourse of pluralism, Novak swells that "no one word, image, or symbol is worthy of all we seek there," and that its emptiness represents "the transcendence which is approached by free consciences from a virtually infinite number of directions." Words like "God" are "pointers," he continues, "which each person must define for himself." If you ignore the rhetoric, the affinity of this vision with the money economy could not be more evident or more lucrative. Like the money that establishes an abstract equivalence among incommensurate commodities, Novak's vacuous "transcendence" fosters a brisk and voluminous trade in the currencies of private fancy and avarice. It's also worth remembering that the "empty shrine" is, in fact, occupied—by the corporation. (Perhaps "sponsored by" would be more apt.) In Novak's intellectual confection, the corporation becomes the ark of a new covenant, an "analogue of the church," our clearest "incarnation of God's presence in the world."[4]

Novak's *apologia pro vita pecunia* finds its complement in the *Strategy*. With all the obligatory rhetorical flourish about cooperation, human dignity, and multilateralism, the *Strategy* articulates the political and military elements of covenant theology. Opening each of its nine sections with a quote from our evangelical president, it gets right to the point in the introduction with the statement that there is "a single sustainable model for national success: freedom, democracy, and free enterprise." Note the assumption that the nation-state is the only legitimate political community, whose global, capitalist replication is the obvious end of historical evolution. This point is reinforced throughout the document, most ominously with the warning that developing nations will not receive economic aid—and may receive something far worse—if they do not "govern themselves wisely." And how do nations exhibit this wisdom? We learn the answers in sections 6 and 7, devoted to "global economic growth," "expanding the circle of development," and "building the infrastructure of democracy." By "opening [their] societies" to "free markets and free trade," and by "follow[ing] responsible economic policies and enabl[ing] entrepreneurship," nations demonstrate their sagacity. The missionary hubris is barely concealed in the imperative of "opening societies," an imperative the authors elevate to the status of "a key priority of our national security strategy."[5] And given the political and moral economy of corporate capitalism, it doesn't take a political scientist to figure out what "responsible" means. (Still, given the triumphalism of contemporary American ideology, there's a curious reluctance on the part of the authors to use the word *capitalism*. Why the inclination to euphemism?)

Much has been made of the doctrine of "preemption" stated in the *Strategy*. Its supporters argue that "just war theory" has always envisioned the possibility of preemptive attack against enemies posing an indisputable and imminent danger. While I won't dispute the veracity of this claim, I will point out that imperial intellectuals have openly acknowledged that "preemption" supplies ideological camouflage for what Richard Perle has, with frightening and admirable candor, dubbed "total war." An adviser to the Reagan and Bush regimes, Perle made the expansively belligerent import of preemption very clear when asked about the limits of the "war on terrorism":

> We are fighting a variety of enemies. There are lots of them out there. All this talk about first we are going to do Afghanistan, then we will do Iraq, then we take a look around and see how things stand. This is entirely the wrong way to go about it. . . . If we just let our vision of the world go forth, and embrace it entirely, and we don't try to piece together clever diplomacy, but just wage a total war . . . our children will sing great songs about us years from now.[6]

(I was watching C-SPAN one night while reflecting on this essay, and there was Perle, flanked by Novak, as if gargoyles on a panel at the American Enterprise Institute.)

This "total war" is being waged or threatened on behalf of a Western capitalist culture that Christian intellectuals should be the loudest in condemning. Despite all the talk about the erasure of class lines in the rubble of the Twin Towers, the liberal-democratic capitalist state idealized in the *Strategy* is the emptiest of human communities. Lacking, *by design*, a collective, substantive good (which each one, remember, "must define for himself"), it exists to facilitate the contractual orchestration of nihilism. Its "freedom," being purely formal, is therefore morally vacuous, the assertion of countless wills-to-power with no telos beyond autonomy. Indeed, without a shared conception or practice of the good, it forces (not "permits") its denizens to be morally empty and endlessly competitive, and since this forced march of autonomy mandates the accumulation of power—in capital or in weapons—power, which confers the capacity for "choice," becomes the sine qua non of "democracy." "Free enterprise" must be understood as the command economy of choice.

Though critics of the Bush regime contend that the expansive doctrines enunciated in the *Strategy* constitute a radical departure from previous military and diplomatic strategy, it arguably marks the culmination not only of theory and practice since the Cold War, but of two centuries of American millennialism. G. K. Chesterton said more than he ever imagined in 1922 when he observed that the United States was "a nation with the soul of a church."[7] As Ernest Tuveson once put it, Americans have always sacralized their homeland as a "Redeemer Nation."[8] Beginning with John Winthrop's Puritan image of a "city on a hill," and continuing through the "Manifest Destiny" of "Indian removal," westward conquest, and Pacific and Caribbean imperialism, American national identity was, until the early twentieth century, christened in the waters of Protestantism. From the Second Great Awakening to well after the Civil War, the nation's political culture formed part of an evangelical dispensation—one could call it "proprietary-Protestant"—that ascribed salvific import to republican democracy and proprietary capitalism. This "progressive patriotic Protestantism," as Henry F. May once dubbed it, was the covenant theology for American nationalism.[9] This proprietary-Protestant dispensation eroded with the solvents of "liberal" Protestantism, of a corporate economy that displaced the proprietary order, and of growing numbers of Catholics and Jews. These pressures transformed the American covenant theology into a more ecumenical-corporate dispensation, which has, through several metamorphoses, remained the American civil religion.

It's a scandal that some secular intellectuals recognize the sacral character of the market state more readily than Christian writers who are supposed to be wary of rendering unto Caesar. Drawing on the work of Emile Durkheim—who, in *The Elementary Forms of Religious Life* (1912), frequently alluded to the totemic qualities of modern nationalism—the anthropologist Michael Taussig observes that the contemporary state "has a deep investment in death," because death "endows the Nation-State with life, a spectral life, to be sure." Consider, he asks, the meaning of the Tomb of the Unknown Soldier. (Christians might recall that their hope begins with an *empty* tomb.)[10] And if we resist Taussig's Marxist twist on this persistence of political enchantment, we have Richard Rorty, who calls on us in *Achieving Our Country* (1998) to construct a "civic religion" that sacralizes the "secular" democratic state. To his credit, Rorty forthrightly asserts that "privatized religious belief" is essential to this sacralizing project, which creates, in effect, not a separation of church and state, but the separation of church and church—which is to say, the establishment of the imperial civil religion.[11]

But the modern secular intellectual most acutely aware of the ecclesial and redemptive aspirations of the nation-state was none other than Bourne, whose unfinished essay "The State" (1918) reads like an exposé of modern nationalism as a religious surrogate for the salvation once offered by the church. Struck by the verbal and visual pageantry of wartime propaganda, Bourne came to believe that the state was primarily "a mystical conception."[12] "The sanctity of the state" inhered in what Bourne perceived as the fetishism of modern political culture.[13] The state was the "invisible grace" of which the government was "the visible sign, the word made flesh."[14] Likening the state to an ecclesia, Bourne summarized what in theological terms would be its soteriology: "As the Church is the medium for the spiritual salvation of men, so the State is thought of as the medium for his political salvation."[15] Bourne feared that the cultural and military strength of the nation-state enabled it to dissolve or destroy all rival devotions. "The State is a jealous God, and will brook no rivals," and its jealousy extended to the taking and sacrifice of life in war.[16] Offering the individual a sense of existential completion through sacrifice on the battlefield, war "achieved almost his apotheosis" and preserved its own facsimile of eternal life.[17] "War is the health of the State," as Bourne put it in a maxim that belongs on the banner of every ROTC recruiting table at every college campus.[18] Bourne ruefully concluded that despite its pretensions to enlightenment, pluralism, and progress, modern democracy was itself a perverse divinity, "no bright and rational creation of a new day."[19] Indeed, its unprecedented capacity to mobilize the most primal impulses of herd-consciousness and violence revealed its essential continuity with the unenlightened irrationality of the past. As "the last decrepit scion of an ancient and hoary stock," democracy clung "tenaciously to its archaic and irrelevant spirit."[20] Even democracy hath no relish of salvation in it.

St. Augustine might have said to Bourne, "I told you so." Augustine's work has been so often and so perversely employed on behalf of imperial belligerence that he might seem an unlikely witness to invoke against the American empire. But if we read *City of God* with eyes unscaled by nationalism, we can see it not only as a survey of Roman imperial culture, but as an eerie premonition of late capitalism in America. Of course, the story of humanity unfolds in *City of God* as the always intermingled and always antagonistic relationship of the earthly and heavenly cities. The earthly city's marvels—evidence, Augustine observed, of "the blessings it enjoys" from God—are corrupted marvels, tokens of its real aspirations to goodness and redemption, all perverted to futility by the love of power *(libido dominandi)*. But especially in his stunning account of "earthly felicity" in book 2, chapter 20, Augustine dilates on the political consequences of this perversion. "So long as it enjoys material prosperity and the glory of victorious war," he writes, the citizens of the earthly city are happy. "We should get richer all the time, to have enough for extravagant spending every day." The earthly city is a boundless marketplace mastered by "providers of material satisfactions" who cultivate not the honor and morality but rather the "docility of their subjects." This managerial paradise rests on a culture of individualism whose first and only commandment is that "anyone should be free to do as he likes about his own, or with his own, or with others, if they consent." The imperial citizens divinize their desires; they make "false gods whom [they] might serve by sacrifice"; they offer their own bodies as sacrifices in the agonistic liturgy of war; they even welcome the iniquity of their enemies, pointing to their evil so as to highlight Roman rectitude and to sanction the subordination of barbarians. "If it was by waging wars that were just that the Romans were able to acquire so vast an empire," Augustine asks with undisguised sarcasm, "surely they should worship the Injustice of others as a kind of goddess?"[21]

Surely, many Christians will object, isn't this comparison old and moldy? I would certainly urge caution against facile parallels between Rome and the United States, if only because they've been staples in the rhetorical arsenal of reaction. But I would nonetheless affirm this oft-belabored analogy. What else is the fuel of "democratic capitalism" but the urge to "get richer all the time"? How else do we judge our rulers—who rule, let's be candid, from Wall Street as well as K Street—than by their provision of commodities? What other word but "docility" describes a populace that, indifferent to the corporate franchising of democracy, supports the invasion and occupation of Iraq while admitting to incomprehension about its rationale?

And what, to put the matter most starkly, is so much of the "War on Terrorism" but the worship of the goddess Injustice? Recall the president's State of the Union address for 2002. "History," we were informed, "has called America to action." How thankful we should be to killers for the chance to prove our goodness. For what could "history" be, in these circumstances, but the devotees of Injustice? And what could "action" be but the "responsibility *and the privilege* to fight freedom's fight"? While "responsibility" betokens an unwanted and unfortunate duty, "privilege" conveys a coveted pleasure. The United States, Bush implies unwittingly, has thirsted after unrighteousness as the bloody occasion for its sanctity. And we covet that privilege so dearly that we will—to conjure another president's clarion summons—pay any price and bear any burden. "The price of freedom and security is never too high"—always an easy and self-deluding claim for those convinced of their unlimited power and secretly determined to pay the bill in the currency of others' lives. (Recall Madeleine Albright's response to the deaths of Iraqi children from sanctions: "*We* think the price is worth it.")[22] Yes indeed, Augustine speaks to our time, and he says things that would scandalize our embedded intellectuals.

Of the many points on which these embedded clerics are vulnerable, one that we need to press concerns the dissonance of their support for military ventures and their visceral disgust at American culture. Jean Bethke Elshtain in particular is worth engaging here, not only because, as she proves in *Just War against Terror* (2003), she is the most powerful and sophisticated apologist for liberal imperialism and the "just-war" tradition it requires, but because she has also been a powerful and sophisticated critic of injustice and corruption within the empire. Unlike Novak, George Weigel, and Richard John Neuhaus (whose pro-war arguments were demolished by William Cavanaugh in *Commonweal*), Elshtain does not collapse the *eschaton* into corporate capitalism or reduce the just-war tradition to a checklist of conditions.[23] She also raises unavoidable issues about intervention in the affairs of "failed states" such as Liberia. Now, on the one hand, I'm not comfortable with the United States marking the pass-fail tests of other states. When I look at the venal and doltish citizenry, or at the ever more plutocratic government, I don't see any functioning "democracy" in this country. Yet I also have to say that in their pointed critique of Elshtain, Stanley Hauerwas and Paul J. Griffiths offer no guidance whatever about what "we" (as "Americans" or as "Christians") are to do when a political order collapses into bloody anarchy.[24]

Yet despite her invocation of Augustine, and despite her identification of real problems in the political thinking of her detractors, Elshtain seems uninterested in a problem addressed with great erudition and elegance by my friend and colleague Michael Hanby: Augustine's oft-forgotten concern with the *character* of those who fight. What sort of person (or community, for that matter) would be capable of identifying and fighting a just war (or, for that matter, identifying and intervening in a "failed state")? Elshtain doesn't seem to read Augustine's account of war in *City of God* (which is not the same thing, Hanby shrewdly contends, as a *theory* of just war) in connection with his reflections on virtue, especially on the culpable quality of a virtue that *requires vice* to enable its presence. ("Surely they should worship the Injustice of others . . .") As Hanby has argued, such a person or community would, at the very least, have to lament the necessity of deadly force, demonstrating this disposition through personal *and public* penitential practices. How would one acquire this disposition? As Cavanaugh reminds us, it comes through "the gifts of the Holy Spirit available in the sacraments of the church and the practices of Christian charity, in communion with the whole people of God and its pastors."[25]

Like Hanby (and, I suspect, Cavanaugh), I certainly don't see any penitential disposition among American leaders or the American people—certainly none that recalls Lincoln's insistence, in his second inaugural address, on "malice toward none and charity for all." I do not see any sackcloth and ashes, and I do not hear any calls for repentance from Bush, Cheney, Rice, or Rumsfeld. What I see is a military-entertainment complex whose ubiquitous imagery fuses the martial, the frivolous, and the mercantile. What I hear from the president is "Let's roll" and "Bring it on" in bellicose ardor, not the beating of his chest in penitent humility. Indeed, by inviting the very evil he professes to abhor, Bush proves that he desires the sort of virtue that covertly delights in iniquity. ("It is a wicked prayer," Augustine asserts, "to ask to have someone to hate or to fear, so that he may be someone to conquer.")[26]

Elshtain's defense of the "War on Terrorism" also passes rather swiftly over the domestic order she's zealous to defend. Though she denies that American expansionism is driven by capitalist imperatives, Elshtain might want to consider this nugget of bluster from Thomas Friedman, the *New York Times'* resident imperialist:

> For globalization to work, America can't be afraid to act like the almighty superpower that it is. The hidden hand of the market will never work without a hidden fist. McDonald's cannot flourish without McDonnell-Douglas, the designer of the F-15, and the hidden fist that keeps the world safe for Silicon Valley's technology is called the United States Army, Air Force, Navy and Marine Corps.[27]

There's a pithy statement of imperial covenant theology: the divinity of the empire (complete with reference to the Golden Arches, those cheesy spires of consumerism); the persistence of the market's invisible hand, "hidden" insofar as we refuse to expose it; and the high-tech terror that stands ready to inflict perdition on all who oppose its will.

Since Friedman shows, in his way, respect for the plain sight of his readers, let us be candid where embedded Christians employ euphemism or change the subject. Our government is a franchise of multinational capital; our political culture is a seller's market in knavery; our economy is a gargantuan galley of imperious executives, harried workers, and stressed-out families; our culture is a cheerful mendacity—irony as a way of life—summarized long ago by Peter Sloterdijk as "cynical reason": "I know what I am doing; nonetheless, I am doing it." To which Slavoj Zizek has made the crucial addition: ". . . because I don't know what I believe."[28] And not knowing what you believe—that vertiginous and beguiling "freedom" so hallowed in imperial theology—is the ideal point of capture by the idols of State and Market. (As Chesterton once mused, the problem when people cease to believe in God is not that they then believe in nothing, but that they then believe in *anything*.) Cynical reason is the instrumental and substantive rationality of wide swaths of the American middle classes, whose only deep conviction is their inalienable right to do as they please. This is what Augustine dubbed *libido dominandi*, the love of domination, draped in the ideological raiment of "choice" and "freedom." From abortion and genome-mapping to the proclamation of total war, the scope and magnitude of this country's culture of death receives only the weakest of chastisements in Elshtain's call-to-arms. I cannot believe that Elshtain has forsworn this kind of critique, and I can only hope that she will remain as critical of this culture of death as she has been in the past.

I suspect that this inattention derives (as Charles Mathewes complained in an otherwise sympathetic response to her book) from Elshtain's neglect of proper and sustained theological reflection. The fundamental flaw in "Christian realism," à la Niebuhr or à la Elshtain, lies not in its refusal of pacifism but in its nonexistent ecclesiology. The *church*, not the nation-state, is the political community within which Christians must not only debate war and peace, but *define* war and peace, as well as violence, justice, and love. Here I concur with John Milbank, whose recent reflections on "violence" should be central to any serious deliberation on the moral and political responsibilities Christians bear in the imperial moment.[29] Although Milbank provides, in my view, a shrewd corrective to the pacifism of Hauerwas, I would propose that following it will entail a position almost indistinguishable from pacifism, because imperial violence will always mean an attempt to impose the well-mannered nihilism of corporate capital on an increasingly unwilling and resistant planet.

We must, in short, recover the *theological* idiom of Christian political intelligence and moral imagination. This mandates, first, remembering that the church has been, for political theologians from Augustine to Hauerwas, an alternative *polis*, a community of pilgrims toward another city, a network of cells whose final allegiance lies with another empire. (It is, in Lenin's parlance, "a strong organization of revolutionaries . . . [prepared for] prolonged and stubborn struggle.") Against the bogus individualism that issues in docility and cynicism, the heavenly *ecclesia* poses a communal ethic that recognizes, in Augustine's words, that "the only real goods are those enjoyed in common." Against the deification of self that ends in its sacrificial offering to a deified imperium, Christians pose the true worship of a God who has already made and accepted the ultimate sacrifice. And against the phony internationalism of liberal globalization, it counters with "a society of aliens speaking all languages, taking no account of difference in customs, laws, and institutions."[30]

This revolutionary vanguard—"the True International" as it was christened by A. J. Muste and Dorothy Day—has long relied on a venerable but now atrophied symbolism and has nurtured visions of "divine economy" that dispute the imperatives of accumulation and purchase. (There is wisdom Christians must harvest from Lenin's dictum that "there is no revolutionary movement without a revolutionary theory.") Just as the increasingly indistinguishable iconographies of corporate advertising and state propaganda form a species of spiritual formation, so we must learn to think again of our practices of common prayer, common study, and eucharistic observance as a spiritual formation that is also a pedagogy in moral and political thought. From that formation, Christians have produced the only remaining alternatives to the empire of capital. In the "Christian" or "sacramental socialism" of Anglo-Catholics from J. N. Figgis and Vida Scudder to Maurice Reckitt and Milbank, and in the Christian anarcho-syndicalist writings of Simone Weil, we have a tradition that affirms the liturgical character of labor and exchange and redeems them from their erosion or perversion under capitalism.[31]

In these times, when death is so readily offered as the solution to inconvenience, loss, injustice, or death, the affirmation of life is our most urgent and emancipating duty. From poverty, unemployment, and alienation, to abortion, capital punishment, and "total war," the empire thrives, not only on death, but on our countless efforts to evade or sacralize it. For all its enlistment of our celestial longings, and for all the solemnities with which it apes true worship, this empire will purchase nothing but fear, ashes, and ruin. A freedom purchased with death is really a servitude; a homeland so secured is really a prison; a security so leveraged is really a terror. Yet our remonstrance to the empire must not conclude on so true but hopeless a note. Chesterton once remarked that he wanted to sing both the *Marseillaise* and the *Magnificat*, and it's his hopeful, loving, and pugnacious spirit that we need to cultivate and exemplify. The *Magnificat*, we should recall, is a hymn of celebration and judgment. "God has remembered God's mercy," Mary proclaims. And how has he remembered it? "He has lifted up the lowly, and cast the mighty from their thrones." Let the empire tremble.

Notes

1. Randolph Bourne, "The War and the Intellectuals" (1917), in Randolph Bourne, *The Radical Will: Selected Writings 1911–1918*, Olaf Hansen, ed., (Berkeley and Los Angeles: University of California Press, 1992), 309.

2. Tariq Ali, *The Clash of Fundamentalisms: Crusades, Jihads, and Modernity* (London and New York: Verso, 2002), esp. 253–313.

3. William Cavanaugh, "The City: Beyond Secular Parodies," in John Milbank, Catherine Pickstock, and Graham Ward, eds., *Radical Orthodoxy: A New Theology* (London and New York: Routledge, 1999), 182.

4. Michael Novak, *The Spirit of Democratic Capitalism* (New York: Simon and Schuster, 1982), 53–54, 56, and *Toward a Theology of the Corporation* (Washington, D.C.: American Enterprise Institute for Public Policy Research, 1981), 45.

5. *The National Security Strategy of the United States of America*, accessible on the Web at www.whitehouse.gov/nsc/nss.html. See the appendix to this volume.

6. Richard Perle, quoted in John Pilger, *The New Rulers of the World* (London and New York: Verso, 2002), 9–10.

7. G. K. Chesterton, *What I Saw in America* (New York: Dodd Mead, 1922), 11–12.

8. Ernest Tuveson, *Redeemer Nation: The Idea of America's Millennial Role* (Chicago: University of Chicago Press, 1980 [1968]). See also Robert T. Handy, *A Christian America: Protestant Hopes and Historical Realities* (New York: Oxford University Press, 1971).

9. Henry F. May, "The Religion of the Republic," in *Ideas, Faiths, and Feelings: Essays on American Intellectual and Religious History, 1952–1982* (New York: Oxford University Press, 1983), 171–80.

10. Michael Taussig, *The Nervous System* (New York: Routledge, 1992), esp. 119–40.

11. Richard Rorty, *Achieving Our Country: Leftist Thought in Twentieth-Century America* (Cambridge: Harvard University Press, 1998), 10–34.

12. Bourne, "The State" (1918), in Hansen, 358–59, 367, 375, 382.

13. Ibid., 355.

14. Ibid., 358.

15. Ibid., 359.

16. Ibid., 367.

17. Ibid., 361.

18. Ibid., 375.

19. Ibid., 382.

20. Ibid., 382.

21. Augustine, *Concerning the City of God against the Pagans*, trans. Henry Bettenson (Harmondsworth, U.K.: Penguin, 1984), 71–75, 154.

22. President George W. Bush, "State of the Union Address" (2002), accessible on the Web at www.whitehouse.gov/news/releases/2002/01.

23. On this score, I ask forgiveness for my haste and unfairness in pairing her with Novak in an earlier essay of mine on the Ekklesia Project website.

24. Jean Bethke Elshtain, *Just War against Terror: The Burden of American Power in a Violent World* (New York: Basic Books, 2003), esp. 49–53 on the "just-war" tradition; William Cavanaugh, "At Odds with the Pope," *Commonweal* 130 (May 23, 2003), 11–13, quote on 13. For the Hauerwas-Griffiths critique, and Elshtain's response, see "War, Peace, and Jean Bethke Elshtain: An Exchange," *First Things* 136 (October 2003): 41–47.

25. Michael Hanby, "War on Ash Wednesday: A Brief Christological Reflection," *New Blackfriars* 84 (April 2003): 168–78, esp. 175–76; and "Democracy and Its Demons," in Kim Paffenroth, Kevin Hughes, and John Doody, eds., *Augustine and Politics* (Lanham, MD: Lexington Books, 2004), which I have read in manuscript. On the ambivalence of virtue, see also Milbank, "Can Morality Be Christian?" in *The Word Made Strange: Theology, Language, Culture* (Oxford: Blackwell, 1997), 220–22.

26. Augustine, *City of God*, 154.

27. Thomas Friedman, *New York Times*, March 19, 1999, quoted in Ali, 260–61.

28. Peter Sloterdijk, *Critique of Cynical Reason*, trans. Michael Eldred (Minneapolis: University of Minnesota Press, 1987); Slavoj Zizek, *The Puppet and the Dwarf: The Perverse Core of Christianity* (Cambridge: MIT Press, 2003), 7. See also Zizek, *Welcome to the Desert of the Real! Five Essays on September 11 and Related Dates* (London and New York: Verso, 2002).

29. Charles Mathewes, Religion and Culture Web Forum, May 2003, accessible at www.marty-center.uchicago.edu/webforum. On the non-ecclesial quality of Niebuhr's ethical thought, see Hauerwas, "The Irony of Reinhold Niebuhr: The Ideological Character of 'Christian Realism,'" in *Wilderness Wanderings: Probing Twentieth-Century Theology and Philosophy* (Boulder, CO: Westview, 1997), 48–61, and Milbank, "The Poverty of Niebuhrianism," in *The Word Made Strange*, 233–54; on the meaning of "violence," see Milbank, *Being Reconciled: Ontology and Pardon* (London and New York: Routledge, 2002), 26–43, esp. 36–40.

30. Lenin, *What Is To Be Done? Burning Questions of Our Movement* (New York: International Publishers, 1969), 102; Augustine, *City of God*, 601–02, 878. I argue for the possibility of an "Augustinian socialism" in "The Enchanted City of Man: Augustine, Politics, and the Fetishes of Modernity," in Paffenroth, *Augustine and Politics*, forthcoming. If any embedded clerics would wail at my citing Lenin, I invoke none other than Peter Maurin and Dorothy Day, neither of whom saw anything perverse or irresponsible in comparing Christianity to a revolutionary movement. Indeed, it's a scandal that Marxist intellectuals are recognizing the revolutionary character of Christianity far more keenly than many Christians, and doing so without the facile compromises of "Marxist-Christian dialogue" in the 1960s. See, for instance, Zizek, *The Ticklish Subject: The Absent Center of Political Ontology* (London and New York: Verso, 1999), esp. 125–70; *The Fragile Absolute: Or, Why is the Christian Legacy Worth Fighting For?* (London and New York: Verso, 2000); *Puppet and the Dwarf*, esp. chaps. 1 and 2; Alain Badiou, *Saint Paul: La foundation de l'universialsme* (Paris: Presses universitaires de France, 1997); *Ethics: An Essay on the Understanding of Evil* (London and New York: Verso, 2001). Some of the recent work of Terry Eagleton is also worth perusing in this regard, and his early work with the British New Left Catholic group *Slant* deserves renewed attention: see especially *The Body as Language: Toward a 'New Left' Theology* (London and New York: Sheed and Ward, 1970).

31. Lenin, *What Is to Be Done?* 25. I am thinking especially of the "guild socialism" examined in Peter D'Alroy Jones, *The Christian Socialist Revival, 1877–1914: Religion, Class, and Social Conscience in Late-Victorian England* (Princeton, NJ: Princeton University Press, 1968), esp. 275–302; Vida Dutton Scudder, *Social Ideals in English Letters* (Boston: Houghton, Mifflin and Co., 1898), and *Socialism and Character* (Boston: Houghton, Mifflin and Co., 1912); Simone Weil, *Oppression and Liberty*, trans. Arthur Wills and John Petrie (Amherst: University of Massachusetts Press, 1973), esp. 37–124; Milbank, "On Complex Space," in *Word Made Strange*, 268–92; "Socialism of the Gift, Socialism by Grace," *New Blackfriars* 77 (December 1996): 532–48; *Being Reconciled*, 162–211.

AND IF THERE'S NO GOING BACK?

9

On the True Globalism and the False, or Why Christians Should Not Worry So Much about American Imperialism

Stephen H. Webb

The Second Gulf War has brought out the best and the worst in America, but what that best and worst are is a matter of much dispute. While American soldiers were giving their lives to liberate Iraq, many representatives of higher education at home were deriding American foreign policy as a barely disguised grab for oil. Only in a democracy can a war be condemned while it is being fought. Much of the debate focuses on the issue of unilateral action. For some, the implosion of the Soviet Union makes it all the more necessary for America to fill the resulting power vacuum by promoting democratic ideals. For others, foreign adventurism is proof that the cowboy mythos is alive and well and being updated for a world without economic borders or unexplored frontiers. Everyone can agree that America uses its status as the only remaining superpower to advance its own interests, and everyone can agree that those interests are largely self-interests, but there is little agreement about how those interests overlap with the interests of other nation-states. There is even less agreement about whether the interests of empire can be made to coincide with the interests of democracy. The question I want to pursue is what interest Christians should have in these questions.

In the midst of all the second-guessing, speculation, and commentary about American motives—much of it laden with the suspicion that America can never be up to any good—the wisest words to come out of this war were delivered by President Bush at Dearborn, Michigan. Speaking to an audience of Iraqi immigrants, President Bush stated an Enlightenment ideal that was worthy of Immanuel Kant: "The desire for freedom is not the property of one culture. It is the universal hope of human beings in every culture." The president can speak with such confidence because he combines the Enlightenment heritage of optimistic humanism with the evangelical fervor of an altar call. Given the fact that the American version of the Enlightenment—which was shaped by Lockean empiricism and the rationality of the market, rather than Voltaire and the virulent anticlericalism of the French Enlightenment—was deeply theological, this evangelical Kantianism, if I can coin a phrase, makes a lot of rhetorical sense.

At least, it makes sense to most Americans who live outside the isolated precincts of the academy. For academics, especially those influenced by the postmodern attack on objective rationality, there are no two discourses more troubling than the Enlightenment dedication to the universal kingdom of reason or the evangelical pursuit of a universal kingdom of God. That President Bush combines these two discourses accounts for much of the outrage over the Second Gulf War that could be heard from university professors.

What I am calling President Bush's evangelical Enlightenment or enlightened evangelicalism should be given careful scrutiny, but it needs scrutiny of the right kind. The problem is not that this theology of foreign affairs depends upon the use of military might. All diplomacy is grounded in the use or threat of force. The well-known and always provocative theologian Stanley Hauerwas portrays pacifism as the only alternative to vengeance, but this is powerful rhetoric rather than clear-eyed politics (or theology). Only if Christians have no investment in any secular order can Christians embrace an absolute pacifism. If God does ordain governments to bring order to the world, and if some forms of government are better than others, then Christians, like everyone else, must do their best to promote the best forms of government and defend the innocent from the worst forms. Hauerwas thinks of the church as a countercultural polis, an island amid the stream of torrential capitalism, and there is much to recommend this ecclesiology. Nevertheless, after 9/11, it seems less persuasive to argue that the church can withdraw from civil society. If 9/11 was born in the prisons of Egypt (or the political abuses of the House of Saud), then American Christians have good reasons to promote not just mutual dialogue between Islam and Christianity but also more democratic forms of government in the Middle East. To do anything less than this is to spiritualize and privatize the great Protestant theme of freedom.

Hauerwas is right, of course, that Christians should work for peace in the world, but the very term *pacifism* denotes an absolute principle that trumps every other theological concern. A better term than *pacifism* for believers would be *peace first Christians*, which suggests that Christians should strive for peace but should not make a god out of it. If Christians choose peace first, then the question becomes not whether military force should ever be used but when it should be used and for what end. What are the goals for which President Bush's evangelical Kantianism is employed? A comparison with the European Enlightenment, with its very different theological foundation, might be helpful. There is little doubt that the European Enlightenment was the philosophical expression of European cultural and economic confidence. The Enlightenment parlayed Europe's rise to worldwide political domination into a cultural and intellectual—indeed, a theological—hegemony. Although it has been fashionable in the academy to equate imperialism with every kind of harm, the political impact of European worldwide domination will not be fully assessed for centuries to come. Those on the political left are loath to admit it, but much good, as well as much harm, came out of the British Empire, for example. Needless to say, without this European expansion, American expansion would not be a topic of conversation today, and, as we will soon see, the explosion of evangelical and Pentecostal forms of Christianity would also not be happening today.

What is clear is that the philosophical basis of European expansion is no longer a viable option in thinking about the future of Christianity. The social and cultural elite of Europe enlisted the Protestant battle against superstition and irrationality as an indispensable tool in the arsenal of European dominance. Protestants joined arm in arm with European expansionists in order to take advantage of new economic markets for the spreading of Christianity, but the reshaping of the world also resulted in the reshaping of Christianity. If religious extremism abroad had to be policed in order to make room for European influence, then the same religious sentiments at home were also quarantined. Enlightenment philosophers defined themselves against religious exuberance of every variety. Christians who wanted to assimilate to the new Enlightenment regime of moderation and perspicuity had to define themselves in opposition to the more preposterous actions of the less liberally educated of their faith.

Given the association between Enlightenment philosophy and theological liberalism, it is easy to understand why President Bush's enlightened evangelicalism, which associates aspects of the Enlightenment with theological conservativism, sounds so strange to so many people in the academy. The president combines a zeal for human rights with an unapologetic faith in the unrivaled lordship of Jesus Christ. He does not try to derive the one from the other, which makes him something less than an Enlightenment thinker. Indeed, for all the criticism he faces for invoking the name of God in public, he has actually been pretty careful about distinguishing between faith and foreign policy. That is why it is so unfair that, in a recent essay, Hauerwas chides President Bush for wanting it both ways: he wants America to be religious, but he does not want the war on terrorism to be a religious war.[1] Hauerwas does not explain why these two goals are incompatible; that apparently seems obvious to him. It seems obvious to me that political leaders can affirm the religious traditions and heritage of their country without thereby turning every war they initiate into a religious war. Hauerwas should know better, but for many liberal critics of the Bush administration, it evidently follows from the fact that he avows faith in Jesus Christ that he takes our troops to war in Jesus' name as well. The president, however, is more careful than his critics. He has thus gone out of his way to make it clear that he thinks Islam is a peaceful religion and that the war on terrorism is not a religious crusade. Nevertheless, he is who he is, and that means that he talks like a true believer. That this bothers so many caretakers of the public square suggests just how far America has fallen in privatizing the faith that was once so essential to our society.

President Bush's public displays of faith stand out only because they depart from the old alliance between the Enlightenment and theological liberalism. That alliance permitted a civil use of religion as long as religious expression remained generic and restrained. Declaring that Jesus Christ is your favorite philosopher, as President Bush did in a public debate, violates the rules about acceptable religious rhetoric for such occasions. This declaration might make sense to a majority of Americans, but it is distasteful to those who think that people in the public eye should not talk about religion in too personal a manner.

Ironically, those who criticize American involvement in Iraq frequently employ a religious rhetoric that goes much more unexamined than President Bush's evangelical Kantianism. Young people in the sixties used to sing liturgical chants conjuring the coming of "one world," and antiwar protestors today are still in their debt. Their dream of universal peace and harmony is made possible by a certain innocence about the use of military force. Rowan Williams, the Archbishop of Canterbury, thinks that the threat of terrorism demands, at best, an international police response, rather than an all-out war.[2] Williams is probably right that to call the fight against terrorism a "war" gives more credit to the terrorists than they deserve, but he seems a bit unrealistic to think that the police could do a better job in Afghanistan or Iraq than the military.

Unlike President Bush's faith in Jesus Christ, Williams's evangelical fervor appears to take the form of an overestimation of the persuasive power of the good and a willed blindness to the pervasive presence of evil in the world. Williams warns Americans against using the theological category of evil because it "lets us off the hook,"[3] and he cannot imagine that the world hates America as much for its virtues as for its vices. Certainly America has done much harm in the world, but America also represents much that is true, and one of the lessons of Christianity is that the good is often subjected to irrational hatred. Williams's utopianism becomes dangerous when it disregards humanity's fallen condition. An inordinate fear of doing unintended harm can paralyze one's responsibilities toward others. The will of decent people alone is insufficient to prevent the cruel from dominating the innocent.

This is not to say that there are no reasons to worry about the new American globalism. I am also not suggesting that President Bush's policies are beyond reproach simply because he is an evangelical Christian. The president himself would not say such nonsense. Nonetheless, I am suggesting that Christians should offer Christian reasons for the concern about American hegemony. The political complexity of the issue suggests that too many Christians have merely adopted the liberal orientation of the academy in place of thoughtful theological analysis. After all, it is far from clear what impact the American empire will have on the world. It is even unclear whether America really will become a global empire. As I write this, Americans are tiring of the sacrifices demanded by the occupation of Iraq. Americans seem willing to take on some of the responsibilities of policing the world, but we prefer to use democracy, human rights, and open markets—rather than colonies and conquest—to achieve our ends. Michael Ignatieff has called this an "empire lite."[4] The global economy is so interconnected that the leftist charge that America went into Iraq to protect its economic interests is a throwback to the days of the United Fruit Company. The elite across the globe have the same interests, and those interests are most efficiently protected through monetary and trade policies, not direct military intervention.

Critics of our invasion of Iraq appear to forget that there are many countries, and not just Japan and Germany, that owe their freedom and prosperity to us. This suggests that it was not simply recklessness or vengeance that motivated our attempt to oust one of the world's most dangerous dictators. The problem with our invasion of Iraq is not that we are too powerful. Rather, we are not powerful enough. Regime change is an enormously risky venture, especially in an area of the world where hatred of America, both justifiable and irrational, is so rampant. If Iraq demonstrates anything, it shows just how far America is from claiming the title of *empire*.

Nonetheless, it is popular among many religious studies professors to compare America to ancient Rome. John Milbank, for example, argues that America is just like Rome—except that it is worse.[5] Milbank acknowledges that the apostle Paul granted at least some measure of legitimacy to Rome. The modern nation-state, however, is beyond such concessions for Milbank, because it exists only to serve the market (Milbank is a socialist). Like Hauerwas, Milbank considers all nation-states to be illegitimate. "Pure liberty is pure power," he writes, "whose other name is evil."[6] He can recognize no positive relationship between Christianity and modern nation-states, nor can he see any positive outcome to the extension of free markets across the globe. Although Milbank is a theologian, much of his analysis of globalization is shaped by economic concerns. There is little doubt that there are many economic reasons to be worried about this new American globalism, but I do not think there are many reasons why Christians, as Christians, should be worried about it.

From a specifically Christian point of view, the comparison of America and Rome is surely limited, if not fatally flawed. Not only were the imperial ambitions of Rome completely different from the global responsibilities of America, but the Romans viciously persecuted Christians, which makes it especially obnoxious to compare Rome to a predominantly Christian America. Sectarian arguments about the Constantinian captivity of the church, while provocative, often go too far in dismissing the providential ways that God has used governments to spread the gospel. This is especially true in America, where a distinctively Protestant rhetoric has developed that is inseparable from the American cultural landscape.

Indeed, the arguments of theologians like Hauerwas and Milbank will make little sense to the evangelical Christian community, which includes President Bush. I still value the account of church history taught to me by the evangelical church of my youth. It involved three basic stages. The early Christians were persecuted, but God chose Constantine to save the church and conquer paganism.[7] The Reformation purified the medieval church in order to set free the Word of God for a renewed mission of proclamation. Finally, America, for all of her faults and limitations, has been chosen by God to spread Protestantism across the globe, thus fulfilling the Great Commission. The straight and narrow line that can be drawn in this account from Constantine, through the Reformation, to America would no doubt send shudders down the spines of the liberal critics of the Bush administration, whether they are Christian or not. It exudes all of the rhetoric of a line drawn in the sand, daring anyone else to cross it. Of course, this evangelical account of history would need to be supplemented by many other developments—many other lines, leading in a variety of directions—to make it convincing. Although today I understand how the story taught to me in my youth deletes much of the richness and variety of church history, I still find it to be a more persuasive account of the workings of the Holy Spirit through history than the account of those who think capitalism and the birth of nation-states mark the utter ruin of the church.

Trusting in providence has always been one of the hardest aspects of the Christian life. Theologians should have a lot to say about the destiny of the world, but it is far from clear what role American globalism will play in God's plan. As Philip Jenkins has shown in his recent book *The Next Christendom*, American influence has enabled America to export homegrown varieties of evangelicalism and pentecostalism to the rest of the world.[8] In fact, there is a good case to be made that there are actually two globalisms competing for the future course of world history, one economic and the other religious. Jenkins observes that Christianity is all but dead in Europe, while the future of Christianity belongs to the Southern Hemisphere, where American-style Protestantism, along with more traditional churches, is flourishing. The economic interconnection of the world's nation-states might even provide some hope for the religious future of the Northern Hemisphere. African priests are helping to keep the Roman Catholic Church functioning in many northern countries, while Great Britain has 1,500 missionaries from more than fifty countries working in it. The Nigeria-based Redeemed Christian Church of God has active parishes in Dallas, Tallahassee, Houston, New York, Chicago, Washington, and many other cities. A religious revolution is afoot that will change America's role in the world as much as the revolution in free trade agreements. Christianity has left Europe behind, which suggests that the United States might have increasingly less in common with Europe and more in common with southern countries.

The coming revolution in Christianity will be deeply divisive. Southern Christianity, as Jenkins points out, is more conservative, more supernatural, and more orthodox in its theology than northern Christianity. Perhaps the shift of Christianity's center of gravity from the north to the south will finally break the hold of the Enlightenment on the life of faith. The forms of Christianity that are spreading most rapidly are technologically sophisticated and skilled in the ways of marketing, but they also represent the only international movement capable of challeng-

ing and shaping global capitalism. Those on the political left are probably just as worried about the spread of evangelicalism as the triumph
of American interests abroad, so my portrait of the future will provide
them with no comfort. Leftist political voices are still tied to the kinds
of criticisms that trace their genealogy back to Marx and other radical
European thinkers, but there is no international socialist or communist
movement to give these voices a platform or an audience. Already, there
are signs that the Southern Hemisphere is not only growing in numbers
but also establishing itself as the intellectual leadership of the Christian
faith. When that happens, a discourse on globalism will commence
that has the potential to become a worldwide drama far exceeding the
analyses of politically radical professors in European and American
higher education.

What role America will play in relationship to global Christianity is
anyone's guess, but American Christians cannot simply turn their back
on the world's best hope for freedom and democracy. Some theologians talk as if Christians should have nothing to do with any modern
nation-state. This ignores the fact that every society needs some form
of religion in order to ensure peace and order as well as to counter the
power of the state. When religion fails to provide a sacred canopy for
a persuasive account of ultimate meaning, communism or consumerism has been the ideology in the modern world most likely to flourish.
To the extent that the world really is becoming a smaller place, in the
sense of becoming more interconnected through the travel of people,
information, and goods, then it is appropriate to ask which religion will
be able to make the most sense of a political and economic globalism.
Some would suggest that it has already revealed itself to be a passive-
aggressive American imperialism, ready to take advantage of every
market in the benign name of freedom and democracy. This, as I have
argued, is an argument that overstates American strength and American
resolve. A better candidate to put forward as the future religion of globalism is evangelicalism in its various forms. Evangelicalism is capable of
spreading rapidly and efficiently due to its lack of institutional baggage.
It preaches a gospel that borders on Pelagianism in its requirements
that believers demonstrate the sanctifying effects of salvation. It thus
mixes easily with the rhetoric of individualism and freedom that drives
market economies.

All of this is not to say that it is necessarily a good thing for religions
to provide the structure that makes societies run smoothly. It is a devil's
bargain, with religions being used by political states as much as they
benefit from them. But in Christianity this awkward and no doubt
compromising relationship cannot be avoided. Christianity claims to
be a universal religion that offers not only happiness in the next life

but also purpose and meaning in this one. Christianity anticipates the kingdom of God, in which all order will be saturated by grace and suffused with God's will. Christianity cannot be marginalized as a church without a political message and mission. Its telos is to inform the world with a shape that is all-encompassing. History does have a direction, and Christ is its consummation. This does not sanction triumphalism, but it also does not excuse sectarianism. Christianity is destined to be reshaped by globalism as much as it will take advantage of globalism to fulfill the gospel's mandate.

In sum, the new globalism today is as much a part of divine providence as was the globalism of the Roman Empire. And just as the two globalisms of Rome and Christianity overlapped but were eventually shown to be separate—with the false globalism of Rome giving way to European Christendom—a similar history will be played out in the centuries to come. There were those in the ancient world who thought that Rome would last forever, just as there are those today who think that America will be an eternal and solo superpower, but I am convinced that God will use America as God used Rome for God's own purposes. Rome withered as the church spread, just as America will probably decline as evangelicalism continues to spread throughout the world, taking advantage of international consumerism and its technology to bring the Word to all peoples in all places, and thus fulfilling the Great Commission that Christ gave the disciples. The decision of the Bush administration to downplay its dependence on European cooperation for foreign affairs might prove, in the long run, to be a remarkably prescient move. Likewise, President Bush's evangelical Kantianism just might prove to be as influential in the centuries ahead as the liberal Enlightenment was in the centuries now behind us.

Notes

1. Stanley Hauerwas and Frank Lentricchia, eds., *Dissent from the Homeland: Essays after September 11* (Durham, NC: Duke University Press, 2003), 7.

2. Ibid., 35.

3. Ibid., 27.

4. Michael Ignatieff, "The Burden," *New York Times Magazine*, Jan. 2, 2003, 24. For more on this perspective, see Charles A. Kupchan, *The End of the American Era: U.S. Foreign Policy and the Geopolitics of the Twenty-first Century* (New York: Knopf, 2002).

5. Hauerwas and Lentricchia, *Dissent from the Homeland*, 64. Milbank not only finds America wanting when compared to Rome but also finds that "American neocolonialism is yet more insidious than the older variety," such as the British Empire (66). For another example of the analogy between Rome and America, see Richard A. Horsley, *Jesus and Empire: The Kingdom of God and the New World Disorder* (Minneapolis: Fortress, 2003).

6. Hauerwas and Lentricchia, *Dissent from the Homeland,* 65.

7. See Robert Louis Wilken, "In Defense of Constantine," *First Things* (April 2001): 36–40.

8. Philip Jenkins, *The Next Christendom: The Coming of Global Christianity* (New York: Oxford University Press, 2002).

10

International Justice as Equal Regard and the Use of Force

Jean Bethke Elshtain

Academic debates about international justice in recent decades have typically ranged over the terrain of distribution and re-distribution. From Dame Barbara Ward's *Rich Nations, Poor Nations*, published in the early 1960s, to calls during the Jubilee Year of 2000 for forgiveness of the Third World debt, justice is thought of in economic terms. The reigning assumption is that all of us are persons who, through neither fault nor merit of our own, happen to be born within the boundaries of a wealthy country or an impoverished one. Justice consists in righting the balance between these cases. I am not going to revisit this question, in part because I believe a more exigent matter lies before the international community, namely, how to bring about the political stability—the minimal civic peace—necessary to attain and to secure fundamental human goods, including, of course, a measure of distributive justice. These are preeminently political questions that involve the good or ill use of power.

The Preeminence of "the Political"

The political question must precede any discussion of distributive justice. Why? Because absent political stability, every attempt to prop up impoverished countries must fail.[1] Justice demands accountability, and there is no political accountability where there is no structure of power and laws. Instead one sees disasters like the recent unrest in the Congo, where human beings are prey to the ruthless, the inflamed, and the irresponsible. Absent such a structure, culminating in some form of political sovereignty, the likelihood of what we now routinely call "humanitarian catastrophes" is magnified many-fold. A paradigm of the ills attendant upon political instability absent a central, legitimate locus of power and authority is the disaster of so-called failed states. It is, of course, the case that states themselves, whose *raison d'être* is maintaining stability and civic peace, may become disturbers of civic peace, hence agents of injustice. An ossified, dictatorial order also qualifies as a violator of minimal civic peace, given the horrors of a state—like the Iraq of Saddam Hussein—in which fear reigns supreme. This latter, however, is a bit off to the side of the question I intend to focus on. What follows is an argument for international justice construed as an equal claim to the use of coercive force, deployed in your behalf, if you are a victim of one of the many horrors attendant upon radical political instability. Most often this instability is instigated by ruthless ideologues or presided over by feckless profiteers.[2] The force to be brought to bear in such cases is lodged within a structure of restraints that I will spell out. Equal regard backed up, if need be, by coercive force, is an ideal of international justice whose time has come.

The burden of this responsibility will be borne disproportionately by the United States, given its unique capability to project power. I realize that some will argue that the kinds of interventions I call for in this essay amount to imperialism. I believe, however, that we simply must get past the almost inevitable initial negative reaction to views that call on the United States to exercise robust powers of intervention. The doctrine that I will defend here differs quite significantly from past imperialisms since it involves neither colonization nor the imposition of any permanent structure of proconsuls (as was the practice of the Roman Empire). Instead of invoking the rather unhelpful imperialist tag, we should reflect on the nature of the interventions and likelihood that the intervening powers will fulfill their mission to assist.

If you are a political theorist, as am I, your starting point is almost invariably the ancient Greeks. Most often political theorists look to how the Athenians understood the life of the citizen in the polis. But what happens if you explore the contrast between the rules that applied to citizens within the polis and the norms and practices that governed dealings with foreigners? An ideal of to whom justice is owed lies at the heart of the matter. According to Athenian thinking—and it is this thinking that lies at the basis of what became known as realism or realpolitik in international relations—different spheres set the boundaries for norms of right and wrong, the just and the unjust. Justice governed relations among citizens within the polis. Force came into play between Athenians and others. What would be counted a wrong against a citizen was not so adjudged if it pertained to an external political entity or a foreigner.

The *locus classicus* of this rule in its most extreme form is the so-called Melian dialogue, familiar to all readers of Thucydides' great work *The History of the Peloponnesian War*. When the citizens of the island of Melos refused to give up their seven-hundred-year-old tradition of civic liberty, the Athenian generals proclaimed that the strong do what they will and the weak suffer what they must. The Athenians attacked the island, slew the men, young and old, and sold the women and children into slavery.[3] To be sure, diplomacy and arbitration might be called upon to mediate this norm of force in relations with external others, but the presumptive divide—justice as internal norm, force as external rule—held, with acts of generosity toward the foreigner embodying an exception.

To Whom Is Justice Owed?

Political and conceptual debate surrounding the concept of justice since the ancient Greeks concerns to whom justice is owed as well as in what justice consists. Over the centuries, there were challenges to the sharp "us" (citizens) versus "them" (foreigners) rule. One was embodied in Christian teaching. Christianity put pressure on the notion that good or ill treatment should be meted out differently, depending on whether or not a human being was or was not a member of one's particular tribe or polity. Instead, hospitality extended to all without exception. One of the most famous of the parables of Jesus of Nazareth illustrating this claim is the story of the Good Samaritan. If a Samaritan, with whom the Jews of Jesus' day had only hostile relations, could treat a beaten and robbed Jew with tenderness and mercy, was it not possible for a Samaritan to be good and for the normative presumptions to be reversed? Hospitality—*caritas*—obliged believers, whether the one to whom aid was proffered or from whom aid was received was a family or tribal member or a stranger.

In many ways, this melting down of the neighbor/stranger divide where moral obligation is concerned is counterintuitive. It is unsurprising that we feel most deeply obligated to family and friends, first and foremost; second, to members of our own culture, clan, or society; with foreigners and strangers coming in a distant third. An injustice meted out against one of our own pains us more keenly than does injustice perpetrated against those far removed from us by language, custom, and belief and separated from us by borders and geographic distance. This is only human and the fact that this "only human" intuition got solidified into enforced practice should not surprise us.

More surprising by far is the insistence that all human beings without distinction deserve consideration and should not be subjected to arbitrary abuse, a claim I have associated with Christian theology, whatever the lamentable shortcomings of Christian practice over the centuries. The ancient Greek distinction between justice and force never disappeared, of course. It made a powerful comeback in the writings of Machiavelli and other so-called civic republicans. It was re-encoded by the Peace of Augsburg (1555) and, most tellingly, the Treaty of Westphalia (1648). With Westphalia, the norm of justice as pertaining to members of a particular territorial entity was given official sanction in its recognizably modern form, marking the beginning of the international state system.

The presumption of state sovereignty held that the state alone was the arbiter of what counted as justice, law, freedom, and everything else within its bounded territory. The alternative—a world with multiple centers of contending self-help and incessant warfare—came to be seen as much less desirable than the alternative, despite the obvious excesses to which sovereigns might be drawn. Efforts at softening sovereign autonomy (associated with Hugo Grotius and the notion of international law) were only partially successful and were observed most often when hewing to international norms and state self-interest could be reconciled.

Just War as Comparative Justice

At the same time, Christian universalism not only remained alive in theological and moral arguments but was present as well in several traditions of theologically grounded political practice. Where the matter of international justice is concerned, the most important of these is the just or justified war tradition. Many will find this a surprising claim. How can a method of assessing whether a resort to war is justified, and going on to evaluate the means used to fight a war, bear directly on contemporary debates about international justice? The argument, simply put, is this: the just war tradition is not just about war. It is a theory of *comparative justice* applied to considerations of war and intervention. Among other things, this means that the post–World War II universalization of human rights deepens and enhances the importance and reach of the just war perspective rather than running counter to it. Just war arguments and universal human rights are not only not incompatible, they can and should be placed within the same frame. In what, then, does the notion of justice with universal applicability, embedded within the just war tradition, consist?

To answer this question, a précis of the basics of just war doctrine is required. Following that, I will argue that the just war tradition helps to secure a *citizenship model* for international justice—this by contrast to the model of victim/victimizer that underlies the humanitarian intervention model, one that invites the use of force as a form of rescue, even welfare, by contrast to the use of force as a way to strengthen or to secure a polity within which accountable officials are responsible for securing civic security, order, and minimal decency.

Just war argument insists that no unbridgeable conceptual and political divide be opened up between domestic and international politics, precisely the cleavage central to the ancient Greek world and, as well, to realpolitik, with its insistence that the rules that govern domestic moral conduct and obligation apply to the body politic internally and are inapplicable to relations between states that function in an international arena construed as a zone of anarchic self-help. Just war politics, by contrast, insists that while it would be utopian to presume that relations between states can be governed by the premises and care apposite in our dealings with family, friends, and fellow citizens, this does not mean that a war of all against all need kick in once one leaves the hearth, the neighborhood, or the borders of one's country.

Here it must also be noted that just war thinkers worry as well that appeals to a cosmopolitan order that minimizes or even aims to eliminate the distinction between the thick moral obligations we owe to those nearest and dearest and the thinner obligations that oblige us where strangers and those far removed from us are concerned, cut so powerfully against ordinary human moral intuitions and are cast so abstractly that they are either unrealizable in principle or unsustainable in practice. The universalism flowing from the obligation of neighbor-regard in the just war tradition, by contrast, *begins* with the concrete, then goes on to embrace members of one's church community as "brothers and sisters," and then extends to a wider circle from this humble beginning. This expanded ideal obliges those who are members of a particular community in relation to others outside their community. The obligation is a concrete one compelled by one's profession of faith that works from basic human experience outward, so to speak: this by contrast to the notion of universal categories and norms that descend from a great height and are supposedly untainted by particular interests or communal experiences.

The typical contrast—either the particular *or* the universal—at least as these are cast philosophically, is an artificial antinomy when assessed from the perspective of the theology that underlies the just war tradition. Within that theology, the world is one of *both . . . and.*

From Just War to Equal Regard

Just war thinking is best known as a cluster of concrete injunctions: what it is permissible to do; what it is not permissible to do, where the resort to, and the use of, force is concerned. For example, a war must be openly and legally pursued; a war must be a response to a specific instance of unjust aggression or the certain threat of such aggression; a war may be triggered by an obligation to protect the innocent (non-combatants), including those who are not members of one's polity, from certain harm; a war should be the last resort: these are the so-called *ad bellum* criteria.

As a set of strictures about war fighting, just war insists that means must be proportionate to ends—the rule of proportionality—and that a war be waged in such a way as to distinguish combatants from non-combatants—the principle of discrimination and the most important *in bello* criterion. Note that one harm that justifies a forceful response, if other criteria such as last resort are also met, is sparing the innocent from certain harm—the innocent being those in no position to defend themselves. A response to a direct attack is similarly exigent. Acts of aggression, whether against one's own people or against those who cannot defend themselves, are stipulated as cases of injustice that warrant the use of force. This does not mean one must respond with force. It does mean that a justice claim has been triggered and that a resort to force is justifiable without being automatic.

Herein lies the rub, the point at which just war and international justice as equal regard make contact. Because the origins of just war thinking lie in Christian theology, a view about human beings as equal in the eyes of God underscores what is at stake when persons are unjustly assaulted, namely, that human beings qua human beings deserve equal moral regard. Equal regard means one possesses an inalienable dignity that is not given by governments and cannot be revoked arbitrarily by governments or other political bodies or actors. It follows that the spectacle of people being harried, deported, slaughtered, tortured, or starved en masse constitutes a prima facie justice claim. Depending on the circumstances on the ground as well as the relative scales of power—who can bring force effectively to bear—an equal regard claim may trigger a movement toward armed intervention in behalf of the hounded, tortured, murdered, and aggrieved.

There are times when the claims of justice may override the reluctance to take up arms. This is a principle sanctified over the centuries in the case of aggrieved states who are the victims of aggression. As a principle applying to all peoples without distinction, however, this claim is by no means universally affirmed. What I am calling for is controversial, namely, the use of force as a remedy under a justice claim based on *equal regard* and *inviolable human dignity*. This principle takes a political form rather than the inviolable form of a Kantian categorical imperative that leaves no room for the operation of prudential and consequential concerns. Prudential considerations enter into all political decisions, including those based on an equal regard justice claim, an issue I say more about below. For now, the basic point is a presumptive case in favor of the use of armed force by a powerful state or alliance of states who have the means to intervene, to interdict, and to punish in behalf of those under assault.

If the claim is universal, some might cavil, ought not an international body respond? Perhaps, but all too often United Nations "peacekeepers"—and they are tagged "peacekeepers," not "soldiers"—are obliged by their rules of engagement (rules of disengagement would be more like it) to stand by as people are being rounded up and slaughtered. International bodies have defaulted on the use of coercive force in behalf of justice as equal regard. Joseph Nye points out that the "power of the veto in the Security Council has prevented it from authorizing the use of force for collective-security operations in all but three cases in the past half-century."[4] This makes the insistence that there are grievances and horrors to which "we" must respond—provided "we" can do so in a manner that avoids, to the extent that this is humanly possible, either deepening the injustice already present or creating new instances of injustice—doubly difficult to sort out.

Equal Regard: What It Means, What It Does Not Mean

Let's tackle the first difficulty—what it means to make a claim under the equal regard norm—before turning to the second vexation, namely, who can be called upon to use coercive force in behalf of justice.

Defining and defending international justice as the equal right to have force deployed in your behalf means that an aggrieved group has the obligation to make the case that theirs is a just cause of substantial gravity. Genocide or ethnic cleansing is the most obvious case in point. But there are others, including many man-made disasters, that are now the occasion for "humanitarian intervention." Devastating famine is a case in point. As Amartya Sen has demonstrated, famine on a catastrophic scale is most often the coming together of natural factors with manipulated starvation engineered by ruthless political actors to further their own ends. In such circumstances, it makes more sense to speak of intervention in a just cause, and to call it justified war, than to fog matters with the term "humanitarian relief." If attack helicopters, armored personnel carriers, automatic weapons, and the like are involved, it is a war of one sort or another. If famine is the *casus belli*, one interdicts and punishes those responsible for preventing food from reaching starving people.[5] Calling these situations humanitarian intervention only clouds the issue. The real problem is a political one, and coercive force remains an extension of politics by other means.

Let's unpack further an equal regard claim to the deployment of armed force in one's behalf. An implication of this claim is that a third party may be justified in intervening with force in order to defend those unable to defend themselves, to fight those who are engaged in unjust acts of harming, and to punish those who have engaged in unjust harm in order to diminish if not destroy their capacity to continue on a path of egregious and limitless violence of the sort embodied in Osama bin Laden's infamous *fatwas*—an example of the limitlessness of so-called holy wars—calling on all Muslims everywhere to kill all Americans wherever they may be found. Force that observes limits is frequently called upon to fight force without limits.

Here it is worth noting that the obligations of *caritas* in Christian theology are defining features of the just war thinking of such theologians as St. Augustine and St. Thomas Aquinas. Each was working and thinking in a pre-Westphalian world. The secularization of just war thinking and its insertion, so to speak, within a Westphalian model—especially if sovereignty becomes something akin to the highest political good—diminishes the neighbor-regard features of the just war tradition. Interestingly enough, scratch the post–World War II universalization of human rights that serves as a background to the neighbor-regard issue, albeit in nontheological terms, and you will find a theological claim lurking underneath.

Because I advance this argument as a form of comparative justice, it is important to note what the equal regard argument does not mean. It does not mean that any one nation or group of nations can or should respond to every instance of violation of the innocent, including that most horrific of all violations—genocide or ethnic cleansing.

It is important to note that the just war tradition incorporates a cautionary note: Be as certain as you can, before you intervene in a just cause, that you have a reasonable chance of success. Don't barge in and make a bad situation worse. Considerations such as these take us to the heart of the *jus in bello* rules, those restraints on the means deployed even in a just cause. Means must be proportionate to ends. The damage must not be greater than the offenses one aims to halt. Above all, non-combatant immunity must be protected, even as one recognizes that, in any armed conflict, noncombatants will fall in harm's way.

A prudential warning that intervention in a just cause might exacerbate the harm, or that the only means available in a given situation will themselves create unacceptable injustice—like massive damage to the civilian population of a country or group being harmed by another country or group—must be addressed within the equal regard–just war framework.[6] In such sad situations, those called upon to intervene are obliged to affirm the equal regard norm even as they spell out explicitly how and why they are unable or unwilling to undertake the risks attendant upon intervention with force. The reasons for standing down must themselves be grounded in the equal regard norm, for example, the high probability that more victims would die as a result of armed intervention in their behalf than would likely suffer if such intervention were not mounted.

This approach is better than the strategies of evasion and denial of the sort visible in the 1994 slaughter by Rwandan Hutus of Rwandan Tutsis, to take one example. Exculpatory strategies at the time included claiming that the full extent of the slaughter was unknown. Or that, as bad as the slaughter was, it wasn't *as* bad as other cases of genocide, so action that might put American (or other) soldiers in harm's way wasn't warranted. In this and other well-known cases, one is confronted frequently with the spectacle of officials speaking boldly about universal human rights and going on to revert to a narrow doctrine of national self-interest in order to evade the implications of embracing these rights. This tension is lodged in the heart of the United Nations itself—a universal body whose members are *sovereign* states, hence the final judges of their own interest. The moral candor and requisite decision making within the just war tradition make it more difficult to slide into the evasive maneuvers of trying to avoid the word "genocide," for example, or minimizing the problem in other ways because one has chosen not to act and would rather not discuss this openly. Killing of the innocent needn't rise to the level of genocide—although Rwanda was, in fact, a case of attempted genocide—to trigger an equal regard claim.

Accounts of the Bosnian war illustrate both evasion and ineptitude. Safe havens under a United Nations umbrella were declared for beleaguered Bosnian Muslims. People flowed into these safe havens and were there shot to pieces as United Nations peacekeepers stood by. Why? Because United Nations peacekeepers were impotent under standing rules of engagement. The United States, fearing unfavorable domestic political reaction, temporized, making promise after promise it never kept. Indeed, according to Samantha Power, word was sent down that administration spokespersons were to avoid using the word "genocide," because that word triggers a reaction of horror and might create pressure to act. She writes:

> First, they [administration officials] wanted to avoid engagement in conflicts that posed little threat to American interests, narrowly defined. And second, they hoped to contain the political costs and avoid the moral stigma associated with allowing genocide.[7]

By turning the issue into one of international peacekeeping rather than just war-making, ethnic cleansing proceeded apace. Refusing to name horrors correctly—calling genocide genocide, for example—is a strategy of evasion that becomes more difficult to mount if a clear commitment to international justice as equal regard attains a status akin to that now enjoyed by the right for a state to defend itself and, further, if the assumption is that the use of coercive force to interdict such violence—to stop its perpetrators—is a reasonable expectation rather than an act akin to moral supererogation.

Humanitarian Intervention or Equal Regard?

Suppose one state, or a coalition of states, intervenes in behalf of a victimized state or people. Does this in and of itself mean that the principle of equal regard is being honored in full? Not necessarily. Take, for example, United States intervention in Kosovo under the rubric of NATO authority.[8] The rules of NATO engagement in Kosovo are an example of a deflection of one central norm of *jus in bello* requirements, namely, that it is morally preferable, albeit politically excruciating, to risk the lives of one's own combatants than those of enemy noncombatants. With its political determination to keep American combatants out of harm's way—to enjoy a zero-casualty war—the Clinton administration embraced a principle I tagged *combatant immunity*, not only for our own combatants but, ironically, for Serbian soldiers, too, as no attempt was made to interdict the Serbian forces on the ground where the damage to Kosovar civilians continued and even escalated with NATO bombing.

The Serbian army operated with impunity for weeks even as plenty of infrastructural damage, harmful to civilian life, was going on.

In a hard-hitting piece, "War and Sacrifice in Kosovo," Paul W. Kahn scored this violation of the equal regard-just war norm. His comments are worth quoting at some length:

> If the decision to intervene is morally compelling, it cannot be conditioned on political considerations *that assume an asymmetrical valuing of human life.* This contradiction will be felt more and more as we move into an era that is simultaneously characterized by a global legal and moral order, on the one hand, and the continuing presence of nation-states, on the other. What are the conditions under which states will be willing to commit their forces to advance international standards, when their own interests are not threatened? Riskless warfare by the state in pursuit of global values may be a perfect expression of this structural contradiction within which we find ourselves. In part, then, our uneasiness about a policy of risk-less intervention in Kosovo arises out of an incompatibility between the morality of the ends, which are universal, and the morality of the means, which seem to privilege a particular community. There was talk during the campaign of a crude moral-military calculus in which the life of one NATO combatant was thought to be equivalent to the lives of 20,000 Kosovars. Such talk meant that those who supported the intervention could not know the depth of our commitment to overcoming humanitarian disasters. Is it conditioned upon the absence of risk to our own troops? If so, are such interventions merely moral disasters—like that in Somalia—waiting to happen? If the Serbs had discovered a way to inflict real costs, would there have been an abandonment of the Kosovars?[9]

It is my contention that the humanitarian intervention doctrine animating the Kosovo war, triggered by the sight of Kosovars fleeing by the thousands, being shoved into trains and expelled, together with eyewitness reports of hundreds, if not thousands, simply "disappearing," not only built in no barriers to the kind of calculus Kahn condemns, it tacitly encouraged a situation of unequal regard.[10] I will say more about just why this is, but first it is important to acknowledge the attractiveness and moral power of the humanitarian relief model. It taps many of our deepest human reactions and sympathies. For some, the cry of pity is natural (Rousseau made such an argument), simply part of our human makeup. For others, a complex capacity for empathy that emerges developmentally is involved. Certainly the backdrop of Christianity and the insistence that one offer the shirt off one's back to one in need; that one give even though one has little oneself; that one sacrifice for those less fortunate—all comes into play here. The problem emerges when such potent human sentiments are refracted as state policy. How so?

The state's primary task is maintaining civic peace. Constitutive of civic peace is justice, especially in its retributive form as punishment for those who prey on others, who violate civic order, whether one construes this order as emerging from a social contract or in some other way. None of the other goods human beings cherish can flourish if one lives in a world in which, in St. Augustine's mordant phrase, people are "devoured like fishes." Beyond order, the state is also the instrument of justice in the sense of just deserts. For a variety of complex cultural reasons, citizens in the modern West, shaped as it is by centuries of Christian belief and practice, feel more "comfortable"—in current parlance—with the compassionate end of politics than with the punitive or coercive end required to make possible the free flow of *caritas* in the first place.[11]

Humanitarian intervention relies on a model of international victimization. Those victimized are represented as in need of relief. We—the more powerful—come to their assistance as an act of pity or, at best, empathy, rather than as a requirement of justice for those perceived as our equals in moral regard. The humanitarian relief model in such circumstances is somewhat analogous to the bureaucratic welfare model of a needy client dependent upon the largesse of a powerful and remote provider. This invites situations in which American soldiers, the best equipped and trained in the world, are deployed as relief workers—tasks that could be undertaken by others, including nonmilitary American personnel. To the extent that stopping violent activities prevents relief from going to victims, to that same extent just war principles come into play. Even here, however, the model that ought to pertain in the use of force *and* in the provision of life is a civic and political one—the model of equal regard.

The equal regard doctrine as an elementary requirement of international justice sets up a *citizenship model*. We—the more powerful—respond to attacks against persons who cannot defend themselves because they, like us, are human beings, hence equal in regard to us, and because they, like us, are members of nations, states, or would-be states whose primary obligation is to protect the lives of those citizens who inhabit their polities. Thus, *all* states or would-be states have a stake in building up an international civic culture in which fewer horrors such as Rwanda or Kosovo take place and in which those that do take place trigger a level of concern that warrants the use of armed force, unless grave and compelling reasons preclude such intervention. We intervene by sending in soldiers who fight under rules of engagement that abide by just war norms, most importantly, noncombatant immunity.

If we cannot intervene, other means must be resorted to immediately. People should not be slaughtered because powerful nations are dithering, hoping the whole thing will soon be over and using domestic political considerations as a trump card in refusing to do the right thing.

Doing the right thing is frequently, if not uniformly, consistent with the interest all states have in preventing the emergence of deadly cycles of violence. As Samantha Power notes, "people victimized by genocide or abandoned by the international community do not make good neighbors, as their thirst for vengeance, their irredentism, and their acceptance of violence as a means of generating change can turn them into future threats."[12]

I have long argued in my work that moral imperatives are not so many nice-sounding nostrums that we can simply ignore when the chips are down in favor of hard-headed evocations of national interest but, instead, that ethical considerations are a core feature of American national interest. It is in our long-term national interest to foster and to sustain an international society of equal regard. An equal regard standard is central to a well-functioning international system composed of decent, if not perfect, states. These states may or may not be democratic in our constitutional and representational sense. But some form of what we usually call democracy is essential in the sense that avenues for public involvement and engagement in the life of a polity must be available. This is no "imposition" of some alien "Western" ideal, a holdover from colonialism. The discourse of human rights and democratic decency is now worldwide: witness the student protests against the Islamic Republic of Iran, with its theocratic stringencies. Stopping brutality and arbitrary violence, including terrorism of international reach, is both a strategic necessity and a moral requirement of the highest priority. There will always be moral heroes who challenge tyrannical regimes, even at the risk of their lives. But for the overwhelming majority of people in any society, the development of genuine political freedom becomes a salient issue when freedom from fear is largely won.

The politics of equal regard, hence the right to make a claim for armed intervention rather than simply humanitarian assistance, establishes a framework for the achievement of a decent, stable international order as the necessary prelude to freedom and to international justice.

Many states are capable of responding to local situations indigenous to a region, even if that means sending their soldiers into a neighboring country. But if you come from a country whose nationals comprise a minority population within a country at some remove, and they are being destroyed, or threats are made to destroy them, your obligation under the equal regard rule is clear. You are obliged to make your case on the grounds of justice rather than mere humanitarian relief as you call upon those with the means to intervene.

Who Enforces Equal Regard?

I argued above that all states or would-be states have a stake in creating and sustaining an international system of equal regard. This is not, of course, entirely true as an empirical fact. It is a normative claim derived from principles that are part of the universal armamentarium of states at present (whether they like it or not), if they are members of the United Nations and signatories of various international conventions. Not all states, however, have the capacity to act to enforce a model of equal regard. Given my argument, the more powerful have greater responsibilities. One might call this the Spider-Man ethic: with great power comes great responsibility.[13] Despite all the clamor about U.S. power, and the resentment it engenders in some quarters, the "we" likely to be called upon to intervene to protect the innocent from harm, the "we" to whom a country without the means to intervene would likely make its case, is the United States. The United Nations cannot be ignored, of course, but it has not proved to be effective in this regard. *Once* a measure of order is restored, United Nations peacekeepers may indeed be the best body to enforce a fragile peace, at least in some situations. But the United Nations habitually temporizes, sends radically mixed signals, and takes so long to gear itself up and put peacekeepers on the ground that its unreliability in this regard needn't be argued at great length. I have already noted that a Security Council veto is the predictable outcome when a "collective security" matter is brought before that body.

The upshot is that the likeliest "we" at present, with both the means to enforce international justice as an equal regard norm and a strong motive to do so, is the United States.

The United States is capable of projecting its power as no other state can. This does *not* mean that the United States should "go it alone." Coalitions of the willing based on issue-specific concerns are one possibility, already part of our repertoire. Surely there are other avenues for multilateral action, perhaps a series of regional security alliances. The United States will have to demonstrate its reliability to the skeptical, of course, by showing that, in a post–Cold War world, principled concerns of equal regard are not going to play second fiddle to geopolitical issues that lead, or have led, to a whole series of unsavory alliances between the U.S. and some very unpleasant people and polities. While understandable contextually, such alliances are now less and less defensible. The United States is itself premised on a set of universal propositions concerning human dignity and equality. There is no conflict *in principle* between our national identity and universal claims and commitments. The conflict lies elsewhere—between what we affirm and aspire to, what we can effectively do, and what we can responsibly do. Here fundamental human moral intuitions will inevitably and invariably come into play. I described these as a powerfully felt human urgency to protect, to care for, and, yes, to seek justice in behalf of those nearest and dearest to us—our families and friends. Second, we feel these obligations keenly toward our fellow countrymen and -women and, third, *toward* a more universal category of all persons without distinction.

If the case can be made—and it isn't just an exculpatory strategy to avoid acting under the equal regard principle—that those nearest and dearest (categories 1 and 2 of family and friends and fellow nationals) will be directly imperiled if one acts, the obligation to act under equal regard may be affirmed even as exigent prudential reasons for why one cannot act in this case are proffered. A reasonable and justifiable departure from the equal regard norm, for example, a claim that substantial harm will come to one's fellow citizens if one acts, not as a remote possibility but as a nigh-certain probability, does not apply to the anticipated harm to military men and women attendant upon any commitment to coercive force: it is their job to go into harm's way. It is also their honor to fight as just warriors rather than as terrorists unleashed like the Athenians at Melos, determined to slay young and old alike or to take them into slavery without exception.

It is extraordinarily difficult to articulate a strong universal justice claim and to assign a particular state and its people a disproportionate burden to enforce that claim. But international justice as coercive force in behalf of equal regard does precisely this. At this critical juncture in human history, the United States is a polity that acknowledges on a foundational level universal premises and is sufficiently powerful to act, or to put pressure on others to act, when and where no other state or states can. The brutal Melian rule is hereby reversed: The strong do what they must in order that the weak not suffer what they too often will.

Notes

1. It is, of course, true that conflict over resources may exacerbate political tension and invite unrest. That said, without a structure of law, a mailing address, and a phone number for what could reasonably be called a "state," tensions over economic maldistribution are likely to erupt into the anomic violence from which so many human beings now suffer. Unless responsible structures of government are in place, it is not possible to foster greater economic equality. The political question precedes the economic one, despite the fact there is a form of economic determinism embedded in many perspectives that put markets prior to law and politics.

2. The instability I refer to is not the disturbance of civic peace attendant upon social and political contestation. In such cases, including those involving widespread civil disobedience, a structure of laws and accountability is in place—and it is precisely this structure that becomes a target for protesters to the extent that they believe the law

encodes specific injustices. I am referring to lawless situations of cruelty, arbitrariness, violence, and caprice, and these abound at present.

3. Thucydides, it must be noted, did not lift up the Melian dialogue as a depiction of exemplary behavior on the part of the Athenian generals; indeed, it presaged disaster for Athens. Oddly enough, however, this extreme case of the use of force is often located by contemporary realists as a case in point for their perspective.

4. Joseph S. Nye Jr., "U.S. Power and Strategy after Iraq," *Foreign Affairs* 82, no. 4 (July/August 2003): 68. As Nye points out, "the UN is torn between the strict Westphalian interpretation of state sovereignty and the rise of international humanitarian and human rights law that sets limits on what leaders can do to their citizens. To complicate matters further, politics has made the UN Charter virtually impossible to amend" (68).

5. I would not use U.S. military personnel to respond to authentic natural disasters, like flood relief. International humanitarian relief agencies, including nonmilitary U.S. personnel, NGOs, should be deployed in such instances. At the same time, U.S. military personnel deployed in the aftermath of a coercive military operation to help restore civic order, repair or build up an infrastructure, police chaotic situations, and the like, makes enormous good sense. Given our likely continuing obligations in this regard, the U.S. military will require additional personnel both for the near and the long term.

6. Here precision guided weaponry has rolled back many arguments that modern war and the just war tradition are by definition incompatible. This is surely true of a total war absent restraint. It is not true of a limited war with restraint and fought in order to punish egregious aggression, to interdict terrible violence, to prevent further harm.

7. Samantha Power, "Genocide and America," *New York Review of Books*, March 14, 2002, 15–18.

8. It is fascinating that the decision by the Clinton administration to by-pass the United Nations *entirely* passed by largely without notice—certainly without the denunciations that were routine fare in op-eds and antiwar arguments in the run-up to the Second Gulf War. It is as if the Bush administration and its allies were punished for *attempting* to act through the UN and finding their way blocked; this despite the fact that Iraq was in material breach of the terms of the 1991 truce concluding the First Persian Gulf War.

9. Paul W. Kahn, "War and Sacrifice in Kosovo," *Philosophy and Public Policy Quarterly* 19, no. 2/3 (spring/summer 1999). An online copy of the essay is available at www.puaf.umd.edu/IPPP/spring_summer99/kosovo.htm.

10. Let me be clear that this was not in any way an explicit policy aim; rather, it is one attendant upon what is now the tradition of so-called humanitarian intervention.

11. This is a complex cultural development. But something has happened over the past four decades that drains the Judeo-Christian tradition, for Christians or "post-Christians," at least, of the powerful images of God as sovereign, as the instigator and enforcer of justice, central to the Old Testament and absorbed, therefore, into New Testament teaching. I grapple with this issue in my recent book *Just War against Terror: The Burden of American Power in a Violent World* (New York: Basic Books, 2003), see especially chapters 7 and 8.

12. Power, "Genocide and America."

13. One of my grandsons is a Marvel and D.C. comics addict, so I am very well acquainted with superheroes at the moment.

WHITHER
THE CHURCH?

11

Who Are We?

Being Christian in an Age of Americanism

Allen R. Hilton

The United States enters the twenty-first century as the world's only superpower. From this august throne, the eyes and aspirations of the government have turned outward toward empire and an expanded vision of manifest destiny. Commitments to allies, which formerly symbolized American security in a dangerous Cold War world, have come into question as U.S. power reaches unrivaled levels. The Iraqi war was the first in what will undoubtedly become a series of initiatives that assert unilateral American will, presence, and influence on the world stage.

In this geopolitical context, American Christians face important decisions about our identity. As the United States government revises its foreign policy in light of changed circumstances, so the churches in the United States must ask what will be our means of carrying out our biblical mandate to bring good news to the nations. The way we churches orient ourselves to the national government will greatly determine the shape of Christian mission in the decades to come. Will we direct our first energies toward persuading the White House and Congress to enact humane international policies, or will we seek rather with our first energies to establish our own separate international policies? Will we continue to pursue the mediated goods of Christendom, or will our activism be directed more immediately toward the people of the world? And even before we can answer this important question, a prior one must be posed: To what extent can American Christians expect the United States government to be a worthy and effective vehicle of the good God hopes to do on earth?

In the pages that follow, we will ask the question of whether internationally interested Christian activism in America should be directed primarily toward the U.S. government or immediately toward the people in need around the world. We will look together at the inherent limitations of a nation-state in intending and carrying out other-interested acts. Then, these limitations will be juxtaposed with the unshackled generosity that lies at the center of the Christian story, toward the end of envisioning a Christian international policy that is appropriate to the new age of American empire.

All roads lead to identity. In these twilight hours of Christendom, it is time to redefine the position of the church vis-à-vis the state—to call into question the church's self-limiting role as a weaker cousin among democracy's power brokers. It is time, in short, for American Christians to ask soul-searchingly and humbly, "Who are we?"

A Case Study in National Identity

On March 17, 2003, President George W. Bush addressed the people of the United States in primetime to announce that he had given Saddam Hussein and his sons the choice to leave Iraq within two days or face a U.S. military invasion. In that speech, President Bush named two reasons for the ultimatum—Iraq's possession of Weapons of Mass Destruction (WMD) and links between Saddam Hussein's government and the al-Qaeda terrorists: "Intelligence gathered by this and other governments leaves no doubt that the Iraq regime continues to possess and conceal some of the most lethal weapons ever devised," and "The [Iraqi] regime . . . has aided, trained and harbored terrorists, including operatives of al-Qaeda . . ." Mr. Bush ultimately drew the two threats into one ominous specter: "The danger is clear: using chemical, biological or, one day, nuclear weapons, obtained with the help of Iraq, the terrorists could fulfill their stated ambitions and kill thousands or hundreds of thousands of innocent people in our country, or any other."[1]

Even before Mr. Bush's speech, the veracity of his claims about WMD and Iraqi links to al-Qaeda had come under heavy scrutiny in the press, and during the wartime months that followed, even the administration itself lost faith in those claims. By September, Mr. Bush would admit that Saddam Hussein had no connection to the September 11 bombings; and by January of 2004, the U.S. secretary of state, Colin Powell, admitted that he saw "no smoking-gun link" between the Iraqi government and al-Qaeda terrorism.[2] As to the WMD, in a primetime interview with ABC's Diane Sawyer during December of 2003, President Bush dismissed the absence of evidence for WMD in Iraq, saying, "What's the difference?"[3] And by January of 2004, the former U.S. chief CIA weapons inspector Dr. David Kay appeared before a congressional panel and averred that WMD had still not been located in Iraq and that the prospect of ever finding them was remote.[4] Whether by mistake or by deceit, then, the claims about weapons and al-Qaeda links appear to have been false.

The rhetorical decisions that went into preparing the March 17 speech might have gone differently. As he prepared, Mr. Bush had another nobler-sounding rationale to offer the nation as cause for going to war. There were undoubtedly many personal, financial, economic, and political motivations at work in Mr. Bush and his policy camp. Among these were retaliation for Saddam's defiance and attempt on the life of the president's father; profiteering considerations for friends of an oil-friendly administration; considerations of the U.S. long-term oil supply; and the political advantage it might lend to the bid for reelection in 2004. However, the president was not going to go to his people and make the case for avenging his father's humiliation, or increasing the profits of American oil companies, or lowering the cost of gasoline to consumers, or winning reelection.

It happens, though, that in this mixed bag of forces that drove the White House toward military action, one salutary motive stood out. It was a badly kept secret in Washington at the time, and it later became patently clear that, for some in the neoconservative camp, the stated motivation toward war was not preemptive defense, but rather the hope of liberating the Iraqi people and building an exemplary democratic government as a starting point to reconstructing the Arab world. Former Treasury Secretary Paul O'Neill would later reveal that Paul Wolfowitz, Richard Perle, and other neoconservatives in the president's policy stable had begun pitching the ouster of Saddam very soon after Mr. Bush took office, citing these very purposes. In fact, once the assertion that Iraq harbored WMD and supported al-Qaeda was undermined, the administration fell back on precisely these claims as political cover. But on the eve of war, with a nation to persuade, Mr. Bush did not even once mention the benefit that war might offer to the Iraqi people or the people of the Middle East.

The natural question in light of these two observations is, "Why?" Why would the Bush administration risk its credibility with the American people by offering what they knew and we now know to have been very flimsy intelligence in order to rationalize this war? Why would Bush not go to his people with the very heartwarming purpose of liberating the oppressed people of Iraq? Or the similarly inspiring plan to build democracies that would provide a structure for social progress in the Middle East? These were the best hopes of some policy makers in the Bush camp. Nonetheless, consistently, right up through the March 17 speech quoted above, President Bush called his people to war as a form of preemptive defense against what turned out to be a very minor military threat. When the chips were down, on the eve of military intervention and on the basis of very thin military intelligence, the Bush administration appealed to Americans' fears for themselves, rather than appealing to American hopes for others. Why? Why lie when you can state a truth that is more inspiring?

The Power of Story

Narratives form persons and narratives form communities. This discovery—which is not really a discovery at all, but a renewed appreciation of a classical understanding—may turn out to be the signature contribution of late-twentieth-century Euro-American intellectual culture. The insight is not new to postmodern thought, but against the backdrop of the isolated choosing self offered up by the Enlightenment, it seems like a new idea. Philosophers of language, sociologists of knowledge, anthropologists, theologians, and political scientists of the last five decades have increasingly come to appreciate the profound role socialization plays in determining individual and communal lives.[5] Enlightenment anthropology pictured a rational, choosing, Kantian self—a self built with the standard equipment of universal categories that allow it objectivity and a vantage for disinterested decision making. In fact, Immanuel Kant so underestimated the role of cultures in producing selves that he could imagine that his categorical imperative—which, of course, amounts to Jesus' Golden Rule put otherwise—was altogether rationally intuited, with no appreciable assistance from a continuous, seventeen-century legacy of Christianity in his own culture.[6]

Twenty-first-century thinkers cannot abide this oversight. In fact, we acknowledge not only that *individuals* are stamped by enculturation, but also that *communities themselves* can and do actually take on a story-formed character. As collectives, human communities not only shape their members but also are shaped by the assumptions their members hold in common. While early Christianity has received a great deal of attention in this regard,[7] it is true of all human communities. Among the

Nuer of Africa, the cargo cults of Melanesia, or the coal miners of West Virginia, the myths a people share with one another shape the ethos they will embody and so form their identity as a culture. Significantly for this discussion, what is true for individuals and for individual clans and cultures is also true of nations.

The Nation's Story

Like the early Christians or Papua New Guinean tribes, the American people are formed by our defining narratives. As such, it is important to examine those stories in order to understand the possibilities open to us as a nation. The formative myths are myriad, of course—stories of pilgrims bravely crossing the Atlantic, of revolutionaries boldly throwing off the yoke of tyranny, of blue-coats freeing African Americans from the tyranny of slavery, of a Horatio Alger-like rise to the pinnacles of national prosperity, of women and African Americans courageously seeking franchise, and now of the one superpower holding the world together by its wisdom. On the other side of the moral ledger, of course, lie the narratives of oppression that necessitated each liberating moment: of Africans enslaved, Japanese interred, "communists" imprisoned, protesters abused, and now of Arab thousands detained, uncharged, in a post-9/11 hysteria. However, the canonical American narratives envision a brave, independent, prosperous, powerful nation that now rightly sits on the throne of twenty-first-century world dominance.

Amid all the American myths, the one "story" that most consistently and enduringly shapes the national character is the story that is embedded in the legal language of the U.S. Constitution. One might discuss the formative influence of the Constitution through its binding nature as law, and that is the most obvious aspect of its governance. However, there is an effective story etched in its pages as well. While it does not take the form of a narrative, in its own language and fashion, the Constitution nonetheless chronicles the highest ideals of its people in a way that can be told as story.

Seeking "a more perfect union . . . justice . . . and domestic tranquility," this people's charter members penned a defining document that would establish the boundaries of its conduct and its aspirations. As the American people evolves, so does the document and its story, so that the Constitution not only governs its people, but records its history as well. Amendments mark watershed change. The proud voice of successful revolution, the glory of emancipation, the franchise of women and then African Americans, and many other amending moments are all spelled out in its pages, making it something of a diary of our nation's best efforts to realize its promise. In that capacity, it registers the story of the nation's formation and progress.

As a register of American identity, the U.S. Constitution offers us a useful lens through which to look again at the White House on the evening of March 17, 2003. As we review President Bush's decision to feature preemptive defense rather than humanitarian intervention in his speech,[8] the pertinent aspect of that august document is the boundary of its beneficence. The beautiful words of the preamble sing out the glories of a government that promises great benefaction *to its citizens*. It does not, in any of its articles or amendments, address the well-being of any person who dwells outside its borders. There has not yet been and will undoubtedly never be an amendment to the U.S. Constitution that provides for the care of Ethiopians or Australians or Koreans or Poles who remain in their homeland. As enlightened as it is, so great a turning point in the history of human governments as the American Constitution intends and tends only to the well-being of Americans.

This discovery is not surprising. Nation-states exist for their own benefit. This may seem like an obvious observation, but it is crucial for helping us understand why an American president with a very flimsy rationale for a defensive war and (perhaps) a much stronger humanitarian rationale for liberating and reorganizing an oppressed people must nonetheless stand on that flimsy ground and declare a war of preemptive defense. As much as it might have brought a proud thrill to some Americans' hearts to do so, Mr. Bush could not go before his nation with a case for spending their money, their sons, and their daughters rescuing Iraqis or insuring the welfare of Middle Eastern peoples for *their own sake*. The benefit to Americans would be far too indirect.

A nation with a humanitarian foreign policy is the stuff of an idealist's fiction. Aaron Sorkin's *The West Wing* arrives at this point in its fourth season. When genocide ravages the fictitious Equatorial Kundu—a nation offering the U.S. no strategic military or economic advantage—and President Bartlet must develop a strategic response, he asks speechwriter Will Bailey a rhetorical question: "Why is it that I value an American life more than a Kundunese life?" Bailey answers accusingly, "I don't know, sir, but you do." In Sorkin's imagined world, President Bartlet sees the error of his ethnocentric ways and responds with a policy plan that is unique in human history: "A nation with a foreign policy based solely on humanitarian principles."[9]

So much for that fictional world where U.S. presidents can be Nobel Prize-winning economists with rhetorical polish and good taste. In the real Pennsylvania Avenue White House, Will Bailey would properly have to answer the president's question, "Because it's your job, sir." The American president, whatever her or his ideals, is vocationally responsible to the American people. The very Americentric Constitution is his or her sworn focus upon inauguration: "I do solemnly swear (or affirm) that I will faithfully execute the office of President of the United States, and will to the best of my ability, preserve, protect and defend the Constitution of the United States." The American president is hired to serve American citizens.

The logic of Mr. Bush's implicit argument in this speech is simple and clear, and it reflects the moral limitation of nation-states. The U.S. Constitution, which the president pledges upon inauguration to "preserve, protect and defend," was ordained and established partly to "provide for the common defense." The purported threat that Iraq posed to American security thus made it the American president's duty to declare and enact a preemptive war, and Mr. Bush closed his speech accordingly. "The United States of America has the sovereign authority to use force in assuring its own national security. That duty falls to me, as Commander-in-Chief, by the oath I have sworn, by the oath I will keep."[10]

The Church's Story

Christian communities purport to be formed by an altogether different constitution. The Christian story pictures a God who creates the world out of nothing for the sake of the created and who later enters human history actively to assist humanity—by calling Abraham's family to be a blessing to all nations, by delivering Abraham's family out of oppression through Moses, by extending the bounds of divine care through the prophets' visions, and finally by entering history in Jesus of Nazareth. Dietrich Bonhoeffer rightly called Jesus "the man for others," for his purpose is "not to be served, but to serve, and to give his life a ransom for many" (Mark 10:45). The Jesus of this story crosses boundaries of race, helping and then commending a Gentile centurion (Matt. 8: 5–13); of gender, offering "living water" to a Samaritan woman (John 4); of nation, extending a healing hand to a woman of Syro-Phoenecia (Mark 7:24–37); of social place, as he walks into the lonely world of a leper (Mark 1:40–45) and a prostitute (John 8); and even of strife, as he forgives those who have engineered his execution (Luke 23:34). The character in whom Christianity finds its identity is eminently oriented to the well-being of others.

This same generous One imparts this identity to the church, "the people for others," commissioning them as his agents to preach the good news to all nations (Matt. 28:19). He issues them the challenge of following him in a pattern of service to one another (Mark 10:

42–45), of moving beyond normal communal boundaries to bring healing to a broken and fragmented world (Acts 1:8), and even of loving enemies and praying for persecutors (Matt. 5:44). The Christian community is constituted, then, not primarily for its own sake but for the sake of others.

We should allow ourselves no pretense or illusion here. The Christian community has not been fully formed by this example and these exhortations at any point in its nearly two-millennia-long history. In fact, Christian groups have shown a discouraging capacity for disastrous failure. This failure is to be expected. In the battle to form persons and peoples, the grand narratives of cultures are pushing a rock up the hill of native self-serving that is the biological deposit of evolution. The attempt to transcend this native self-serving, family-serving, and clan-serving should be expected to meet with incomplete and spotty success. However, postmodernism helps us to realize that a culture will begin to counter this self-serving instinct only to the extent that its grandest myths empower it to do so.

The grand narratives of Christianity do precisely this, and they have not been spoken for 2,000 years without effect. It is normal Christian behavior to gather on a Sunday and hear an exhortation to feed poor people for the poor people's sake, to make peace for the sake of the disputants, to entertain strangers, and to resist the urge to retaliate. This is normal Christian conversation, and it often produces normal Christian behavior. While it is not uncommon to hear ministers sound forth the joy that will attend Christian lives lived generously for others' sake, a survey of pulpits will quickly demonstrate that these ministers feel no obligation to ground their plea in the motivational structure of self-interest or to apologize for calling their congregations to acts and attitudes of self-sacrifice. This premise of other-interested life and conduct is the central identifying characteristic of Christianity, embedded in the primal narratives of creation and cross. It exists often as an unmet hope, but it remains the story-formed aspiration of the Christian people. Christians are, in the terms of their constitution, "the people for others," and they know that because the Bible tells them so.

Living into Our Stories

This comparison of national and ecclesial stories poses a challenge to the rarely questioned assumption of American Christians, right-wing and left-wing, that a democratic state ought to and is able to serve as a primary vehicle of the good God will accomplish through

God's church in the world. This governmentally activist approach
to Christian citizenship is a product of marrying Christendom and
democracy. It is seen most vividly in organizations like the Moral
Majority and the Christian Coalition on the right, and on the other
end of the spectrum in the National Council of Churches and its most
recent left-leaning progeny, the Clergy Leadership Network; but it is
prevalent in denominational offices and in congregations across the
nation. While they strongly disagree on what Christian good looks
like, liberals and conservatives in the church seem to share this one
assumption: the church should devote considerable resources of time,
energy, and money to raise its voice among others in a democracy,
in order to exert pressure on the government to carry out Christian
good by means of its foreign policy.

One purpose of this essay is to point out that these strategies of
Christendom are bound to end in frustration. We have seen that if
postmodern insights into character and community formation are to
be believed, the conservative or liberal Christian hope can expect only
accidental successes. Communities rarely transcend their stories. The
United States government will continue to enact policies and develop
strategies that can be presented to the American people as serving
their own self-interest.

Attempting to run an ethic of justice and mercy and peace and love
for all peoples through the alien filter of a government charged to
serve only its own people will lead to one of two ends: either it will
entail cleverly disguising policies that are shaped by the cross and
trying to pass them off as prudent and sound national self-interest,
or it will involve abandoning the cross and settling for other more
prudent ways of being in the world.

Trying to dress up the Christian way of the cross to look like self-
interested American foreign policy is a project bound for failure. As
an example, Christian leaders in the United States routinely expend
a great deal of time, money, and energy attempting to guide the administration and Congress one way or another on this war and other
foreign policy issues. For example, in an ecumenical letter to the
president, dated September 12, 2002, fifty undersigned "leaders of
American churches and church-related organizations . . . oppose[d]
on moral grounds the United States taking further military action
in Iraq" at that time.[11] Of the five paragraphs in the ecumenical letter, four might have been written by any military or policital adviser
to the president, Christian or non-Christian. Despite a brief nod to
morality, the letter's opposition is put in strategic and international-
political terms, rather than moral terms. Thrice it references "U.S.

interests" as a worthy consideration for fifty Christian leaders and denominational heads.

Letters like these have become *pro forma* duties for denominational heads and other church leaders. They are undoubtedly seen by these leaders and by some of their flock as a function of their prophetic role. However, as with this one, these prophecies almost always prove manifestly ineffective and take on an aspect, at best, of token gestures and, at worst, of pathetic armchair quarterbacking. The five-paragraph letter of September 12 quickly trots through a few moral considerations before spending most of its words on the "national interests" of the United States. However, even had the letter been skillfully crafted and elegantly persuasive, it carried no political clout in an age when left-wing clergy find themselves unable to carry their congregations with them. It was an empty act that is emblematic of an approach to "world mission" that is doomed to fail.

Compare the effectiveness of activists in the Christendom model to that of direct Christian activists on the issue of AIDS in Africa. The former approach lobbies Congress and the White House to appropriate aid money. After years of lobbying, last spring Christian lobbyists celebrated what they thought was a victory when President Bush pledged in his 2003 State of the Union address to appropriate over $20 billion to help poor African nations in their battle against AIDS. But then on January 27, 2004, facing an election year and feeling deficit pressures, President Bush demoted this initiative on his priority scale and announced that the promised AIDS funding would be cut considerably. In other words, these American Christians entreated the government leaders of their quasi-Christian nation to send money to non-Christian organizations and governments who would then be asked to increase their own budget for combating the disease and distribute it to various service outlets. The first link in that considerable chain weakened, so the aid remains in doubt.

In contrast to this contingent and mediated activism, there is the more direct international policy of American Christian missionaries in Africa. *New York Times* op-ed columnist Nicholas Kristof, a very outspoken critic of conservative Christianity in America, nonetheless had to marvel and applaud when he visited Africa in the summer of 2003 and observed the salutary role that evangelical missionaries were playing in those AIDS-ravaged societies. He quotes Helene Gayle, head of the AIDS project for the Bill and Melinda Gates Foundation, calling their Christian orphanages, schools, clinics, and hospitals a veritable "cornerstone" of the African health system. These direct missions continue, unblessed (and unfettered) by money or policy statements from the United States government or the governments of African states, and, according to Ms. Gayle, "in some countries they serve more people than the government health system."[12] Even skeptics stop and take notice when the church attends to the business of being the church for others. More importantly, though, people in need actually get help and Christian love is delivered directly, person to person.

The grand narratives of Christianity do not call upon Christians to take steps to ensure that their neighbors receive love. In those narratives, Christians are commanded to love their neighbors themselves. What I have referred to here as the Christendom model of Christian activism hopes to extend love to neighbor in a very contingent and mediated form: "If we can convince the massive and powerful American government that our Christian policy is in their best interest, or if its policies and ours happen to overlap, then big government will carry out our end for us." This approach to Christian mission ends with Christians reading the newspapers to see whether God is getting things done in the world, rather than finding our way to the poor or the sick or the war-torn and extending our own hand of love.

If we continue to place hope in our power incrementally to alter the direction of an inherently self-serving state, we will continue to experience the frustration of ineffectiveness and identity compromise. On the other hand, by living into our defining stories, we can be set free from the shackles of national self-interest actually to be the church in the world.

Teresa of Avila lived during a time when Christendom prevailed. In fact, the fabric of her culture was so deeply formed by it that her heroic vision as a young girl was to walk out with her little brother and seek martyrdom in battle with the Moors. This unfortunate merger of temporal power and church mission did not, however, keep her from imagining the missionary function of the church in the world. She put this vision into words in her famous lines

> Christ has no body now on earth but yours,
> no hands but yours, no feet but yours.
> Yours are the eyes through which to
> look out Christ's compassion to the world;
> yours are the feet with which He is to go about doing good;
> yours are the hands with which He is to bless others now.

Unshackled by the constraints and dependency of co-opting a self-interested government, American Christians will be set free to live out our story-formed, regenerative vocation directly in the world.

Notes

1. George W. Bush, "President Says Saddam Hussein Must Leave Iraq Within 48 Hours," March 17, 2003, the official White House website, www.whitehouse.gov/news/releases/2003/03/20030317-7.html.

2. Mr. Powell admitted in a press conference that the link to al-Qaeda had not been proved; reported in the *New York Times* by Christopher Marquis in a story entitled "The Struggle for Iraq: Diplomacy," January 9, 2004.

3. Reported by Richard W. Stevenson, "The Struggle for Iraq: White House Memo," *New York Times*, December 18, 2003.

4. Kirk Semple, "Ex-Inspector Calls for Inquiry on Prewar Intelligence," *New York Times*, January 28, 2004.

5. For a collection of L. Wittgenstein's writings on language as a social and communal phenomenon, see R. J. Fogelin, *Wittgenstein* (London: Routledge & Kegan Paul, 1980), 153ff.; for the constructive role of culture in forming individuals, see P. Berger and T. Luckmann, *The Social Construction of Reality* (Garden City, NY: Anchor, 1966); for the role of shared myths and stories in forming a culture and its members, see C. Geertz's essay "Religion as a Cultural System," in his collection, *The Interpretation of Cultures* (New York: Basic Books, 1973), 87-125; and for a development of the concept that religion is a story-formed culture, see G. Lindbeck, *The Nature of Doctrine* (Louisville: John Knox Press, 1984).

6. Kant's point of view is perhaps most apparent in the title of his treatise "Religion within the Bounds of Reason Alone" (*Die Religion innerhalb der Grenzen der blossen Vernunft*).

7. As an early example of this now-pervasive approach to the early Christian communities, see W. Meeks, *The First Urban Christians* (New Haven: Yale, 1984). Meeks presents a profile of the social world constructed in earliest Pauline Christianity.

8. Editor's note: Or just intervention solely on the basis of equal regard for the oppressed, as Jean Bethke Elshtain suggests elsewhere in this volume.

9. *The West Wing*, NBC Television, Episode: "Inauguration: Over There," Original Airing: February 12, 2003.

10. Bush, "President Says Saddam Hussein Must Leave Iraq."

11. Churches for Middle East Peace website (www.cmep.org/letters/2002Sep12_Bush ReIraq.htm).

12. Nicholas Kristof, "God on Their Side," *New York Times*, op-ed, September 27, 2003.

12

Pastors, Prophets, and Patriotism

Leading Pastorally during These Times

Arthur Paul Boers

When the Twin Towers fell in 2001, I was pastoring a rural congregation in Ontario, Canada. I remained in Canada until the following February, when I began my new seminary position in Elkhart, Indiana. My location is relevant to these reflections because being in Canada during the first months after September 11 gives me a slightly different perspective on matters than if I had lived in the United States that whole time.

While I am about the business of discrediting my *American* credibility, let me say a little more about nationality. Although my children are American citizens, I am not. Their status comes from the fact that we lived in the United States two decades ago. While Canadian by birth, I am the oldest son of Dutch immigrants. Dutch is my first language, my mother tongue. When in Canada, I think of myself as Dutch. But when I go to the Netherlands, I realize that I am not actually Dutch. I have a typical immigrant child's problem of identity: I do not feel that I have a nationality. I do not lament my uncertain nationality but celebrate it. My remove from national citizenship is a good parallel for a Christian stance toward *any* nation where we happen to reside or hold citizenship.

I tie this conviction to baptism. At age 19, I was immersed in the cold, turbulent waters of Lake Ontario (on the feast of the beheading of St. John the Baptist, no less, although I did not know that at the time). I stood where the Niagara River, a border between the U.S. and Canada, empties into that Great Lake. From there I could see the soil of both nations and also, as it happens, historical military forts in both countries. In my baptism into the Reign of God, I stood apart from those two countries.

The location was symbolically appropriate. On the border, the periphery, of two countries, my baptism declared that my primary citizenship is not in earthly kingdoms but in God's reign, and here I am a sojourner, pilgrim, and resident alien. (The latter image is more telling for me now, when I see that even for a Canadian it is far harder to be a foreigner in the U.S. than it was twenty years ago.) A Christian's first loyalty is to God's Reign, and when that loyalty gets eroded, we are in deep, deep trouble.

My baptism is relevant to these matters in another way too. One of the most difficult aspects of my conversion to the Mennonite faith was the peace position. At first, I was reluctant to study the peace stance because I rejected it. But the catechetical process converted me to seeing that reconciliation is at the heart of the Christian gospel. It is not just a quirky idea of Mennonites and other fringe believers.

This conviction came at personal cost. My parents and grandparents lived and suffered through the Nazi occupation of the Netherlands. My great-grandmother, I am told, died as a result of a Nazi-enforced evacuation. My father and grandfathers were all active in risky underground resistance. After the Second World War, my father volunteered for the army to defend Dutch empirical interests in Indonesia, an experience that haunted him until the end of his life. So questions of war, militarism, resistance, nationality, empire, and peace are deeply important to my family. They were not impressed that I embraced the peace position.

Thus I write as a Mennonite Christian. And I write as one who was a pastor for over sixteen years, one who tried to keep central peace and justice concerns in ministry and church life. And I write as one who was a pastor on September 11 and during the following months as well and as one who now trains and supports pastors.

September 11 has become a cliché. I reject the claim that "everything changed" or everything should change because of that day. Rather, I see it in its truest sense as an *apocalyptic* moment, an opening or revelation where truths are made clear and are suddenly hard to ignore. The truths revealed, however, are not necessarily those being drawn by political leaders, the military, the media, or even many church folks, alas.

One concern I have as a pastor is how God-language and Christian vocabulary are usurped for the purposes of war and patriotism. This is especially striking now. I was not listening to the radio on September 11 but was informed of the events by my born-again auto mechanic, who promptly proceeded to make hateful remarks about Muslims. I later watched with great sorrow as outspoken Christians and churches supported U.S. violent responses in Afghanistan and Iraq. The largest American flag I have ever seen (make that the largest *flag* I have ever seen) is draped on the outside wall of a local church. One bumper sticker reads: "It's God's job to forgive Osama bin Laden. It's our job to arrange the meeting." God is being called on to bless all things American and, I might add, all things *commercial*. I am perplexed when I see patriotic slogans and claims about God's blessings on stores and gas stations.

Thus, in absolute seriousness, I say we must *for God's sake* bear a different witness. We must not coast along with such agendas. Christians need to take a stand on the national urge to violence. If we do not, our loathing and denunciation of the violence on September 11 is hypocrisy.

On Sunday, September 16, our church—like churches throughout North America—faced the question of how to respond to the events of the previous week. We made an important decision to proceed with our usual order of worship. We did add early in the service a special prayer to respond to our horror and grief and to lift up to the Lord our longings for peace. This prayer freed people from preoccupations and released them appropriately into the hands of God. It was our custom to share concerns and petitions later in the service, and during that time there was also appropriate attention given by people to the unfolding events.

In the service, we did *not* choose our Bible text. We had discerned six months earlier that that was a good day to begin a series on the book of Jonah. The first verses connected readily with the week's events. It was appropriate to proceed with the day's text. That week and since I had many good conversations with pastors who proceeded with a given text (especially lectionary preachers) and who found that God spoke *more* powerfully when the preacher was not in charge of Scripture selection but allowed the assigned passage to speak to us.

I have never had so many people respond to a single sermon. We were overwhelmed with requests for copies of the tape. That worship service functioned in the way Christian worship is intended. It reoriented people to God's Reign. It grounded us in God's purposes. It reminded us not to be shaped, formed, and molded by what others told us was true and important. Amid the clamor of calls for war and revenge, we were invited to hear God's still, small voice urging us toward healing and reconciliation.

Later, some in the media (but not in our congregation) said that preachers should have confined themselves to consolation. But Christian comforting is not the same as making comfortable, putting people at ease. And when politicians and the media rushed to exploit the terrible events as a call to war and revenge, it would be poor stewardship of the pulpit to avoid addressing such concerns.

Many spoke to me of the worship service on that day, in the subsequent weeks and months, and at my farewell to the church on Epiphany, January 6. There was a common refrain throughout these messages.

People felt alone and vulnerable in the days after September 11. It was not vulnerability to terrorists and anthrax, but to misunderstandings as friends, relatives, coworkers, and neighbors called for revenge and uttered hateful remarks. Our people were afraid to ask questions, let alone offer other perspectives. They did not know where to turn, even as in their hearts they knew that there were deeply wrong things in what they were told.

Thus many looked forward to Sunday worship. They knew that there they would be called to pay attention to God's perspective. There they could feel safe in proclaiming their faith and be reinforced in their convictions. There they would be heartened and encouraged to stand for God's values. Many, many people told me on that day and subsequently: "There was no place I would rather be than at church."

For many, this was the *first* time and place where they felt at home and safe. They were alone and troubled in various settings all week long. They looked for different perspectives than those offered by the media and by too many acquaintances. They found alternative perspectives at church, which is precisely where they should find them. At church, they were renewed and inspired. And rightly so. They found resources, resonance, reinforcement, and a resting place when much that was around them felt unsafe and dangerous.

Such testimonies are music in a pastor's ear at any time.

But it was not just a matter of stroking the pastor's ego. There was an important theological truth at stake. I was saddened when esteemed friends at Christian Peacemaker Teams (CPT) suggested churches cancel or interrupt Sunday worship services and attend or create protests to make clear how serious these issues were. CPT does much admirable work, but on this count they were wrong. In times of trouble, even and especially serious trouble, Christians belong in worship. To cancel Sunday worship to attend a demonstration is to let the bad, bad news of the world and the world's ways set our agenda. It could not be more important on such occasions to remember and celebrate that our agenda is set by the life, death, and resurrection of our Lord and Savior Jesus Christ. Thus worship is the most important thing we do and the most important thing we can do in the face of trauma and tragedy. Our congregation recognized that worship is the place where we most needed to be.

During the September 11 aftermath (as during the first Gulf War), many were glued to their televisions and completely taken in by what others said was real and of ultimate value and importance. Yet it is vital that we not be ruled by the media setting our priorities and interpreting reality for us. At such times, one of the most faithful things we can do is to continue to immerse ourselves in worship and prayer. As John called believers to worship in the Book of Revelation, drawing them to focus on God's ultimate reality, even and *especially* in light of Roman oppression, we are called to do the same.

Recent events raised important questions for Christians about what we believe. I am grateful for believers (not only in the so-called historic peace churches) who unapologetically assert that peace witness and nonviolence are at the heart of the gospel's priorities and means. The gospel is all about God's first-strike disarmament strategies and initiatives with us and all God's enemies. It reconciles us to God and calls us to be reconciled with others.

While many claim something new happened on September 11, urges to nationalism and vengeance, desires to bless the death-dealing prerogatives of Caesar and empire, and temptations to forget the primacy of God's Reign have tempted Christians for centuries. These were the issues at the heart of Constantinianism. They were issues when sixteenth-century Anabaptists were asked how they would respond to the enemies of state in their day. And these were issues in the twentieth century as well.

In *Preachers Present Arms*, Ray Abrams showed how churches, Christians, and Christian leaders were scandalously coopted for the American war effort in the First World War. Then too "holy war" and "crusade" terminology were adopted. Christian leaders said: "It is neither a travesty nor exaggeration to call this war on the part of America, a truly Holy War"; "The man who is disloyal to the flag is disloyal to Christianity; the State must be obeyed under pain of incurring the guilt of mutiny against God"; "We must keep the flag and the Cross together, for they are both working for the same ends."[1] Churches contributed to wartime hysteria, many peace societies collapsed, and war brought a revival of religion. This sounds all too familiar. German opponents, of course, at the very same time wore belts with the logo that read, "God with us."

This so-called Great War, "the war to end all wars," was so successful that it was the major cause of the Second World War. There, too, churches were tempted to set aside the gospel in favor of this "Good War."

In each war, we are told that this one is exceptional, this one is just and holy. Of course, each time we learn in retrospect that the governments withheld truth and even lied to stir up war. And each time the church cooperates, we corrupt the gospel.

We Mennonites face our own challenges and temptations in such circumstances. We have long been fringe, even second-class citizens. Partly we chose such a position. Partly it was imposed on us. But during the last half of the twentieth century, we found a measure of respectability and recognition among other Christians and even in the public generally. We get good press, whether it is for disaster relief and development work or for the picturesque quaintness of Old Order communities, be they in Indiana, Ohio, Pennsylvania, or Ontario.

But in time of war, we find ourselves thinking differently from neighbors, coworkers, and schoolmates who display American flags, call for revenge and retaliation, speak casually of the need for war, and intimidate those who think differently. Our seminary's opposition to war provoked at least one phoned-in hate message that made my blood run cold; I wondered whether I should invest in a bullet-proof Kevlar vest.

Mennonites are, if anything, respectable. So it is tempting to give up the places where we are "out of step" with wider culture. Ironically, this would be to surrender the very aspect that made us attractive to many Christians. Douglas John Hall, Stanley Hauerwas, William Willimon, and Rodney Clapp (to name just a few mainline Christians who admire Anabaptist witness and priorities) turned to us because Anabaptism sets us apart from the blending of church and state in Constantinianism and provides theological resources for resistance. In our temptation to become like other Christians, to be respectable, we lose a gospel treasure that too few others hold dear and that the wider world and the wider church sorely needs.

Critical issues are at stake. Mennonite theologian J. Denny Weaver cautions: "In the vast majority of cases throughout Mennonite history, when Mennonites have become culturally assimilated, they have also lost their commitment to nonviolence and ultimately their identity as Mennonites."[2]

The apocalyptic events of September 11 remind us that Christian faith is—and needs to be—radically other than what the world proposes. Mennonite Christians know that the gospel makes us different. Flannery O'Connor, hardly an Anabaptist, was onto something when she said, "You shall know the truth and the truth will make you odd." It is getting harder to bear witness to what we know. But as tough as these times are, there is both challenge and gift. The gift is in making our identity and mission clearer.

We need to proclaim that nonviolence, unilateral reconciliation, and the rejection of violence are central to Jesus' teaching, life, death, and resurrection and to the gospel as it is given to us. While this may not befit our ecumenical reticence (often a good quality), we should insist that these are not negotiable values, petty ideas, or a Mennonite frill. Christians should reject violence, we believe.

When that poetic soul Louis Armstrong remembered his baptism, he recalled another story, when "a large, imposing fellow was forced into the baptizing waters by the even larger, more imposing deacons." The insistent deacons kept demanding to know whether or not he believed. Yet he conscientiously refused to answer. They dunked him again and again, holding him under the water for longer and longer periods. Finally, when asked once more whether or not he believed, he responded: "Yes — I believe you [expletives deleted] are *trying to drown me*."[3]

Christians throughout history have been tempted by coercion, whether it is coercion by the state (which so many sixteenth-century Christians used against Anabaptists) or coercion by the church itself. No, issues and *temptations* of coercion are not new, unusual, or unique. September 11 did not change that.

Strangely enough, I took heart recently from *The Lord of the Rings*, which, for all its battles, decries illusions of effectiveness, of the ends justifying the means, of might making right. In a story of world-scale wars and unmitigated evil, it is the small and humble, peripheral and weak, unlikely and unremarkable who are crucial because they know their role. The story hopes in the small and least powerful. It believes in the power and fruitfulness of little acts of faithfulness.

An innkeeper at a key point in the story, who, upon hearing bad news of how desperate conditions are, is asked, "Are you still willing to help

. . . ?" He responds: "More than ever. Though I don't know what the likes of me can do . . ." He is told matter-of-factly that against such evil one's assistance does "*not much, . . . but every little helps*."

Later, an elf ruler says: "The road must be trod, but it will be very hard. And neither strength nor wisdom will carry us far upon it. This quest may be attempted by the weak with as much hope as the strong. Yet such is oft the course of deeds that move the wheels of the world: small hands do them because they must, while the eyes of the great are elsewhere."[4] That is a call Mennonites can understand.

This vision we can understand and embrace *as Christians*. We are not called to overcome all evil (whether in Afghanistan or in the U.S. or in Iraq). We are not called to win at all costs or to lend our support to killing and evil means. Indeed the ethical center of *Lord of the Rings* is a cautionary tale that good, well-meaning folks must not use the Ring of Power even for good, well-meant ends. Tolkien might just as well have quoted Jeremiah (or numerous other Original Testament prophets): "Do not let the wise boast in their wisdom, do not let the mighty boast in their might" (Jer. 9.23).

Pacifist pastors often worry that such unpopular points of view might negatively affect evangelism. As a former pastor and church planter myself, I understand the concern. But we must refuse to compromise the truth of our faith for other ends. And more than that, I can testify that God can use such truth-telling fruitfully.

The Sunday after the First Gulf War bombing began, I decided that even as I was cautious about politics and partisan points of view in the pulpit, it was crucial to present a Christian voice that countervailed that which political leaders and media proclaimed.

That congregation was a struggling new church. It was small and fragile, always longing and looking for newcomers. And on that particular Sunday, wouldn't you know it, a newcomer appeared in our midst. When I saw him, I wished that he had come the week before or might have waited a week. That war was so popular. Why did he have to hear the most scandalous and offensive part of the gospel on his first Sunday in our church? I was tempted to temper my words but did not.

Then, wonder of wonders, he kept coming, studied Scriptures with me, and became more and more involved in our congregation. Finally, after I knew him a long while, I asked about what that first Sunday had been like for him.

He reminded me that just prior to that he had been laid off from work. He spent entire days watching television and seeing those same old battle and bombing scenes over and again. He did not question anything he saw or heard. But when he stepped into our worship, for the first time he heard a different point of view. Worship pulled him away from the mesmerization of media. He saw things differently.

In the same church, a Dutchman, Steve, started attending and took catechism with me. His accent and age reminded me of my parents. He had survived the Second World War, in which a young brother had been killed by Nazis. He was bitter, understandably enough. I was slow to come finally to the question of nonviolence. He was angry and resistant about this issue. How I wished I could avoid the subject. It was like arguing with my parents. Besides, we could always use another convert in our little church, even if one part of his doctrine was not quite in order. But I persisted and he wrestled hard with such ideas. Eventually, he asked for baptism into the faith.

A couple of years ago, Steve was buried. We heard many testimonies about his life and witness that day. One story that touched me was the importance he put on his difficult conversion to nonviolence and how he learned to forgive those who had killed his brother.

To those who fear that advocating nonviolence will make us unpopular (something Jesus predicted, by the way), I must say that in every church I served as pastor it was precisely our commitment to the gospel, our lifting high of God's priorities of peace and justice on earth as in heaven, that brought people through our doors. Such stories hearten me into faithfulness, though I urge truth-telling even without such successes.

Those giving pastoral leadership in this day, then, must ask what it takes for our churches to proclaim and live out the radical implications and costly demands of gospel. Several elements and practices are needed for faithful living.

We certainly need to *worship*, for reasons I already discussed above.

We need *community*. It is impossible to counteract larger trends and persuasive forces on our own. People in my former congregation had more courage in countering rumors of wars and of the necessity of war because they fellowship with one another, study together, and worship as a body.

We need *mentors*, saints, and models. We need to know and tell stories in which we see people live with integrity, where actions and practices mesh with convictions. We need witnesses and *testimony* of many stripes. I was heartened by the PBS special in January 2002, "The Good War and Those Who Refused to Fight It," the story of conscientious objectors in World War II. Mennonites would be wise and do well to tap elders in our congregations who lived through wars and learn from them. They know what it means to be different and to suffer as a minority for one's convictions. It is also time to engage Old Order believers about ways and strategies of being separate from the world, embracing again opportunities of nonconformity.

We need strategies for dealing with *media*, including critical questioning, developing other media, selective engagement, and also at times fasting and abstinence. Too easily our hearts and minds are shaped by false urgencies and destructive hates. Our very souls are at stake. Thus a pastoral duty is to resist. People's hearts are being eaten up by retaliation, revenge, idolatry, and anxiety. Given the strong and seductive powers of the media, a strong counterwitness is needed.

Thomas Merton was a monk when Hiroshima and Nagasaki were bombed. Merton and his brother monks did not learn about the A-bombs until months later. Though monks were not allowed to know daily news, he was an incisive visionary on matters of nuclear weapons, race, and all manner of social issues. His prayerful distance from the media helped him see better. We are called to the same.

We need to be people of *prayer* and discernment. We need to listen to God so that what Jesus said would be true of us: "My sheep hear my voice. I know them, and they follow me" (John 10:27). I worry that not only are spiritual disciplines waning, but that we may be losing our ability for them. Technology forms us to be intolerant of anything that takes time, is difficult, or is not easily accessible because of its depth of meaning. The spiritual life is obviously at risk. Accustomed to being bombarded by a host of images and information, we grow less tolerant with disciplines that demand patience and focus.

Rather than act from or be driven by desperation and fear or mesmerized into hate and violence, whether in daily life or reflecting on larger world events, we live in and with conviction, deliberation, discernment, compassion, and discipline "on earth as in heaven."

September 11 provoked and provokes all manner of pastoral issues. Our congregation had an important meeting scheduled the next day, but a key leader could not attend. His spouse felt panicky, fearing that their family might be a victim of a terrorist attack on their isolated rural farm. Fear is a pastoral and theological issue.

One way of looking at the temptations before us is to use an old theological term, *idolatry*. Idolatry can mean relying too much on something that is not God, but it can also mean attributing disproportionate fear where it does not belong.

Idolatry is rife among Christians. When I joined the peace movement over two decades ago, we focused on and challenged idolatrous reliance on nuclear weapons. Authorities expected too much good from them: safety and security. We correctly said, "It's a sin to build a nuclear weapon." While glad for our work, in retrospect I see that we antinuclear activists also made idols of those weapons, because of how much we feared them and were obsessed by and preoccupied with them.

Too often believers of both liberal and conservative bents make idols of the same thing or person. Some idolize George W. Bush or other presidents as virtual messiah figures. Others see them as evil. Both sides miss the mark. We are called to pray for our government's leaders, to acknowledge their humanity and limitations, and to be aware that they too can be victims of powers and principalities. They are neither Messiah nor Antichrist.

Ever since September 11, media and politicians perpetuate fears. The regular color-coded "cry wolf" alerts about terrorist threats fulfill this function. Fear makes for strange priorities. Thus the State Department paid more sustained attention to anthrax (which, inconveniently, looks more like domestic crime than something that can be laid at the doorstep of foreign terrorists) than it does to far higher daily casualty rates in the U.S. resulting from the use of legal weapons here.

Fear shuts down imagination and creativity and flies in the face of the gospel. Paul commends courage and confidence when he says: "For I am convinced that neither death, nor life, nor angels, nor rulers, nor things present, nor things to come, nor powers, nor height, nor depth, nor anything else in all creation, will be able to separate us from the love of God in Christ Jesus our Lord" (Rom. 8:38–40). Likewise, Jesus says: "Do not fear those who kill the body" (Matt. 10:28), and I presume he would include terrorists abroad and our governments.

"Do not fear" or "be not afraid" are prevailing themes throughout the Scriptures.

September 11 raises other pastoral issues too.

A devoted, friendly, and hospitable Christian and well-educated professional told his Sunday school class of his new-found fear of and even hatred toward neighboring Muslims. He never actually met and conversed with his neighbors; just seeing them provoked such reactions. Hatred of the other is a pastoral and theological issue.

I mentioned that our congregation was formed and informed by Jonah in Fall 2001. One of the shortest books in the Bible, it spoke powerfully to events of our day.

When Jonah was written, Jews were still trying to come to grips with exile. The temple, the center of their faith, was destroyed. This destruction was lamented and mourned for hundreds of years and carried an impact as great as or greater than that of the loss of the World Trade Center. Many died in that exile. And many never came back. After some returned, they struggled with trying to understand the *meaning* of their suffering and exile.

Meanwhile, Jonah was commanded to go and preach to Nineveh. It was highly unusual for prophets to go elsewhere. The book of Jonah is one of twelve in the Original Testament called Prophets. Sometimes those prophets prophesied *against* other countries, but *none went* to a foreign country.

Nineveh, as it happens, was not just a heathen foreign country. It was the *epitome* of enmity. It was the capital of Assyria, Israel's oppressor. It is often described negatively in the Bible as a symbol of wickedness, like Sodom and Gomorrah, only with a strong army too. In recent terminology, it could be considered part of the "axis of evil."

It is completely understandable that Jonah did not want to go there. For one thing, no other prophet had done such a thing. For another, Nineveh truly was an enemy of Jews. For still another, Nineveh was known for its *war crimes*, brutality, evil ways, and crimes against humanity. Who wants to hang out with these people? Finally, Jonah might also have realistic *fears* that they would respond to him with violence.

Nineveh as symbol holds meaning for us as we consider the terrible events of recent months. If Nineveh means nothing more than an enemy, a capital of war crimes, a source of wickedness, then it is easy for us to point fingers elsewhere. We can name places and people that are Nineveh today: Iraq or Afghanistan, Saddam Hussein or bin Laden. Ironically, Nineveh is literally in what we now call Iraq! Like Jonah, we would not be too eager to go to those places or people. Not only would we be *afraid*, but we are not really sure whether we want to be in heaven with such war criminals, truth be told. That is understandable enough, but it is not Christian.

A careful reading of Jonah warns us against identifying and writing off others as Nineveh. Such texts call us to take a hard look at ourselves. We should realize that there are violence, sin, evil, and war crimes on both sides. Jonah teaches us to *beware* of writing off others as enemies. It teaches that God loves *even* our enemies (and loves even us when we are enemies). God pleads with us, as God pleaded with Jonah, to do the right thing with enemies, even if they are war criminals.

Jonah also teaches that not only should we not treat our enemies as enemies but we should examine *ourselves*. Compared to pagan, multi-god-worshiping sailors (Jonah 1:5) and the wicked Ninevites (1:2), the biggest and most obvious sinner and slowest to repent (two times!) is Jonah, a faithful, pious, and religious believer who hears from God directly. So when we read Jonah, rather than condemn others, we need to examine ourselves and confess our own sins.

Ironically, it is the wicked people of Nineveh who repent, but it is never clear that Jonah himself is faithful. So often in Scriptures it is the stranger, the other, the foreigner, even the enemy, who reveals God or is faithful to God. So it is the daughter of the oppressing Pharaoh who saves Moses. And Moses himself is a privileged adopted son of the oppressor. Or think of Naaman, the Syrian military man (resident of another "axis of evil") who owns an Israelite slave but is miraculously healed of leprosy and even more incredibly converted to humility and monotheism (2 Kings 5). Do not underestimate the scandal of such stories. When Jesus, centuries later, preached in his hometown synagogue, he gave a host of examples, but when he cited the healing of Naaman (Luke 4: 27), then his congregants "were filled with rage" and tried to kill him. Jesus scandalized later when he spoke of a Samaritan as "good." Imagine the controversy today of trying to translate Jesus' parable into the "good Iraqi" or the "good terrorist." Such uncomfortable reversals of perspective are frequent in the Scriptures.

Aleksandr Solzhenitsyn once said: "If only there were evil people somewhere, insidiously committing evil deeds and it were necessary only to separate them from the rest of us and destroy them. But the line dividing good and evil cuts through the heart of every human being."[5] This is an eloquent summation of much of Jonah: good and evil are in everyone. That means that faithful people are called to two things: examination of self for one's own sins and mercy and compassion to others, even enemies.

Jonah speaks *directly* to recent events, if only we would have ears to hear. God is not saying that Nineveh is misunderstood, understandable, or justifiable. Clearly the city is evil; "their wickedness has come up before me" (Jonah 1:2b). Yet in Jonah all bets are off as to whom God favors and blesses: pagan sailors who ultimately do the right thing, the greatly wicked city of Nineveh, which is capable of repentance, or the pious, God-believing prophet who does not finally repent. So God says to the sullen Jonah and to us: stop hating and stop cycles of violence.

As the West makes war on the East, I recall a legend about St. Francis. During the Crusades, Francis, a former soldier, was horrified by conflict between Christians and Muslims. So he crossed battle lines to meet the enemy, an important Muslim leader, Al-Kamil. By the end of their time together, Al-Kamil said that he would be willing to be baptized and be a Christian if he ever met another Christian like St. Francis. "But that will never happen," he was sure. Apocryphal or not, this story reveals an intrinsic Christian message.[6]

Being willing to cross battle lines and enemy lines is intrinsically biblical. It is a call that Jonah resisted but one that Jesus embraced. In fact, the Gospels report powerful examples of Jesus going to "the other side of the sea" (e.g., Mark 5:1 KJV). That is not just a geographical description but a "symbolic transit to a symbolic locale, a journey to the unknown, the foreign, the 'other side' of humanity."[7]

Jonah is a good biblical text these days. For we are both Jonah and Nineveh. Like Jonah, we too are called to reach out to and listen to those "on the other side." Here the work of solidarity groups—Voices in the Wilderness and Christian Peacemaker Teams—who send delegations to "enemies" truly fulfill an important aspect of the gospel.

Sometimes when I am discouraged by dealing with conflicts—whether in congregations, or our denominations, or wider church structures, or our world—I am tempted to quote Shakespeare and utter a curse of dismissal: "A pox on both your houses." But as I reflect on events of these last months, and the violence and evil and hurt and suffering and tragedy on all sides, I believe that the Christian response is to offer a blessing and testimony. That is the Christian thing to do. That is the pastoral thing to do.

So I urge us rather to rework this as a Benedictine blessing: "A *pax* on all our houses."

Notes

1. Ray H. Abrams, *Preachers Present Arms* (Scottdale, PA: Herald Press), 50.

2. J. Denny Weaver, "Anabaptist Theology in the Face of Postmodernity: Why Theology Matters," *Preservings*, no. 19 (December 2001): 4.

3. Krin Gabbard, *Louis and the Good Book*, liner notes, Verve CD, 2001.

4. J. R. R. Tolkien, *The Fellowship of the Ring* (Toronto: Methuen, 1971), 181, 283. Italics added.

5. *The Gulag Archipelago*, trans. Thomas P. Whitney (New York: Harper & Row, 1973), 168.

6. Editor's note: See David Johnston's treatment of the same story elsewhere in this volume.

7. Ched Myers, *Binding the Strong Man: A Political Reading of Mark's Story of Jesus* (Maryknoll, NY: Orbis, 1988), 195.

13

Empire's Sleepy Embrace

The View from the Pew

Lillian Daniel

Prelude

The sun comes through the tall, clear windows of our sanctuary, casting gentle yellow streaks across the white-painted pews with their faded red cushions. The organ prelude is the dramatic piece of music that calls people into church as church bells once did. Our organist plays his prelude with the idea that people are listening, and indeed some are. They sit quietly in the pews, using this time of music to pray; they are already engaged in the worship service.

Others rush around the back of the church during the prelude and chatter with one another. To them the prelude is background music to the busy lives they are in the process of setting aside for this next hour. When the organ swells, they seem to be annoyed and speak even louder to be heard above it. They in turn annoy the people who are listening quietly in the pews.

It raises the question for me, as their pastor, of when worship actually begins. Is the organ prelude a warning that worship is about to begin, or is it the first piece of our worship as a community? And then comes another question: What if the people who chatter during the prelude are worshiping? Could it be that they are simply bringing their lives into worship, as we all do—just more obviously? Whether our mouths are moving or not, when we worship our heads are full of the questions of life, some of them personal, some of them related to the world we live in, a world that is increasingly dominated by an American empire most of us do not see coming. It is sneaking up on us, but we feel it in the questions we ask of God as we walk into church to worship.

When does one war end and another begin? When will gas prices go down? When will the economy improve? Why are so many people getting laid off? Why are we told that wars are over, but still our loved ones do not come home? Why do people in other countries hate us? Why do people drive their daughters to soccer practice in military-style Hummers? What exactly is the American way of life?

And here, writing from the perspective of a local church pastor whose job description gets crystalized once a week, it occurs to me that these questions are nothing new. The writings of the Old and New Testaments were forged under the white-hot pressures of real-world empires, and so these questions are woven throughout our tradition, and our worship. While others may debate the political nuances, and while we may struggle to understand and wonder where we can discuss such matters, Christians have only to take a look at a Sunday worship service to see that many of the questions about empire get hit upon with frightening regularity. This is a conversation God means for us to have.

Built into our worship, through text and liturgy, are powerful pointers to a God who is greater than any empire, and a savior who saved us from the bottom up. While these weekly worship times may seem small in number next to the barrage of news and media and nation building, they have on their side the truth that Jesus died not for the world's winners, but for us all. So they might be suspicious of anyone who equates victory on the cross to victory on the battlefield. Regular worship within a tradition, in consistent patterns with regular practices, has always had a catechetical function. In worshiping, we are learning what we believe. And we are learning what we do not believe.

The Wake-Up Call to Worship

Each week, as our nation grows stronger in the ways of the world, extending tendrils around the necks of nations that may or may not want to be embraced, we are called to worship something greater than ourselves. Usually in our American churches, the first words of a worship service call us into worship and the presence of God.

Sitting in churches in the wealthiest nation in the world, we may feel connected to that wealth, smugly satisfied that the goodness of our nation's affluence is somehow related to our own goodness. Let's imagine that we are sitting in a church where Volvo station wagons sit parked like sentries outside, those cars whose advertisements promise safety against wind, rain, and other drivers.

Perhaps among the members of this church there exists a sleepy satisfaction with life, nipped around the edges by vague impulses for small social reforms that stay away from that nastier question of the gap between the rich and the poor. Here, at this American church, that same sleepy satisfaction may extend to the nation's place in the world. We may see ourselves as specially blessed to take care of the other nations, singled out for a special purpose and a special responsibility. It's a responsibility that lies just on the other side of a dream, lost in the vagaries of newscasts and lofty editorials that replace the language of humanity with that of machines and assembly lines, and we become numb under the weight of words like "collateral damage" as one war bleeds into another.

This is empire's sleepy embrace that creeps up on us softly and lures us in with the whispered promise of duty without real sacrifice, privilege without the appearance of greed. As we get all the oil we need, we act as though we are carrying a heavy burden, but really we are all being lulled into sleep. Softly and tenderly, empire is calling.

And then suddenly, just a few minutes after arriving in church, we hear the words of the call to worship. Often they come from the words of a psalm, and perhaps the pastor included not just words of praise but words of lament as well. There in the words of the psalm we hear from people who were not sleepy, but wide awake in their discomfort. They railed against their enemies, gnashing their teeth and cussing out the God who left them at the bottom of the realpolitik ladder.

In the call to worship, the unspeakable happens. In the words of a psalm, we in the empire are reminded that despite our current comfort, we come from a long lineage of life's losers.

Welcome to church, America.

Good morning, Vietnam. And Iraq, North Korea, Saudi Arabia, Palestine, Israel, and Myanmar. Every week, when we allow them their full rant, the Psalms remind those of us who may be tempted to smugness that we're not in Kansas anymore.

The Announcements and the Prayer Requests

The announcements put the ball back in our court. Get the attention back off of God, and back to ourselves. Perhaps it's the pastor, or perhaps a lay leader, who tells the story of the congregation's life. A silver tea to celebrate the beginning of Holy Week. The pastor's anniversary dinner; tickets are still available from Deacon Smith. Has anybody lost a pair of green wool gloves? Sign up to buy a birthday present for a child whom the Department of Child and Family Services has removed from his home. Attend the peace rally against the war this Saturday.

Oops. The car of community life screeches to a halt. Someone has made a faux pas and crossed the line from general announcement to partisan call to action, at least by the standards of the world. Not to worry. Someone will respond with a parry from the other side during prayer request time, with a call for prayers for the troops. Then another will volley back with a call to pray for peace, for all people, with a self-conscious twang on the "all." Eyes that were closed during prayer time will open covertly to look for reactions.

At our local church, the announcements time and the prayer requests taken from the floor of the church open the floodgates of our free church democracy with occasionally bizarre results. Prayers for the healing of a beloved church member's inoperable cancer have to stand awkwardly next to a teenager with a fondness for show tunes' prayer of thanksgiving for the life of Gene Kelly.

Some churches are too large for this chaos, and they limit the random input of ordinary Christians into worship time with screened written announcements. Some pastors prefer the lofty and general prayers that cover illness as a concept rather than speaking directly to that tumor on Mr. Jones's liver. But I've always loved the outbreak of humanity in the middle of worship when we solicit announcements and prayer requests from the floor. It's messy, sticky, and sometimes involves damage control for church leaders, but it's our reminder each Sunday of the beating heart of the church. And issues of empire get mapped out in their messiness every time.

How do you pray for our president? Some want prayers of thanksgiving for his leadership, while others are praying for a well-timed lightning bolt. How do you announce on the one hand a peace rally and, on the other, the collection of toiletries for the troops?

One week we pray with thanksgiving that a beloved nephew will return from Iraq. The next week we are asked to continue to pray for his safety, for he has been told he must stay for another eight months. We do not know this man, but we ride the family's rollercoaster with them.

To my mind, the minefield of congregational chaos is an opportunity for teaching about the body of Christ and the fact that Jesus chose not to assemble an army of clones but rather a ragtag group of dissenters who railed against each other as much as against the forces of evil. It's a chance to remind the church that Paul wrote his letters to vital, arguing churches for a reason, and that we saved his letters for the same reason. Worship is the meta-conversation, but when our earthly conversations, however clumsy, break into worship, my hunch is that God delights in the relationship. To cut off human hurts, pains, politics, and faux pas from the liturgy of worship is to excise a body part that needs to be there.

Besides, the discussion after church of who said what is a rich one. One person might find the peace rally announcement to be political, while another sees it as a basic part of the Christian faith. The visiting missionary, agreed by even the most traditional members to be in a cause above politics, may deliver a blistering harangue against globalization and shock the adult education group. Empire, by its nature, clamps down on dissent. Church conversation grounded in our tradition offers an alternative. It's often in our prayers of deepest longing that the door is opened.

In the Puritan tradition, our churches were once called meetinghouses. They were places where the worship of God was not to be separated from the concerns of the community. We New England Congregationalists once believed that all the windows in the church should be tall and absolutely clear. True, as Protestant dissenters we were reacting against the stained glass of the churches we were running from, but the theology that grew up around those plain, clear windows still moves me. The windows were to be clear so that in worship, the concerns of the world would always be visible from inside the church and the light of the gospel would always be able to shine out into the world.

Confession

Worship is not meant to be a solitary, private experience of faith, but one that shapes communities and makes them different. The flow from calling, to praying, to confession, to passing, to hearing, toward the communion meal transforms us, so that when we leave the abundance of that table, its image will be emblazoned on our minds, so that when we encounter the imbalance of tables in the world, we will be convicted. On the way there, the words of confession we share remind us that while we are broken, in Christ we can still have new life. We are meant to enter worship, move through it, and be sent from it not just convicted, but repentant and forgiven too. It is in this state of grace that we might have the strength to take on life's hard questions and to continue the conversation about empire that God begins with here.

The Passing of the Peace

In a nation that engages in war, in a church that prays for both the end of war and for those who serve in the military, in a congregation in which we differ in our political views, each Sunday we are called upon to take one another's hands in our own and wish the other the peace of Christ.

"Peace be with you," we are called to say, not to our friends but to those whom God has seated near us in the pews.

"And also with you," we are called to respond, without regard to whom we are speaking. God's peace, passed through people of faith, is to be offered freely. Every week the warriors are reminded that our first wish for one another in Christian community is peace. Every week the peace activists are reminded that God's peace is extended to the warriors as well. This is no ordinary peace we share. No wonder we call it the "peace that passes all human understanding."

We are not supposed to use this liturgical time to make chitchat, although of course we often do. The quirkiness of human relationships in community breaks into the liturgical moment, with strange results.

"Peace be with you. Oh! I love your hair. When did you get it cut?"

"Thanks. And also with you. Say, don't forget the trustee meeting this Thursday."

"Is it this Thursday? We need to address that leak in the men's room." And now he turns to greet the stranger. "And peace be with you too."

Yet in times of war, or military expansion, that moment of exchanging God's peace becomes a shaping practice. In and of itself, it may not convert anyone, but the consistent sharing of a peace that passes human understanding reminds us that peace is not just a luxury for the powerful, wealthy, and mighty to enforce and then enjoy. God's peace is for everybody, and we are the ones expected to pass it around.

To those who suggest that war is a way of maintaining peace in the world, it is interesting that in two thousand years of Christian history no one has thought to exchange the passing of the peace with a slap. While we may have steered away from the holy kisses exchanged in the early church, our Christian peace has always been shared through the extension and touching of hands. This action combines generosity and vulnerability, and it bears within itself a critique of one tenet of empires: that one party "brings" peace to another.

The passing of the peace in worship is reciprocal. In the church, peace is not the possession of one party who can then give it to another party who lacks it. The only one capable of that sort of gift of peace from above is God. Notice also that we do not use threats or bargains when we exchange the peace. We don't say, "I'll pass you the peace once I've received it from you." Nor do we say, "Pass me the peace or else." When we human beings pass the peace to one another we do so as equal parties to peace, without threats or bargains. We simply exchange it.

So in the church our peace is radically communal. Unless we all have it, we can't exchange it. One person cannot receive the peace unless the other has it to give. So for Christians, if we share peace like that in church, we might consider sharing it like that in the world. It certainly gives pause to people of faith who are told that our nation, in its invasions, is "bringing" peace. Peace, when delivered by human beings, is exchanged, not brought.

Preaching the Word

As the American empire grows, and the world's resentment of us grows with it, the task of the preacher gets a new push. Preachers can't ignore the elephants in the living rooms in which our people live. But we still must guard against the sermon becoming the latest "reality show," merely reflecting back to the people the views they already hold, or that have been fed to them by marketing forces who have an empire-building agenda of their own that has a big head start on our government's.

As the world changes and empire grows, I know that some preachers will be tempted to give the congregation information they "do not get to hear from the media." This is a temptation from both the left and the right wings of our country. "If only they could learn what I have learned from this website . . . ," we pastors wonder. But ultimately, this politically correct information exchange from the pulpit is another step in the devil's dance. How do we make the preaching moment different from a National Public Radio discourse on the one hand, or a Drudge Report alert on the other?

How do we not play the games of verbal swordplay and partisan shots into hot air that now pass for broadcast news? And how, in avoiding that, do we not collapse into a vague spirituality that calls for good things for good people everywhere but pays no attention to the fact that so far the world's wealth looks more like a pointy pyramid than a puddle?

Here, I would suggest we entrust ourselves to the Word. Lately, in light of world events, I have found myself struck with the news that almost every great biblical hero spends time as an immigrant, from

Jesus' parents fleeing to Egypt, to Moses leading the people out of that same land, to the psalms written by outcasts, to the early churches in the Roman Empire. God has provided plenty of preaching material within Scripture that can indeed offer people a world they will not read in either *The Nation* or *The Wall Street Journal*.

These stories, in which God blesses the wandering immigrant but understands our human longing for our own land, set up a debate that speaks not primarily of one nation's role in history, but of God's preeminence. When God broke into history in Christ, it was not as a member of the empire's ruling class. It was as one who lived, worked, and struggled like the people our own nation tends to bomb. These stories don't need an NPR commentary running alongside them. They speak for themselves and remind us that sometimes when empires think they are right, they are wrong.

Offertory

Most calls to offering begin or end with a prayer of thanksgiving. It is out of our blessing that we are able to give. It is in giving that we receive a blessing. The moment of offering is the moment when we are reminded that nowhere in the Christian liturgy do we take things away from one another, but central to our worship is a moment of giving.

Despite the constant struggle the church has had in dealing with issues of money and wealth, despite those sad moments when our theology of money boils down to a sticky sweet prosperity gospel, and despite the many times preachers consider but duck away from talking about the mighty gap between the rich and the poor, we still are reminded of the hard issues every week at the moment of the offering. Even if the preacher doesn't address these issues, this moment of giving in the midst of worship confronts the worship of money and material things with a call to generosity.

Surely questions of empire are really questions of money. We usually expand our territories not to bring an ideology but to ensure our own standard of wealth and power on the world's scales. Biblical empires were portrayed with the same skepticism American Christians hold in their hearts today. Deep within, we know we have more of our share of the world's stuff, and part of why we control other countries is to postpone the moment when we will be forced to share.

As we struggle to maintain the unmaintainable imbalance of the world's wealth, our measures become more extreme. More jobs move overseas as we create a national economy in which goods must get cheaper so that our own lower paid or underemployed workers can buy them. Domestic budgets begin to show the wear and tear of maintaining a military presence around the world, as state budgets get cut to fund our activities abroad. The budget cuts are made in services to those who have the least ability to protest: the sick, the poor, the old, and the very young. But each week the offertory reminds us that these are the very people Jesus calls Christians to care for.

The Table

If the offertory leaves us wondering if we can never do enough, or leaves us with the impression that the church has to do it all, the eucharistic feast reminds us that the heavenly banquet is prepared by God, not human hands. Still, the extravagance of that table, the extravagance of God's gift to us in Christ calls us to a radical generosity in which all are fed.

At our church, the Communion Table is open to all who wish to know the love of Christ. But the American economic table is not so open. Increasingly our economy depends upon immigrants whom we allow to work for us but do not allow the rights of citizenship. As the gap between the rich and the poor grows in our country, it is but a sliver of the gap that exists between us and the rest of the world. As we struggle to keep our table piled higher than everyone else's, could the communion table remind us that our striving is ridiculous, in that we have already been fed?

The struggle for Americans about empire is not just abstract and political. It is a personal struggle related to our lifestyle, to what we consider to be necessities in life, but which God might reveal to be mere luxuries. It is at the table that our unceasing hunger and anxiety to have more is met head on by a generous God. We, like the disciples, will never be free of the human condition of sin, but we, like them, can be touched by God's grace, for we have been promised that "he had been made known to them in the breaking of the bread" (Luke 24:35).

Benediction

As America has slipped into empire's sleepy embrace, it has been to the background noise of political leaders who have listed into the lofty language of good and evil usually reserved for the worship hours. We're being called to unity in response to an "axis of evil." As the geographic boundaries of "the enemy" shift so rapidly, from Afghanistan one day, to Iraq the next, to Iran or North Korea tomorrow, how convenient it is to consider evil to be an axis, a topologically indistinct shute through the world that only the experts can keep track of.

As Christians, we understand the words of good and evil differently. We've heard in our own Scriptures the cries of nations who want to see other nations go down, but we also follow a savior who trumped all of that on the cross. Our words of goodness proclaim that evil is vanquished only in Christ, which is why we share his blessing as our sending out into the world at the conclusion of our worship.

Our politicians identify us as ones who will eliminate evil. To some, this current call to unity is necessary. But the history of Protestant dissent that leads some to this fire leads others to question. Many of us suspect that in promising to rid the world of evil, our politicians mistake themselves for the One most of them claim to follow.

Churches are on the front lines of these conversations, if they dare to be. And for those who choose not to have the conversations, there is no neutrality. Some of our churches may sit on old town greens that were once the church green when the church was what made the town. Some may sit in the middle of ample suburban parking lots with attendants who direct you to a building that looks more like a mall than a cathedral. Some may sit in neighborhoods surrounded by the boarded-up houses of absentee landlords who would rather rent to no one than move the crackheads along. But wherever we worship as Christians, we worship in the context of a nation that grows more powerful every day. Whether we openly discuss that or not, we are interpreting it every time we gather to praise the God who gave us life in such a place.

Within the bones of worship each Sunday, we find the tools with which to recognize blasphemy when we walk the streets on Monday or watch the news on Tuesday. Within the words of life that we hear on Sunday, we hear an answer to the words of death that might come our way on Wednesday. And by Thursday, when the world is full of angry speech in which battle lines are drawn that prevent conversation, we might look with longing to Sunday where we can enter into a conversation that started long before we were born and will continue long after, and that can only take place within the community of faith. Until suddenly, Friday and Saturday's stories have found their place within Sunday's and our empire stands next to the Roman Empire, which stands next to the Babylonian Empire, which stands next to whatever empire will rise up next. Our salvation will not be played out on that stage, or on an axis of evil on a spinning political top. No, our salvation lies in the practices of worship that subvert the paltry promise of empire with the more profound promise of new life, where all will be fed and none of us will starve.

Postlude

As the organist plays the final piece of music, we mostly listen, but a few begin to talk.

"Did you hear in the prayers that Jessica's nephew has been called up again?"

"Did you get the half and half for the coffee hour?"

"Did you see the news about the bus in Jerusalem?"

"What is this piece? Did we hear it at Easter?"

Some of us sit, some of us talk, but hopefully we're all still listening for God in the midst of all these questions that others have had before us about violence, power, and the longing for a better community. And so the conversation continues.

Sharing the Word

In my church, we've gathered in that back room after worship over many issues. Sometimes it's the newspaper that pulls us. Mostly, it's the cries of a congregation that wants its world discussed. A parent of a gay teen wants a meeting. A former missionary despairs about a certain country and our government's treatment of it. A musician wants a hearing for a new kind of beauty that tickles some ears more than others. A mugging prompts a discussion of homelessness and the call to hospitality.

But empire isn't that obvious. Most of us don't bump up against it. Empire's nature is such that within the strongest nation you don't realize you're strong. It's like the wealthy ladies in New England who wear hand-made sweaters, carry PBS tote bags, and swear to the world that their economic status is merely "comfortable," when all the statistics would call them "rich." Empires seldom feel like empires from the inside out. And so we respond to the jeers and taunts of the outside world, to those who ridicule our comparative wealth, with a puzzled tug at a tasteful cashmere sweater and, "Why, this old thing? I've had it for years."

For this reason, there has never been a better time for Christians to consider the fact that we are truly an international church. There has never been a better time to remind ourselves that Christianity is not a state religion. If one listens to political rhetoric, you would think the church was a "team" religion in which, in this odd conflation of roles, we are both playing for the winning side and acting as referee. Christianity as a team sport may rally a few, but there has never been a better time to offer the counterargument. As the American empire grows, the church in America can remind people that Jesus' death and resurrection marked the end of a chosen people with a single zip code.

For American churches, contact with congregations around the world can provide the insight we miss from the inside. The world's church can remind us how jarring our American church triumphalism sounds to the faithful who watch for our falling bombs. The churches around the world might remind us of our wealth in light of their lack. They might point out that it is a luxury to have so much that we keep money in the bank—not just individuals, but congregations, too. And that the old sweater we've had for years may well have been sewn by a child in a sweatshop.

I know that in my congregation the emails from members who have moved away to other countries seem to get fired back to me like God's angry angels. On the same day a church member complained that my sermons were "biased" in favor of peace, on the same day I was urged to preach "support for the troops and support for the president," an email arrived from a Sri Lankan member who had moved to Australia, asking me if our church has considered trying to have George W. Bush tried as a war criminal. It was a great wake-up call from the wider church.

Even our denominational missionaries' formulaic letters of greetings to the churches who support them carry words of rebuke, in terms of naming the wealth and power that Christians on the fat side take for granted. The words of Christians around the world may be the most revolutionary force in the empire these days, and it wouldn't be the first time the missionary field gave the good news a radical spin.

Responding to the Word

In my Congregationalist tradition, we love our words. Our older sanctuaries often put the pulpit in the center, so that the word is central and marks the high point of a worship service designed around it, often focused on a minister who gives the word from a pulpit with a high stairway, in case anyone missed the point.

The power of God's Word and leisurely liturgy sometimes gets transferred to merely human words, at the risk of trivializing. Whenever we gather in large groups nationally, we rush through the worship so we can get to the really exciting work of gathering in committees to debate word choice on resolutions. When most Christians hear "In the beginning was the Word," some folks may think "Jesus," but my particular tribe thinks "by-laws!" So it came as no surprise that when faced with a nation on the brink of war, my congregation went to words, and to resolutions.

A while back, with the approval of the church's governing board, our associate minister stood to announce that at an after-church gathering we would debate a resolution that we would send on, if approved, to our Connecticut Conference's annual meeting. It called upon our nation to stop its march toward unilateral war against Iraq. It was not a now-and-forever call to pacifism, but a word for a church and a nation at one point in history. The gathering after church was packed.

As people began to raise their hands to speak, I worried, as a pastor, that we would be simply staging our own church version of the partisan yelling matches our members watch on television. So before people began giving their opinions on the resolution, I told them that I trusted they were knowledgable on the issues on either side and that most of us were fairly familiar with not only our own arguments but of those we disagreed with. So the question I posed to them was this: "What can you say about this issue of impending war here in a church setting? What can you say here that you can say nowhere else? We can all talk politics. But what can you say or ask here as a Christian in a Christian community that you can't say or ask out there?"

There was a silence, as people who had prepared to speak reconsidered. And then what came forth was remarkable, not so much in content as in tone. There was a reverence in the conversation, as people spoke of how they prayed for peace—or of times they had prayed for vengeance. People mentioned their desire to understand pacifism and just war theory better, their lack of confidence in their own understanding of the theological debates on the issue of war. They spoke of Christian pacifists they admired or of their own experience of God's grace when they had served in the military. People on all sides spoke of being afraid and of being angry. The resolution passed with a few abstentions and no "nays."

Later, at the Connecticut Conference meeting, it passed again. But this time there was debate, not from the World War II generation but from a teenager. He worried, passionately and thoughtfully, that we as a great and powerful nation had a moral responsibility to defend the people of Iraq from a cruel leader. I noticed the young people watching him, those who had never lived through Vietnam, and as he spoke of rescuing the Iraqi people from a leader he likened to Hitler there were tears in their eyes and in the eyes of others. Yet our congregation's resolution passed nearly unanimously.

There at that meeting, when the adult minds were caught up in signs and weariness of war, I caught my first glimpse of what history will see as much more important. In a room full of people pursuing peace, that teenager was discussing empire, and he was not weary, but inspired. As we adults reacted to the latest news, he was already reading between the lines. As we ran in circles breathlessly trying to prevent a war that had been planned long before we started organizing, the teenager was voicing a theology of empire. And so he should be. His generation will inherit that empire and its consequences, just as the adult generation may create it and pass away.

The church must discuss empire, not in the way we discuss so many other things—by hiring a few academics to lecture to a few interested clergy and calling it a day—but in the way the early church must have discussed Caesar. We need to talk as Christians, not the way the world talks.

I'll never forget returning to church the following Sunday, when our moderator stood to tell the congregation that the resolution had passed. The majority of the congregation applauded, but a significant number did not. In the months that followed, in the debates in church class-rooms and the informal debates over cookies and coffee after church, we learned that while support for the congregational resolution against the war was not unanimous, it was not particularly painful to those who disagreed. After all, we are a church that prides itself on its diversity. But we did indeed have a painful aftermath, and it was related not to the vote, but to that moment of applause. Even in a critique of a nation that seemed more intent on winning than discerning, we had fallen into our own moment of triumphalism. We have since promised ourselves as a congregation not to applaud at moments like that, but I'm not sure we'll be able to stick to it. After all, we are only human. We really do like to win. This is messy work.

Appendix

*T*he *National Security Strategy of the United States of America* was published by the White House on September 17, 2002, prefaced by President George W. Bush. Principles invoked, issues raised, and policies promoted in the *Strategy* are in some respects specific to the administration that produced it and its time. In other respects, however, the *Strategy* reaches well beyond one administration to principles, issues, and policies that will remain open to reasoned discussion and democratic debate for much of the twenty-first century. The essays in this book take up that call to reasoned discussion and democratic debate. They do so from positions of commitment to the church and its mission and particular burden for how American Christians might engage these times. As an aid to this ongoing discussion and debate, the *Strategy* is included as an appendix to this collection.

The National Security Strategy of the United States of America

The great struggles of the twentieth century between liberty and totalitarianism ended with a decisive victory for the forces of freedom—and a single sustainable model for national success: freedom, democracy, and free enterprise. In the twenty-first century, only nations that share a commitment to protecting basic human rights and guaranteeing political and economic freedom will be able to unleash the potential of their people and assure their future prosperity. People everywhere want to be able to speak freely; choose who will govern them; worship as they please; educate their children—male and female; own property; and enjoy the benefits of their labor. These values of freedom are right and true for every person, in every society—and the duty of protecting these values against their enemies is the common calling of freedom-loving people across the globe and across the ages.

Today, the United States enjoys a position of unparalleled military strength and great economic and political influence. In keeping with our heritage and principles, we do not use our strength to press for unilateral advantage. We seek instead to create a balance of power that favors human freedom: conditions in which all nations and all societies can choose for themselves the rewards and challenges of political and economic liberty. In a world that is safe, people will be able to make their own lives better. We will defend the peace by fighting terrorists and tyrants. We will preserve the peace by building good relations among the great powers. We will extend the peace by encouraging free and open societies on every continent.

Defending our Nation against its enemies is the first and fundamental commitment of the Federal Government. Today, that task has changed dramatically. Enemies in the past needed great armies and great industrial capabilities to endanger America. Now, shadowy networks of individuals can bring great chaos and suffering to our shores for less than it costs to purchase a single tank. Terrorists are organized to penetrate open societies and to turn the power of modern technologies against us.

To defeat this threat we must make use of every tool in our arsenal—military power, better homeland defenses, law enforcement, intelligence, and vigorous efforts to cut off terrorist financing. The war against terrorists of global reach is a global enterprise of uncertain duration. America will help nations that need our assistance in combating terror. And America will hold to account nations that are compromised by terror, including those who harbor terrorists—because the allies of terror are the enemies of civilization. The United States and countries cooperating with us must not allow the terrorists to develop new home bases. Together, we will seek to deny them sanctuary at every turn.

The gravest danger our Nation faces lies at the crossroads of radicalism and technology. Our enemies have openly declared that they are seeking weapons of mass destruction, and evidence indicates that they are doing so with determination. The United States will not allow these efforts to succeed. We will build defenses against ballistic missiles and other means of delivery. We will cooperate with other nations to deny, contain, and curtail our enemies' efforts to acquire dangerous technologies. And, as a matter of common sense and self-defense, America will act against such emerging threats before they are fully formed. We cannot defend America and our friends by hoping for the best. So we must be prepared to defeat our enemies' plans, using the best intelligence and proceeding with deliberation. History will judge harshly those who saw this coming danger but failed to act. In the new world we have entered, the only path to peace and security is the path of action.

As we defend the peace, we will also take advantage of an historic opportunity to preserve the peace. Today, the international community has the best chance since the rise of the nation-state in the seventeenth century to build a world where great powers compete in peace instead of continually prepare for war. Today, the world's great powers find ourselves on the same side—united by common dangers of terrorist violence and chaos. The United States will build on these common interests to promote global security. We are also increasingly united by common values. Russia is in the midst of a hopeful transition, reaching for its democratic future and a partner in the war on terror. Chinese leaders are discovering that economic freedom is the only source of national wealth. In time, they will find that social and political freedom is the only source of national greatness. America will encourage the advancement of democracy and economic openness in both nations, because these are the best foundations for domestic stability and international order. We will strongly resist aggression from other great powers—even as we welcome their peaceful pursuit of prosperity, trade, and cultural advancement.

Finally, the United States will use this moment of opportunity to extend the benefits of freedom across the globe. We will actively work to bring the hope of democracy, development, free markets, and free trade to every corner of the world. The events of September 11, 2001, taught us that weak states, like Afghanistan, can pose as great a danger to our national interests as strong states. Poverty does not make poor people into terrorists and murderers. Yet poverty, weak institutions, and corruption can make weak states vulnerable to terrorist networks and drug cartels within their borders.

The United States will stand beside any nation determined to build a better future by seeking the rewards of liberty for its people. Free trade and free markets have proven their ability to lift whole societies out of poverty—so the United States will work with individual nations, entire regions, and the entire global trading community to build a world that trades in freedom and therefore grows in prosperity. The United States will deliver greater development assistance through the New Millennium Challenge Account to nations that govern justly, invest in their people, and encourage economic freedom. We will also continue to lead the world in efforts to reduce the terrible toll of HIV/AIDS and other infectious diseases.

In building a balance of power that favors freedom, the United States is guided by the conviction that all nations have important responsibilities. Nations that enjoy freedom must actively fight terror. Nations that depend on international stability must help prevent the spread of weapons of mass destruction. Nations that seek international aid must govern themselves wisely, so that aid is well spent. For freedom to thrive, accountability must be expected and required.

We are also guided by the conviction that no nation can build a safer, better world alone. Alliances and multilateral institutions can multiply the strength of freedom-loving nations. The United States is committed to lasting institutions like the United Nations, the World Trade Organization, the Organization of American States, and NATO as well as other long-standing alliances. Coalitions of the willing can augment these permanent institutions. In all cases, international obligations are to be taken seriously. They are not to be undertaken symbolically to rally support for an ideal without furthering its attainment.

Freedom is the non-negotiable demand of human dignity; the birthright of every person—in every civilization. Throughout history, freedom has been threatened by war and terror; it has been challenged by the clashing wills of powerful states and the evil designs of tyrants; and it has been tested by widespread poverty and disease. Today, humanity holds in its hands the opportunity to further freedom's triumph over all these foes. The United States welcomes our responsibility to lead in this great mission.

George W. Bush
THE WHITE HOUSE,
September 17, 2002

I. Overview of America's International Strategy

"Our Nation's cause has always been larger than our Nation's defense. We fight, as we always fight, for a just peace—a peace that favors liberty. We will defend the peace against the threats from terrorists and tyrants. We will preserve the peace by building good relations among the great powers. And we will extend the peace by encouraging free and open societies on every continent."

President Bush
West Point, New York
June 1, 2002

The United States possesses unprecedented—and unequaled—strength and influence in the world. Sustained by faith in the principles of liberty, and the value of a free society, this position comes with unparalleled responsibilities, obligations, and opportunity. The great strength of this nation must be used to promote a balance of power that favors freedom.

For most of the twentieth century, the world was divided by a great struggle over ideas: destructive totalitarian visions versus freedom and equality.

That great struggle is over. The militant visions of class, nation, and race which promised utopia and delivered misery have been defeated and discredited. America is now threatened less by conquering states than we are by failing ones. We are menaced less by fleets and armies than by catastrophic technologies in the hands of the embittered few.We must defeat these threats to our Nation, allies, and friends.

This is also a time of opportunity for America. We will work to translate this moment of influence into decades of peace, prosperity, and liberty. The U.S. national security strategy will be based on a distinctly American international-ism that reflects the union of our values and our national interests. The aim of this strategy is to help make the world not just safer but better. Our goals on the path to progress are clear: political and economic freedom, peaceful relations with other states, and respect for human dignity.

And this path is not America's alone. It is open to all. To achieve these goals, the United States will:

- champion aspirations for human dignity;
- strengthen alliances to defeat global terrorism and work to prevent attacks against us and our friends;
- work with others to defuse regional conflicts;
- prevent our enemies from threatening us, our allies, and our friends, with weapons of mass destruction;
- ignite a new era of global economic growth through free markets and free trade;
- expand the circle of development by opening societies and building the infrastructure of democracy;

- develop agendas for cooperative action with other main centers of global power; and

- transform America's national security institutions to meet the challenges and opportunities of the twenty-first century.

II. Champion Aspirations for Human Dignity

"Some worry that it is somehow undiplomatic or impolite to speak the language of right and wrong. I disagree. Different circumstances require different methods, but not different moralities."

President Bush
West Point, New York
June 1, 2002

In pursuit of our goals, our first imperative is to clarify what we stand for: the United States must defend liberty and justice because these principles are right and true for all people everywhere. No nation owns these aspirations, and no nation is exempt from them. Fathers and mothers in all societies want their children to be educated and to live free from poverty and violence. No people on earth yearn to be oppressed, aspire to servitude, or eagerly await the midnight knock of the secret police.

America must stand firmly for the nonnegotiable demands of human dignity: the rule of law; limits on the absolute power of the state; free speech; freedom of worship; equal justice; respect for women; religious and ethnic tolerance; and respect for private property.

These demands can be met in many ways. America's constitution has served us well. Many other nations, with different histories and cultures, facing different circumstances, have successfully incorporated these core principles into their own systems of governance. History has not been kind to those nations which ignored or flouted the rights and aspirations of their people.

America's experience as a great multi-ethnic democracy affirms our conviction that people of many heritages and faiths can live and prosper in peace. Our own history is a long struggle to live up to our ideals. But even in our worst moments, the principles enshrined in the Declaration of Independence were there to guide us. As a result, America is not just a stronger, but is a freer and more just society.

Today, these ideals are a lifeline to lonely defenders of liberty. And when openings arrive, we can encourage change—as we did in central and eastern Europe between 1989 and 1991, or in Belgrade in 2000.When we see democratic processes take hold among our friends in Taiwan or in the Republic of Korea, and see elected leaders replace generals in Latin America and Africa, we see examples of how authoritarian systems can evolve, marrying local history and traditions with the principles we all cherish.

Embodying lessons from our past and using the opportunity we have today, the national security strategy of the United States must start from these core beliefs and look outward for possibilities to expand liberty.

Our principles will guide our government's decisions about international cooperation, the character of our foreign assistance, and the allocation of resources. They will guide our actions and our words in international bodies.

We will:

- speak out honestly about violations of the nonnegotiable demands of human dignity using our voice and vote in international institutions to advance freedom;
- use our foreign aid to promote freedom and support those who struggle non-violently for it, ensuring that nations moving toward democracy are rewarded for the steps they take;
- make freedom and the development of democratic institutions key themes in our bilateral relations, seeking solidarity and cooperation from other democracies while we press governments that deny human rights to move toward a better future; and
- take special efforts to promote freedom of religion and conscience and defend it from encroachment by repressive governments.

We will champion the cause of human dignity and oppose those who resist it.

III. Strengthen Alliances to Defeat Global Terrorism and Work to Prevent Attacks Against Us and Our Friends

"Just three days removed from these events, Americans do not yet have the distance of history. But our responsibility to history is already clear: to answer these attacks and rid the world of evil. War has been waged against us by stealth and deceit and murder. This nation is peaceful, but fierce when stirred to anger. The conflict was begun on the timing and terms of others. It will end in a way, and at an hour, of our choosing."

President Bush
Washington, D.C. (The National Cathedral)
September 14, 2001

The United States of America is fighting a war against terrorists of global reach. The enemy is not a single political regime or person or religion or ideology. The enemy is terrorism—premeditated, politically motivated violence perpetrated against innocents.

In many regions, legitimate grievances prevent the emergence of a lasting peace. Such grievances deserve to be, and must be, addressed within a political process. But no cause justifies terror. The United States will make no concessions to terrorist demands and strike no deals with them. We make no distinction between terrorists and those who knowingly harbor or provide aid to them.

The struggle against global terrorism is different from any other war in our history. It will be fought on many fronts against a particularly elusive enemy over an extended period of time. Progress will come through the persistent accumulation of successes—some seen, some unseen.

Today our enemies have seen the results of what civilized nations can, and will, do against regimes that harbor, support, and use terrorism to achieve their political goals. Afghanistan has been liberated; coalition forces continue to hunt down the Taliban and al-Qaeda. But it is not only this battlefield on which we will engage terrorists. Thousands of trained terrorists remain at large with cells in North America, South America, Europe, Africa, the Middle East, and across Asia.

Our priority will be first to disrupt and destroy terrorist organizations of global reach and attack their leadership; command, control, and communications; material support; and finances. This will have a disabling effect upon the terrorists' ability to plan and operate.

We will continue to encourage our regional partners to take up a coordinated effort that isolates the terrorists. Once the regional campaign localizes the threat to a particular state, we will help ensure the state has the military, law enforcement, political, and financial tools necessary to finish the task.

The United States will continue to work with our allies to disrupt the financing of terrorism. We will identify and block the sources of funding for terrorism, freeze the assets of terrorists and those who support them, deny terrorists access to the international financial system, protect legitimate charities from being abused by terrorists, and prevent the movement of terrorists' assets through alternative financial networks.

However, this campaign need not be sequential to be effective, the cumulative effect across all regions will help achieve the results we seek. We will disrupt and destroy terrorist organizations by:

- direct and continuous action using all the elements of national and international power. Our immediate focus will be those terrorist organizations of global reach and any terrorist or state sponsor of terrorism which attempts to gain or use weapons of mass destruction (WMD) or their precursors;
- defending the United States, the American people, and our interests at home and abroad by identifying and destroying the threat before it reaches our borders. While the United States will constantly strive to enlist the support of the international community, we will not hesitate to act alone, if necessary, to exercise our right of self-defense by acting preemptively against such terrorists, to prevent them from doing harm against our people and our country; and
- denying further sponsorship, support, and sanctuary to terrorists by convincing or compelling states to accept their sovereign responsibilities.

We will also wage a war of ideas to win the battle against international terrorism. This includes:

- using the full influence of the United States, and working closely with allies and friends, to make clear that all acts of terrorism are illegitimate so that terrorism will be viewed in the same light as slavery, piracy, or genocide: behavior that no respectable government can condone or support and all must oppose;
- supporting moderate and modern government, especially in the Muslim world, to ensure that the conditions and ideologies that promote terrorism do not find fertile ground in any nation;
- diminishing the underlying conditions that spawn terrorism by enlisting the international community to focus its efforts and resources on areas most at risk; and
- using effective public diplomacy to promote the free flow of information and ideas to kindle the hopes and aspirations of freedom of those in societies ruled by the sponsors of global terrorism.

While we recognize that our best defense is a good offense, we are also strengthening America's homeland security to protect against and deter attack. This Administration has proposed the largest government reorganization since the Truman Administration created the National Security Council and the Department of Defense. Centered on a new Department of Homeland Security and including a new unified military command and a fundamental reordering of the FBI, our comprehensive plan to secure the homeland encompasses every level of government and the cooperation of the public and the private sector.

This strategy will turn adversity into opportunity. For example, emergency management systems will be better able to cope not just with terrorism but with all hazards. Our medical system will be strengthened to manage not just bioterror, but all infectious diseases and mass-casualty dangers. Our border controls will not just stop terrorists, but improve the efficient movement of legitimate traffic.

While our focus is protecting America, we know that to defeat terrorism in today's globalized world we need support from our allies and friends. Wherever possible, the United States will rely on regional organizations and state powers to meet their obligations to fight terrorism. Where governments find the fight against terrorism beyond their capacities, we will match their willpower and their resources with whatever help we and our allies can provide.

As we pursue the terrorists in Afghanistan, we will continue to work with international organizations such as the United Nations, as well as nongovernmental organizations, and other countries to provide the humanitarian, political, economic, and security assistance necessary to rebuild Afghanistan so that it will never again abuse its people, threaten its neighbors, and provide a haven for terrorists.

In the war against global terrorism, we will never forget that we are ultimately fighting for our democratic values and way of life. Freedom and fear are at war, and there will be no quick or easy end to this conflict. In leading the campaign against terrorism, we are forging new, productive international relationships and redefining existing ones in ways that meet the challenges of the twenty-first century.

IV. Work with Others to Defuse Regional Conflicts

"We build a world of justice, or we will live in a world of coercion. The magnitude of our shared responsibilities makes our disagreements look so small."

President Bush
Berlin, Germany
May 23, 2002

Concerned nations must remain actively engaged in critical regional disputes to avoid explosive escalation and minimize human suffering. In an increasingly interconnected world, regional crisis can strain our alliances, rekindle rivalries among the major powers, and create horrifying affronts to human dignity. When violence erupts and states falter, the United States will work with friends and partners to alleviate suffering and restore stability.

No doctrine can anticipate every circumstance in which U.S. action—direct or indirect—is warranted. We have finite political, economic, and military resources to meet our global priorities. The United States will approach each case with these strategic principles in mind:

- The United States should invest time and resources into building international relationships and institutions that can help manage local crises when they emerge.
- The United States should be realistic about its ability to help those who are unwilling or unready to help themselves. Where and when people are ready to do their part, we will be willing to move decisively.

The Israeli-Palestinian conflict is critical because of the toll of human suffering, because of America's close relationship with the state of Israel and key Arab states, and because of that region's importance to other global priorities of the United States. There can be no peace for either side without freedom for both sides. America stands committed to an independent and democratic Palestine, living beside Israel in peace and security. Like all other people, Palestinians deserve a government that serves their interests and listens to their voices. The United States will continue to encourage all parties to step up to their responsibilities as we seek a just and comprehensive settlement to the conflict.

The United States, the international donor community, and the World Bank stand ready to work with a reformed Palestinian government on economic development, increased humanitarian assistance, and a program to establish, finance, and monitor a truly independent judiciary. If Palestinians embrace democracy, and the rule of law, confront corruption, and firmly reject terror, they can count on American support for the creation of a Palestinian state.

Israel also has a large stake in the success of a democratic Palestine. Permanent occupation threatens Israel's identity and democracy. So the United States continues to challenge Israeli leaders to take concrete steps to support the emergence of a viable, credible Palestinian state. As there is progress towards security, Israel forces need to withdraw fully to positions they held prior to September 28, 2000. And consistent with the recommendations of the Mitchell Committee, Israeli settlement activity in the occupied territories must stop. As violence subsides, freedom of movement should be restored, permitting innocent Palestinians to resume work and normal life. The United States can play a crucial role but, ultimately, lasting peace can only come when Israelis and Palestinians resolve the issues and end the conflict between them.

In South Asia, the United States has also emphasized the need for India and Pakistan to resolve their disputes. This Administration invested time and resources building strong bilateral relations with India and Pakistan. These strong relations then gave us leverage to play a constructive role when tensions in the region became acute. With Pakistan, our bilateral relations have been bolstered by Pakistan's choice to join the war against terror and move toward building a more open and tolerant society. The Administration sees India's potential to become one of the great democratic powers of the twenty-first century and has worked hard to transform our relationship accordingly. Our involvement in this regional dispute, building on earlier investments in bilateral relations, looks first to concrete steps by India and Pakistan that can help defuse military confrontation.

Indonesia took courageous steps to create a working democracy and respect for the rule of law. By tolerating ethnic minorities, respecting the rule of law, and accepting open markets, Indonesia may be able to employ the engine of opportunity that has helped lift some of its neighbors out of poverty and desperation. It is the initiative by Indonesia that allows U.S. assistance to make a difference.

In the Western Hemisphere we have formed flexible coalitions with countries that share our priorities, particularly Mexico, Brazil, Canada, Chile, and Colombia. Together we will promote a truly democratic hemisphere where our integration advances security, prosperity, opportunity, and hope. We will work with regional institutions, such as the Summit of the Americas process, the Organization of American States (OAS), and the Defense Ministerial of the Americas for the benefit of the entire hemisphere.

Parts of Latin America confront regional conflict, especially arising from the violence of drug cartels and their accomplices. This conflict and unrestrained narcotics trafficking could imperil the health and security of the United States. Therefore we have developed an active strategy to help the Andean nations adjust their economies, enforce their laws, defeat terrorist organizations, and cut off the supply of drugs, while—as important—we work to reduce the demand for drugs in our own country.

In Colombia, we recognize the link between terrorist and extremist groups that challenge the security of the state and drug trafficking activities that help finance the operations of such groups. We are working to help Colombia defend its democratic institutions and defeat illegal armed groups of both the left and right by extending effective sovereignty over the entire national territory and provide basic security to the Colombian people.

In Africa, promise and opportunity sit side by side with disease, war, and desperate poverty. This threatens both a core value of the United States—preserving human dignity—and our strategic priority—combating global terror. American interests and American principles, therefore, lead in the same direction: we will work with others for an African continent that lives in liberty, peace, and growing prosperity. Together with our European allies, we must help strengthen Africa's fragile states, help build indigenous capability to secure porous borders, and help build up the law enforcement and intelligence infrastructure to deny havens for terrorists.

An ever more lethal environment exists in Africa as local civil wars spread beyond borders to create regional war zones. Forming coalitions of the willing and cooperative security arrangements are key to confronting these emerging transnational threats.

Africa's great size and diversity requires a security strategy that focuses on bilateral engagement and builds coalitions of the willing. This Administration will focus on three interlocking strategies for the region:

- countries with major impact on their neighborhood such as South Africa, Nigeria, Kenya, and Ethiopia are anchors for regional engagement and require focused attention;
- coordination with European allies and international institutions is essential for constructive conflict mediation and successful peace operations; and
- Africa's capable reforming states and sub-regional organizations must be strengthened as the primary means to address transnational threats on a sustained basis.

Ultimately the path of political and economic freedom presents the surest route to progress in sub-Saharan Africa, where most wars are conflicts over material resources and political access often tragically waged on the basis of ethnic and religious difference. The transition to the African Union with its stated commitment to good governance and a common responsibility for democratic political systems offers opportunities to strengthen democracy on the continent.

V. Prevent Our Enemies from Threatening Us, Our Allies, and Our Friends with Weapons of Mass Destruction

"The gravest danger to freedom lies at the crossroads of radicalism and technology. When the spread of chemical and biological and nuclear weapons, along with ballistic missile technology—when that occurs, even weak states

and small groups could attain a catastrophic power to strike great nations. Our enemies have declared this very intention, and have been caught seeking these terrible weapons. They want the capability to blackmail us, or to harm us, or to harm our friends—and we will oppose them with all our power."

President Bush
West Point, New York
June 1, 2002

The nature of the Cold War threat required the United States—with our allies and friends—to emphasize deterrence of the enemy's use of force, producing a grim strategy of mutual assured destruction. With the collapse of the Soviet Union and the end of the Cold War, our security environment has undergone profound transformation.

Having moved from confrontation to cooperation as the hallmark of our relationship with Russia, the dividends are evident: an end to the balance of terror that divided us; an historic reduction in the nuclear arsenals on both sides; and cooperation in areas such as counterterrorism and missile defense that until recently were inconceivable.

But new deadly challenges have emerged from rogue states and terrorists. None of these contemporary threats rival the sheer destructive power that was arrayed against us by the Soviet Union. However, the nature and motivations of these new adversaries, their determination to obtain destructive powers hitherto available only to the world's strongest states, and the greater likelihood that they will use weapons of mass destruction against us, make today's security environment more complex and dangerous.

In the 1990s we witnessed the emergence of a small number of rogue states that, while different in important ways, share a number of attributes. These states:

- brutalize their own people and squander their national resources for the personal gain of the rulers;
- display no regard for international law, threaten their neighbors, and callously violate international treaties to which they are party;
- are determined to acquire weapons of mass destruction, along with other advanced military technology, to be used as threats or offensively to achieve the aggressive designs of these regimes;
- sponsor terrorism around the globe; and
- reject basic human values and hate the United States and everything for which it stands.

At the time of the Gulf War, we acquired irrefutable proof that Iraq's designs were not limited to the chemical weapons it had used against Iran and its own people, but also extended to the acquisition of nuclear weapons and biological agents. In the past decade North Korea has become the world's principal purveyor of ballistic missiles, and has tested increasingly capable missiles while developing its own WMD arsenal. Other rogue regimes seek nuclear, biological, and chemical weapons as well. These states' pursuit of, and global trade in, such weapons has become a looming threat to all nations.

We must be prepared to stop rogue states and their terrorist clients before they are able to threaten or use weapons of mass destruction against the United States and our allies and friends. Our response must take full advantage of strengthened alliances, the establishment of new partnerships with former adversaries, innovation in the use of military forces, modern technologies, including the development of an effective missile defense system, and increased emphasis on intelligence collection and analysis.

Our comprehensive strategy to combat WMD includes:

- *Proactive counterproliferation efforts.* We must deter and defend against the threat before it is unleashed. We must ensure that key capabilities—detection, active and passive defenses, and counterforce capabilities—are integrated into our defense transformation and our homeland security systems. Counterproliferation must also be integrated into the doctrine, training, and equipping of our forces and those of our allies to ensure that we can prevail in any conflict with WMD-armed adversaries.

- *Strengthened nonproliferation efforts to prevent rogue states and terrorists from acquiring the materials, technologies, and expertise necessary for weapons of mass destruction.* We will enhance diplomacy, arms control, multilateral export controls, and threat reduction assistance that impede states and terrorists seeking WMD, and when necessary, interdict enabling technologies and materials. We will continue to build coalitions to support these efforts, encouraging their increased political and financial support for nonproliferation and threat reduction programs. The recent G-8 agreement to commit up to $20 billion to a global partnership against proliferation marks a major step forward.

- *Effective consequence management to respond to the effects of WMD use, whether by terrorists or hostile states.* Minimizing the effects of WMD use against our people will help deter those who possess such weapons and dissuade those who seek to acquire them by persuading enemies that they cannot attain their desired ends. The United States must also be prepared to respond to the effects of WMD use against our forces abroad, and to help friends and allies if they are attacked.

It has taken almost a decade for us to comprehend the true nature of this new threat. Given the goals of rogue states and terrorists, the United States can no longer solely rely on a reactive posture as we have in the past. The inability to deter a potential attacker, the immediacy of today's threats, and the magnitude of potential harm that could be caused by our adversaries' choice of weapons, do not permit that option. We cannot let our enemies strike first.

In the Cold War, especially following the Cuban missile crisis, we faced a generally status quo, risk-averse adversary. Deterrence was an effective defense. But deterrence based only upon the threat of retaliation is less likely to work against leaders of rogue states more willing to take risks, gambling with the lives of their people, and the wealth of their nations.

- In the Cold War, weapons of mass destruction were considered weapons of last resort whose use risked the destruction of those who used them. Today, our enemies see weapons of mass destruction as weapons of choice. For rogue states these weapons are tools of intimidation and military aggression against their neighbors. These weapons may also allow these states to attempt to blackmail the United States and our allies to prevent us from deterring or repelling the aggressive behavior of rogue states. Such states also see these weapons as their best means of overcoming the conventional superiority of the United States.

- Traditional concepts of deterrence will not work against a terrorist enemy whose avowed tactics are wanton destruction and the targeting of inno-cents; whose so-called soldiers seek martyrdom in death and whose most potent protection is statelessness. The overlap between states that sponsor terror and those that pursue WMD compels us to action.

For centuries, international law recognized that nations need not suffer an attack before they can lawfully take action to defend themselves against forces that present an imminent danger of attack. Legal scholars and international jurists often conditioned the legitimacy of preemption on the existence of an imminent threat—most often a visible mobilization of armies, navies, and air forces preparing to attack.

We must adapt the concept of imminent threat to the capabilities and objec-tives of today's adversaries. Rogue states and terrorists do not seek to attack us using conventional means. They know such attacks would fail. Instead, they rely on acts of terror and, potentially, the use of weapons of mass destruc-tion—weapons that can be easily concealed, delivered covertly, and used without warning.

The targets of these attacks are our military forces and our civilian population, in direct violation of one of the principal norms of the law of warfare. As was demonstrated by the losses on September 11, 2001, mass civilian casualties is the specific objective of terrorists and these losses would be exponentially more severe if terrorists acquired and used weapons of mass destruction.

The United States has long maintained the option of preemptive actions to counter a sufficient threat to our national security. The greater the threat, the greater is the risk of inaction— and the more compelling the case for taking anticipatory action to defend ourselves, even if uncertainty remains as to the time and place of the enemy's attack. To forestall or prevent such hostile acts by our adversaries, the United States will, if necessary, act preemptively.

The United States will not use force in all cases to preempt emerging threats, nor should nations use preemption as a pretext for aggression. Yet in an age where the enemies of civilization openly and actively seek the world's most destructive technologies, the United States cannot remain idle while dangers gather. We will always proceed deliberately, weighing the consequences of our actions. To support preemptive options, we will:

- build better, more integrated intelligence capabilities to provide timely, accurate information on threats, wherever they may emerge;
- coordinate closely with allies to form a common assessment of the most dangerous threats; and
- continue to transform our military forces to ensure our ability to conduct rapid and precise operations to achieve decisive results.

The purpose of our actions will always be to eliminate a specific threat to the United States or our allies and friends. The reasons for our actions will be clear, the force measured, and the cause just.

VI. Ignite a New Era of Global Economic Growth through Free Markets and Free Trade

"When nations close their markets and opportunity is hoarded by a privileged few, no amount—no amount—of development aid is ever enough. When nations respect their people, open markets, invest in better health and education, every dollar of aid, every dollar of trade revenue and domestic capital is used more effectively."

President Bush
Monterrey, Mexico
March 22, 2002

A strong world economy enhances our national security by advancing prosperity and freedom in the rest of the world. Economic growth supported by free trade and free markets creates new jobs and higher incomes. It allows people to lift their lives out of poverty, spurs economic and legal reform, and the fight against corruption, and it reinforces the habits of liberty.

We will promote economic growth and economic freedom beyond America's shores. All governments are responsible for creating their own economic policies and responding to their own economic challenges. We will use our economic engagement with other countries to underscore the benefits of policies that generate higher productivity and sustained economic growth, including:

- pro-growth legal and regulatory policies to encourage business investment, innovation, and entrepreneurial activity;
- tax policies—particularly lower marginal tax rates—that improve incentives for work and investment;
- rule of law and intolerance of corruption so that people are confident that they will be able to enjoy the fruits of their economic endeavors;

- strong financial systems that allow capital to be put to its most efficient use;
- sound fiscal policies to support business activity;
- investments in health and education that improve the well-being and skills of the labor force and population as a whole; and
- free trade that provides new avenues for growth and fosters the diffusion of technologies and ideas that increase productivity and opportunity.

The lessons of history are clear: market economies, not command-and-control economies with the heavy hand of government, are the best way to promote prosperity and reduce poverty. Policies that further strengthen market incentives and market institutions are relevant for all economies—industrialized countries, emerging markets, and the developing world.

A return to strong economic growth in Europe and Japan is vital to U.S. national security interests. We want our allies to have strong economies for their own sake, for the sake of the global economy, and for the sake of global security. European efforts to remove structural barriers in their economies are particularly important in this regard, as are Japan's efforts to end deflation and address the problems of non-performing loans in the Japanese banking system. We will continue to use our regular consultations with Japan and our European partners—including through the Group of Seven (G-7)—to discuss policies they are adopting to promote growth in their economies and support higher global economic growth.

Improving stability in emerging markets is also key to global economic growth. International flows of investment capital are needed to expand the productive potential of these economies. These flows allow emerging markets and developing countries to make the investments that raise living standards and reduce poverty. Our long-term objective should be a world in which all countries have investment-grade credit ratings that allow them access to international capital markets and to invest in their future.

We are committed to policies that will help emerging markets achieve access to larger capital flows at lower cost. To this end, we will continue to pursue reforms aimed at reducing uncertainty in financial markets. We will work actively with other countries, the International Monetary Fund (IMF), and the private sector to implement the G-7 Action Plan negotiated earlier this year for preventing financial crises and more effectively resolving them when they occur.

The best way to deal with financial crises is to prevent them from occurring, and we have encouraged the IMF to improve its efforts doing so. We will continue to work with the IMF to streamline the policy conditions for its lending and to focus its lending strategy on achieving economic growth through sound fiscal and monetary policy, exchange rate policy, and financial sector policy.

The concept of "free trade" arose as a moral principle even before it became a pillar of economics. If you can make something that others value, you should be able to sell it to them. If others make something that you value, you should be able to buy it. This is real freedom, the freedom for a person—or a nation—to make a living. To promote free trade, the Unites States has developed a comprehensive strategy:

- *Seize the global initiative.* The new global trade negotiations we helped launch at Doha in November 2001 will have an ambitious agenda, especially in agriculture, manufacturing, and services, targeted for completion in 2005. The United States has led the way in completing the accession of China and a democratic Taiwan to the World Trade Organization. We will assist Russia's preparations to join the WTO.

- *Press regional initiatives.* The United States and other democracies in the Western Hemisphere have agreed to create the Free Trade Area of the Americas, targeted for completion in 2005. This year the United States will advocate market-access negotiations with its partners, targeted on agriculture, industrial goods, services, investment, and government procurement. We will also offer more opportunity to the poorest continent, Africa, starting with full use of the preferences allowed in the African Growth and Opportunity Act, and leading to free trade.

- *Move ahead with bilateral free trade agreements.* Building on the free trade agreement with Jordan enacted in 2001, the Administration will work this year to complete free trade agreements with Chile and Singapore. Our aim is to achieve free trade agreements with a mix of developed and developing countries in all regions of the world. Initially, Central America, Southern Africa, Morocco, and Australia will be our principal focal points.

- *Renew the executive-congressional partnership.* Every administration's trade strategy depends on a productive partnership with Congress. After a gap of 8 years, the Administration reestablished majority support in the Congress for trade liberalization by passing Trade Promotion Authority and the other market opening measures for developing countries in the Trade Act of 2002. This Administration will work with Congress to enact new bilateral, regional, and global trade agreements that will be concluded under the recently passed Trade Promotion Authority.

- *Promote the connection between trade and development.* Trade policies can help developing countries strengthen property rights, competition, the rule of law, investment, the spread of knowledge, open societies, the efficient allocation of resources, and regional integration—all leading to growth, opportunity, and confidence in developing countries. The United States is implementing The Africa Growth and Opportunity Act to provide market-access for nearly all goods produced in the 35 countries of sub-Saharan Africa. We will make more use of this act and its equivalent for the Caribbean Basin and continue to work with multilateral and regional institutions to help poorer countries take advantage of these opportunities. Beyond market access, the most important area where trade intersects with poverty is in public health. We will ensure that the WTO intellectual property rules are flexible enough to allow developing nations to gain access to critical medicines for extraordinary dangers like HIV/AIDS, tuberculosis, and malaria.

- *Enforce trade agreements and laws against unfair practices.* Commerce depends on the rule of law; international trade depends on enforceable agreements. Our top priorities are to resolve ongoing disputes with the European Union, Canada, and Mexico and to make a global effort to address new technology, science, and health regulations that needlessly impede farm exports and improved agriculture. Laws against unfair trade practices are often abused, but the international community must be able to address genuine concerns about government subsidies and dumping. International industrial espionage which undermines fair competition must be detected and deterred.

- *Help domestic industries and workers adjust.* There is a sound statutory framework for these transitional safeguards which we have used in the agricultural sector and which we are using this year to help the American steel industry. The benefits of free trade depend upon the enforcement of fair trading practices. These safeguards help ensure that the benefits of free trade do not come at the expense of American workers. Trade adjustment assistance will help workers adapt to the change and dynamism of open markets.

- *Protect the environment and workers.* The United States must foster economic growth in ways that will provide a better life along with widening prosperity. We will incorporate labor and environmental concerns into U.S. trade negotiations, creating a healthy "network" between multilateral environmental agreements with the WTO, and use the International Labor Organization, trade preference programs, and trade talks to improve working conditions in conjunction with freer trade.

- *Enhance energy security.* We will strengthen our own energy security and the shared prosperity of the global economy by working with our allies, trading partners, and energy producers to expand the sources and types of global energy supplied, especially in the Western Hemisphere, Africa, Central Asia, and the Caspian region. We will also continue to work with our partners to develop cleaner and more energy efficient technologies.

Economic growth should be accompanied by global efforts to stabilize greenhouse gas concentrations associated with this growth, containing them at a level that prevents dangerous human interference with the global climate. Our overall objective is to reduce America's greenhouse gas emissions relative to the size of our economy, cutting such emissions per unit of economic activity by 18 percent over the next 10 years, by the year 2012. Our strategies for attaining this goal will be to:

- remain committed to the basic U.N. Framework Convention for international cooperation;

- obtain agreements with key industries to cut emissions of some of the most potent greenhouse gases and give transferable credits to companies that can show real cuts;

- develop improved standards for measuring and registering emission reductions;
- promote renewable energy production and clean coal technology, as well as nuclear power—which produces no greenhouse gas emissions, while also improving fuel economy for U.S. cars and trucks;
- increase spending on research and new conservation technologies, to a total of $4.5 billion—the largest sum being spent on climate change by any country in the world and a $700 million increase over last year's budget; and
- assist developing countries, especially the major greenhouse gas emitters such as China and India, so that they will have the tools and resources to join this effort and be able to grow along a cleaner and better path.

VII. Expand the Circle of Development by Opening Societies and Building the Infrastructure of Democracy

"In World War II we fought to make the world safer, then worked to rebuild it. As we wage war today to keep the world safe from terror, we must also work to make the world a better place for all its citizens."

President Bush
Washington, D.C. (Inter-American Development Bank)
March 14, 2002

A world where some live in comfort and plenty, while half of the human race lives on less than $2 a day, is neither just nor stable. Including all of the world's poor in an expanding circle of development—and opportunity—is a moral imperative and one of the top priorities of U.S. international policy.

Decades of massive development assistance have failed to spur economic growth in the poorest countries. Worse, development aid has often served to prop up failed policies, relieving the pressure for reform and perpetuating misery. Results of aid are typically measured in dollars spent by donors, not in the rates of growth and poverty reduction achieved by recipients. These are the indicators of a failed strategy.

Working with other nations, the United States is confronting this failure. We forged a new consensus at the U.N. Conference on Financing for Development in Monterrey that the objectives of assistance—and the strategies to achieve those objectives—must change.

This Administration's goal is to help unleash the productive potential of individuals in all nations. Sustained growth and poverty reduction is impossible without the right national policies. Where governments have implemented real policy changes, we will provide significant new levels of assistance. The United States and other developed countries should set an ambitious and specific target: to double the size of the world's poorest economies within a decade.

The United States Government will pursue these major strategies to achieve this goal:

- *Provide resources to aid countries that have met the challenge of national reform.* We propose a 50 percent increase in the core development assistance given by the United States. While continuing our present programs, including humanitarian assistance based on need alone, these billions of new dollars will form a new Millennium Challenge Account for projects in countries whose governments rule justly, invest in their people, and encourage economic freedom. Governments must fight corruption, respect basic human rights, embrace the rule of law, invest in health care and education, follow responsible economic policies, and enable entrepreneurship. The Millennium Challenge Account will reward countries that have demonstrated real policy change and challenge those that have not to implement reforms.

- *Improve the effectiveness of the World Bank and other development banks in raising living standards.* The United States is committed to a comprehensive reform agenda for making the World Bank and the other multilateral development banks more effective in improving the lives of the world's poor. We have reversed the downward trend in U.S. contributions and proposed an 18 percent increase in the U.S. contributions to the International Development Association (IDA)—the World Bank's fund for the poorest countries—and the African Development Fund. The key to raising living standards and reducing poverty around the world is increasing productivity growth, especially in the poorest countries. We will continue to press the multilateral development banks to focus on activities that increase economic productivity, such as improvements in education, health, rule of law, and private sector development. Every project, every loan, every grant must be judged by how much it will increase productivity growth in developing countries.

- *Insist upon measurable results to ensure that development assistance is actually making a difference in the lives of the world's poor.* When it comes to economic development, what really matters is that more children are getting a better education, more people have access to health care and clean water, or more workers can find jobs to make a better future for their families. We have a moral obligation to measure the success of our development assistance by whether it is delivering results. For this reason, we will continue to demand that our own development assistance as well as assistance from the multilateral development banks has measurable goals and concrete benchmarks for achieving those goals. Thanks to U.S. leadership, the recent IDA replenishment agreement will establish a monitoring and evaluation system that measures recipient countries' progress. For the first time, donors can link a portion of their contributions to IDA to the achievement of actual development results, and part of the U.S. contribution is linked in this way. We will strive to make sure that the World Bank and other multilateral development banks build on this progress so that a focus on results is an integral part of everything that these institutions do.

- *Increase the amount of development assistance that is provided in the form of grants instead of loans.* Greater use of results-based grants is the best way to help poor countries make productive investments, particularly in the social sectors, without saddling them with ever-larger debt burdens. As a result of U.S. leadership, the recent IDA agreement provided for significant increases in grant funding for the poorest countries for education, HIV/AIDS, health, nutrition, water, sanitation, and other human needs. Our goal is to build on that progress by increasing the use of grants at the other multilateral development banks. We will also challenge universities, nonprofits, and the private sector to match government efforts by using grants to support development projects that show results.

- *Open societies to commerce and investment. Trade and investment are the real engines of economic growth.* Even if government aid increases, most money for development must come from trade, domestic capital, and foreign investment. An effective strategy must try to expand these flows as well. Free markets and free trade are key priorities of our national security strategy.

- *Secure public health.* The scale of the public health crisis in poor countries is enormous. In countries afflicted by epidemics and pandemics like HIV/AIDS, malaria, and tuberculosis, growth and development will be threatened until these scourges can be contained. Resources from the developed world are necessary but will be effective only with honest governance, which supports prevention programs and provides effective local infrastructure. The United States has strongly backed the new global fund for HIV/AIDS organized by U.N. Secretary General Kofi Annan and its focus on combining prevention with a broad strategy for treatment and care. The United States already contributes more than twice as much money to such efforts as the next largest donor. If the global fund demonstrates its promise, we will be ready to give even more.

- *Emphasize education.* Literacy and learning are the foundation of democracy and development. Only about 7 percent of World Bank resources are devoted to education. This proportion should grow. The United States will increase its own funding for education assistance by at least 20 percent with an emphasis on improving basic education and teacher training in Africa. The United States can also bring information technology to these societies, many of whose education systems have been devastated by HIV/AIDS.

- *Continue to aid agricultural development.* New technologies, including biotechnology, have enormous potential to improve crop yields in developing countries while using fewer pesticides and less water. Using sound science, the United States should help bring these benefits to the 800 million people, including 300 million children, who still suffer from hunger and malnutrition.

VIII. Develop Agendas for Cooperative Action with the Other Main Centers of Global Power

"We have our best chance since the rise of the nation-state in the 17th century to build a world where the great powers compete in peace instead of prepare for war."

President Bush
West Point, New York
June 1, 2002

America will implement its strategies by organizing coalitions—as broad as practicable—of states able and willing to promote a balance of power that favors freedom. Effective coalition leadership requires clear priorities, an appreciation of others' interests, and consistent consultations among partners with a spirit of humility.

There is little of lasting consequence that the United States can accomplish in the world without the sustained cooperation of its allies and friends in Canada and Europe. Europe is also the seat of two of the strongest and most able international institutions in the world: the North Atlantic Treaty Organization (NATO), which has, since its inception, been the fulcrum of transatlantic and inter-European security, and the European Union (EU), our partner in opening world trade.

The attacks of September 11 were also an attack on NATO, as NATO itself recognized when it invoked its Article V self-defense clause for the first time. NATO's core mission—collective defense of the transatlantic alliance of democracies—remains, but NATO must develop new structures and capabilities to carry out that mission under new circumstances. NATO must build a capability to field, at short notice, highly mobile, specially trained forces whenever they are needed to respond to a threat against any member of the alliance.

The alliance must be able to act wherever our interests are threatened, creating coalitions under NATO's own mandate, as well as contributing to mission-based coalitions. To achieve this, we must:

- expand NATO's membership to those democratic nations willing and able to share the burden of defending and advancing our common interests;
- ensure that the military forces of NATO nations have appropriate combat contributions to make in coalition warfare;
- develop planning processes to enable those contributions to become effective multinational fighting forces;
- take advantage of the technological opportunities and economies of scale in our defense spending to transform NATO military forces so that they dominate potential aggressors and diminish our vulnerabilities;
- streamline and increase the flexibility of command structures to meet new operational demands and the associated requirements of training, integrating, and experimenting with new force configurations; and

- maintain the ability to work and fight together as allies even as we take the necessary steps to transform and modernize our forces.

If NATO succeeds in enacting these changes, the rewards will be a partnership as central to the security and interests of its member states as was the case during the Cold War. We will sustain a common perspective on the threats to our societies and improve our ability to take common action in defense of our nations and their interests. At the same time, we welcome our European allies' efforts to forge a greater foreign policy and defense identity with the EU, and commit ourselves to close consultations to ensure that these developments work with NATO. We cannot afford to lose this opportunity to better prepare the family of transatlantic democracies for the challenges to come.

The attacks of September 11 energized America's Asian alliances. Australia invoked the ANZUS Treaty to declare that September 11 was an attack on Australia itself, following that historic decision with the dispatch of some of the world's finest combat forces for Operation Enduring Freedom. Japan and the Republic of Korea provided unprecedented levels of military logistical support within weeks of the terrorist attack. We have deepened cooperation on counterterrorism with our alliance partners in Thailand and the Philippines and received invaluable assistance from close friends like Singapore and New Zealand.

The war against terrorism has proven that America's alliances in Asia not only underpin regional peace and stability, but are flexible and ready to deal with new challenges. To enhance our Asian alliances and friendships, we will:

- look to Japan to continue forging a leading role in regional and global affairs based on our common interests, our common values, and our close defense and diplomatic cooperation;
- work with South Korea to maintain vigilance towards the North while preparing our alliance to make contributions to the broader stability of the region over the longer term;
- build on 50 years of U.S.-Australian alliance cooperation as we continue working together to resolve regional and global problems—as we have so many times from the Battle of the Coral Sea to Tora Bora;
- maintain forces in the region that reflect our commitments to our allies, our requirements, our technological advances, and the strategic environment; and
- build on stability provided by these alliances, as well as with institutions such as ASEAN and the Asia-Pacific Economic Cooperation forum, to develop a mix of regional and bilateral strategies to manage change in this dynamic region.

We are attentive to the possible renewal of old patterns of great power competition. Several potential great powers are now in the midst of internal transition—most importantly Russia, India, and China. In all three cases, recent developments have encouraged our hope that a truly global consensus about basic principles is slowly taking shape.

With Russia, we are already building a new strategic relationship based on a central reality of the twenty-first century: the United States and Russia are no longer strategic adversaries. The Moscow Treaty on Strategic Reductions is emblematic of this new reality and reflects a critical change in Russian thinking that promises to lead to productive, long-term relations with the Euro-Atlantic community and the United States. Russia's top leaders have a realistic assessment of their country's current weakness and the policies—internal and external—needed to reverse those weaknesses. They understand, increasingly, that Cold War approaches do not serve their national interests and that Russian and American strategic interests overlap in many areas.

United States policy seeks to use this turn in Russian thinking to refocus our relationship on emerging and potential common interests and challenges. We are broadening our already extensive cooperation in the global war on terrorism. We are facilitating Russia's entry into the World Trade Organization, without lowering standards for accession, to promote beneficial bilateral trade and investment relations. We have created the NATO-Russia Council with the goal of deepening security cooperation among Russia, our European allies, and ourselves. We will continue to bolster the independence and stability of the states of the former Soviet Union in the belief that a prosperous and stable neighborhood will reinforce Russia's growing commitment to integration into the Euro-Atlantic community.

At the same time, we are realistic about the differences that still divide us from Russia and about the time and effort it will take to build an enduring strategic partnership. Lingering distrust of our motives and policies by key Russian elites slows improvement in our relations. Russia's uneven commitment to the basic values of free-market democracy and dubious record in combating the proliferation of weapons of mass destruction remain matters of great concern. Russia's very weakness limits the opportunities for cooperation. Nevertheless, those opportunities are vastly greater now than in recent years—or even decades.

The United States has undertaken a transformation in its bilateral relationship with India based on a conviction that U.S. interests require a strong relationship with India. We are the two largest democracies, committed to political freedom protected by representative government. India is moving toward greater economic freedom as well. We have a common interest in the free flow of commerce, including through the vital sea lanes of the Indian Ocean. Finally, we share an interest in fighting terrorism and in creating a strategically stable Asia.

Differences remain, including over the development of India's nuclear and missile programs, and the pace of India's economic reforms. But while in the past these concerns may have dominated our thinking about India, today we start with a view of India as a growing world power with which we have common strategic interests. Through a strong partnership with India, we can best address any differences and shape a dynamic future.

The United States relationship with China is an important part of our strategy to promote a stable, peaceful, and prosperous Asia-Pacific region. We welcome the emergence of a strong, peaceful, and prosperous China. The democratic development of China is crucial to that future. Yet, a quarter century after beginning the process of shedding the worst features of the Communist legacy, China's leaders have not yet made the next series of fundamental choices about the character of their state. In pursuing advanced military capabilities that can threaten its neighbors in the Asia-Pacific region, China is following an outdated path that, in the end, will hamper its own pursuit of national greatness. In time, China will find that social and political freedom is the only source of that greatness.

The United States seeks a constructive relationship with a changing China. We already cooperate well where our interests overlap, including the current war on terrorism and in promoting stability on the Korean peninsula. Likewise, we have coordinated on the future of Afghanistan and have initiated a comprehensive dialogue on counterterrorism and similar transitional concerns. Shared health and environmental threats, such as the spread of HIV/AIDS, challenge us to promote jointly the welfare of our citizens.

Addressing these transnational threats will challenge China to become more open with information, promote the development of civil society, and enhance individual human rights. China has begun to take the road to political openness, permitting many personal freedoms and conducting village-level elections, yet remains strongly committed to national one-party rule by the Communist Party. To make that nation truly accountable to its citizen's needs and aspirations, however, much work remains to be done. Only by allowing the Chinese people to think, assemble, and worship freely can China reach its full potential.

Our important trade relationship will benefit from China's entry into the World Trade Organization, which will create more export opportunities and ultimately more jobs for American farmers, workers, and companies. China is our fourth largest trading partner, with over $100 billion in annual two-way trade. The power of market principles and the WTO's requirements for transparency and accountability will advance openness and the rule of law in China to help establish basic protections for commerce and for citizens. There are, however, other areas in which we have profound disagreements. Our commitment to the self-defense of Taiwan under the Taiwan Relations Act is one. Human rights is another. We expect China to adhere to its nonproliferation commitments. We will work to narrow differences where they exist, but not allow them to preclude cooperation where we agree.

The events of September 11, 2001, fundamentally changed the context for relations between the United States and other main centers of global power, and opened vast, new opportunities. With our long-standing allies in Europe and Asia, and with leaders in Russia, India, and China, we must develop active agendas of cooperation lest these relationships become routine and unproductive.

Every agency of the United States government shares the challenge. We can build fruitful habits of consultation, quiet argument, sober analysis, and common action. In the long term, these are the practices that will sustain the supremacy of our common principles and keep open the path of progress.

IX. Transform America's National Security Institutions to Meet the Challenges and Opportunities of the Twenty-First Century

"Terrorists attacked a symbol of American prosperity. They did not touch its source. America is successful because of the hard work, creativity, and enterprise of our people."

President Bush
Washington, D.C. (Joint Session of Congress)
September 20, 2001

The major institutions of American national security were designed in a different era to meet different requirements. All of them must be transformed.

It is time to reaffirm the essential role of American military strength. We must build and maintain our defenses beyond challenge. Our military's highest priority is to defend the United States. To do so effectively, our military must:

- assure our allies and friends;
- dissuade future military competition;
- deter threats against U.S. interests, allies, and friends; and
- decisively defeat any adversary if deterrence fails.

The unparalleled strength of the United States armed forces, and their forward presence, have maintained the peace in some of the world's most strategically vital regions. However, the threats and enemies we must confront have changed, and so must our forces. A military structured to deter massive Cold War-era armies must be transformed to focus more on how an adversary might fight rather than where and when a war might occur. We will channel our energies to overcome a host of operational challenges.

The presence of American forces overseas is one of the most profound symbols of the U.S. commitments to allies and friends. Through our willingness to use force in our own defense and in defense of others, the United States demonstrates its resolve to maintain a balance of power that favors freedom. To contend with uncertainty and to meet the many security challenges we face, the United States will require bases and stations within and beyond Western Europe and Northeast Asia, as well as temporary access arrangements for the long-distance deployment of U.S. forces.

Before the war in Afghanistan, that area was low on the list of major planning contingencies. Yet, in a very short time, we had to operate across the length and breadth of that remote nation, using every branch of the armed forces. We must prepare for more such deployments by developing assets such as advanced remote sensing, long-range precision strike capabilities, and transformed maneuver and expeditionary forces. This broad portfolio of military capabilities must also include the ability to defend the homeland, conduct information operations, ensure U.S. access to distant theaters, and protect critical U.S. infrastructure and assets in outer space.

Innovation within the armed forces will rest on experimentation with new approaches to warfare, strengthening joint operations, exploiting U.S. intelligence advantages, and taking full advantage of science and technology. We must also transform the way the Department of Defense is run, especially in financial management and recruitment and retention. Finally, while maintaining near-term readiness and the ability to fight the war on terrorism, the goal must be to provide the President with a wider range of military options to discourage aggression or any form of coercion against the United States, our allies, and our friends.

We know from history that deterrence can fail; and we know from experience that some enemies cannot be deterred. The United States must and will maintain the capability to defeat any attempt by an enemy—whether a state or non-state actor—to impose its will on the United States, our allies, or our friends. We will maintain the forces sufficient to support our obligations, and to defend freedom. Our forces will be strong enough to dissuade potential adversaries from pursuing a military build-up in hopes of surpassing, or equaling, the power of the United States.

Intelligence—and how we use it—is our first line of defense against terrorists and the threat posed by hostile states. Designed around the priority of gathering enormous information about a massive, fixed object—the Soviet bloc—the intelligence community is coping with the challenge of following a far more complex and elusive set of targets.

We must transform our intelligence capabilities and build new ones to keep pace with the nature of these threats. Intelligence must be appropriately integrated with our defense and law enforcement systems and coordinated with our allies and friends. We need to protect the capabilities we have so that we do not arm our enemies with the knowledge of how best to surprise us. Those who would harm us also seek the benefit of surprise to limit our prevention and response options and to maximize injury.

We must strengthen intelligence warning and analysis to provide integrated threat assessments for national and homeland security. Since the threats inspired by foreign governments and groups may be conducted inside the United States, we must also ensure the proper fusion of information between intelligence and law enforcement.

Initiatives in this area will include:

- strengthening the authority of the Director of Central Intelligence to lead the development and actions of the Nation's foreign intelligence capabilities;
- establishing a new framework for intelligence warning that provides seamless and integrated warning across the spectrum of threats facing the nation and our allies;
- continuing to develop new methods of collecting information to sustain our intelligence advantage;

- investing in future capabilities while working to protect them through a more vigorous effort to prevent the compromise of intelligence capabilities; and

- collecting intelligence against the terrorist danger across the government with all source analysis.

As the United States Government relies on the armed forces to defend America's interests, it must rely on diplomacy to interact with other nations. We will ensure that the Department of State receives funding sufficient to ensure the success of American diplomacy. The State Department takes the lead in managing our bilateral relationships with other governments. And in this new era, its people and institutions must be able to interact equally adroitly with non-governmental organizations and international institutions. Officials trained mainly in international politics must also extend their reach to understand complex issues of domestic governance around the world, including public health, education, law enforcement, the judiciary, and public diplomacy.

Our diplomats serve at the front line of complex negotiations, civil wars, and other humanitarian catastrophes. As humanitarian relief requirements are better understood, we must also be able to help build police forces, court systems, and legal codes, local and provincial government institutions, and electoral systems. Effective international cooperation is needed to accomplish these goals, backed by American readiness to play our part.

Just as our diplomatic institutions must adapt so that we can reach out to others, we also need a different and more comprehensive approach to public information efforts that can help people around the world learn about and understand America. The war on terrorism is not a clash of civilizations. It does, however, reveal the clash inside a civilization, a battle for the future of the Muslim world. This is a struggle of ideas and this is an area where America must excel.

We will take the actions necessary to ensure that our efforts to meet our global security commitments and protect Americans are not impaired by the potential for investigations, inquiry, or prosecution by the International Criminal Court (ICC), whose jurisdiction does not extend to Americans and which we do not accept. We will work together with other nations to avoid complications in our military operations and cooperation, through such mechanisms as multilateral and bilateral agreements that will protect U.S. nationals from the ICC. We will implement fully the American Servicemembers Protection Act, whose provisions are intended to ensure and enhance the protection of U.S. personnel and officials.

We will make hard choices in the coming year and beyond to ensure the right level and allocation of government spending on national security. The United States Government must strengthen its defenses to win this war. At home, our most important priority is to protect the homeland for the American people.

Today, the distinction between domestic and foreign affairs is diminishing. In a globalized world, events beyond America's borders have a greater impact inside them. Our society must be open to people, ideas, and goods from across the globe. The characteristics we most cherish—our freedom, our cities, our systems of movement, and modern life—are vulnerable to terrorism. This vulnerability will persist long after we bring to justice those responsible for the September 11 attacks. As time passes, individuals may gain access to means of destruction that until now could be wielded only by armies, fleets, and squadrons. This is a new condition of life. We will adjust to it and thrive—in spite of it.

In exercising our leadership, we will respect the values, judgment, and interests of our friends and partners. Still, we will be prepared to act apart when our interests and unique responsibilities require. When we disagree on particulars, we will explain forthrightly the grounds for our concerns and strive to forge viable alternatives. We will not allow such disagreements to obscure our determination to secure together, with our allies and our friends, our shared fundamental interests and values.

Ultimately, the foundation of American strength is at home. It is in the skills of our people, the dynamism of our economy, and the resilience of our institutions. A diverse, modern society has inherent, ambitious, entrepreneurial energy. Our strength comes from what we do with that energy. That is where our national security begins.

Contributors

Wes Avram is the Stephen Merrell Clement-E.William Muehl Assistant Professor of Communication at Yale Divinity School. He has served as a parish pastor and a college chaplain, and has taught at Northwestern University and Bates College. He is the author of a forthcoming collection of essays on the work of the Holy Spirit in Christian life.

Robert N. Bellah is Elliott Professor of Sociology, Emeritus, University of California, Berkeley. He has published numerous articles on sociology and religion, and his books include *Habits of the Heart*, which was a 1986 Jury Nominee for the Pulitzer Prize, and *The Good Society*.

Wendell Berry is a noted essayist, novelist, poet, and agrarian philosopher, and a frequent contributor to *Orion* magazine. His numerous books include *The Gift of Gravity*, *Life Is a Miracle*, and *Place on Earth*.

Arthur Paul Boers, a Mennonite minister and Benedictine Oblate, teaches pastoral theology at Associated Mennonite Biblical Seminary, Elkhart, Indiana. He has served as a pastor to Canadian congregations. His latest book is *The Rhythm of God's Grace: Uncovering Morning and Evening Hours of Prayer*.

Michael L. Budde is professor of political science and director of the Center for Church-State Studies at DePaul University in Chicago. He was founding director of the Ekklesia Project and writes on the interaction of political economy, ecclesiology, and culture. His books include *Two Churches*, and *The (Magic) Kingdom of God: Christianity and the Global Culture Industries*.

Stephen B. Chapman is assistant professor of Old Testament at Duke Divinity School and author of *The Law and the Prophets: A Study in Old*

Testament Canon Formation. He is also an American Baptist minister and a former legislative assistant to U.S. Rep. Robert A. Young (D-Missouri).

Lillian Daniel is the senior minister of the Church of the Redeemer, United Church of Christ, in New Haven, Connecticut. She is a founding member and co-chair of the Connecticut Center for a New Economy and co-chairs Elm City Congregations Organized. She writes for various periodicals and lectures in homiletics at Yale Divinity School.

Jean Bethke Elshtain is the Laura Spelman Rockefeller Professor of Ethics at the University of Chicago, where she teaches in the Divinity School. A noted political theorist and commentator on contemporary culture, she is also the author of several books, including *Democracy on Trial*, *Augustine and the Limits of Politics*, and *Just War Against Terror*.

Allen R. Hilton is the minister of Christian formation at Congregational Church of New Canaan, Connecticut. He has served as assistant professor of New Testament at Yale Divinity School and has taught at St. Mary's College in Oakland, California. His New Testament research is on early Christian illiteracy and Pagan criticism. He co-edited *In Search of the Early Christians: Selected Essays*.

James Hudnut-Beumler is the Anne Potter Wilson Distinguished Professor of American Religious History at Vanderbilt University and dean of the Vanderbilt Divinity School. He is the author of several books, including *Looking for God in the Suburbs*, an analysis of the religion of the American dream after World War II.

David L. Johnston served as a pastor (Conservative Congregational Christian Conference) and teacher for over fifteen years in Algeria, Egypt, and the West Bank. He obtained his PhD in Islamics at Fuller Seminary and continued his postdoctoral research at Yale University, where he is a lecturer in religious studies. His research concentrates on the doctrine of Creation in Islam and Christianity.

Eugene McCarraher is assistant professor of humanities and history at Villanova University. He is the author of *Christian Critics: Religion and the Impasse in Modern American Social Thought*. His current project is a cultural history of corporate business entitled *The Enchantments of Mammon: Corporate Capitalism and the American Moral Imagination*.

Stephen H. Webb is professor of religion and philosophy at Wabash College. His interests include religion and culture, Christian theology, and rhetorical studies. His books include *Refiguring Theology*, *On God and Dogs*, and *Gifting God*.